W9-BRC-618

100 THINGS ORIOLES FANS
SHOULD KNOW & DO BEFORE THEY DIE

Dan Connolly

TRIUMPH
BOOKS

Copyright © 2015 by Dan Connolly

No part of this publication may be reproduced, stored in a retrieval system, or transmitted in any form by any means, electronic, mechanical, photocopying, or otherwise, without the prior written permission of the publisher, Triumph Books LLC, 814 North Franklin Street, Chicago, Illinois 60610.

Library of Congress Cataloging-in-Publication Data

Connolly, Dan, 1969–
    100 things Orioles fans should know & do before they die / Dan Connolly.
        pages cm
    ISBN 978-1-62937-041-5
1. Baltimore Orioles (Baseball team)—History. 2. Baltimore Orioles (Baseball team)—Miscellanea.   I. Title. II. Title: One hundred things Orioles fans should know and do before they die.
    GV875.B2C66 2015
    796.357'64097526—dc23

                                    2014044588

This book is available in quantity at special discounts for your group or organization. For further information, contact:
    Triumph Books LLC
    814 North Franklin Street
    Chicago, Illinois 60610
    (312) 337-0747
    www.triumphbooks.com

Printed in U.S.A.
ISBN: 978-1-62937-041-5
Design by Patricia Frey
Photos courtesy of Getty Images unless otherwise indicated

To my late mother, Ann, who taught me
to love words and to laugh often.

To my dad, Jerry Sr., who taught me about
hard work and baseball, in that order.

To my four siblings, Jerry Jr., Chuck, Ann,
and Marnie, who taught me what I initially
needed to know about the Orioles and life.

And to my wife, Karen, and my children,
Alex, Annie, and Grace, who teach me
about life and love every single day.

To Marty,
Thanks for making
Chapter 69 "Wild Bill"
So much better. Enjoy!

Contents

Foreword

I played for almost 20 years—counting time on the disabled list—all with the Orioles. And we had the best winning percentage in baseball during that time. We didn't win all of our World Series, but we won half. And we were in six. We made the playoffs two other times. So being an Oriole was about continuity. And when you played for Cal Ripken Sr. in the minors, it was all about doing things the right way, The Oriole Way.

It sounds funny now, but you are 18 years old, and you are making $414.14 every month after taxes. During my first year playing professionally, I think I made $2,039. So obviously everybody wanted to go to the next level. I learned that to do that—to get to the next level—you had to be a good teammate. Cal Sr. helped me understand that. It's not about practice; it is about perfect practice. There are no such things as shortcuts. You had a lot of guys—like Davey Leonhard, Eddie Watt—on the same page as you were going forward.

So I feel very fortunate to have played with the Orioles and I played here at the right time. I had Hall of Famer Robin Roberts as my first roommate, even though he was only there for about three months after my debut. He helped me. And I sat in the bullpen with guys like Harvey Haddix and Stu Miller and Sherm Lollar and Charlie Lau and John Orsino, guys who had been around a little bit. And then there was Dick Hall. When I got to the big leagues, you had to run and condition on your own, and the only guy who really ran was Dick Hall. So we became friends, and he became the godfather of my oldest daughter, Jamie, and my kids grew up with his kids.

I got here at the right time. We had continuity and we had great coaches. We had continuity in the way players were taught. The Oriole Way was to sign talented players, to coach them up, to have a commonality of teamwork and work ethic. Cal Sr. used to tell us, "We are never going to let anybody outwork us. You can have fun. But you have to have a passion of getting better every day." And Earl Weaver certainly had a lot to do with that. He was an easy guy to play for because we won. But he was not an easy guy in that he expected you to be maybe even better than you were. And if you were already pretty good, it made for some difficulties.

But we had a great organization. We developed guys. We had a lot of guys who knew the game and would go on to manage: Jimmy Frey, Billy Hunter, Davey Johnson. George Bamberger managed two teams. The Oriole Way was the universal way. Maybe the New York Yankees were doing a similar thing, but we weren't a large-market team. And yet every year we seemed to be playing really competitive baseball.

The great thing about playing professional sports when you are young is you can look around and say, "Okay, who do I want to be like?" And when I looked at the Orioles when I came up, I was like, *Geez, who could be better than Brooks Robinson? Good guy, everybody likes him. Great player. Great personality.* Some other players come in and are nice on Monday but are total jerks the other six days. And you figure in the same amount of time, you can be nice to people. Part of the process of being here in Baltimore so many years is that I have had a lot of role models, people to emulate. Robin Roberts probably knew I was going to take his place. I was 19, and he was 38. And yet he told me everything I needed to know, so it was a great lesson.

It gave me great pleasure to win 20 games eight times and to win three Cy Young Awards, but it gave me just as much pleasure to mentor the younger guys and see them go out there and make our lives easier and keep the tradition going. You did pitch for the name on the front of your uniform and not the one on the back. Because you won. It didn't have to be about you. It was always about us.

—Jim Palmer

Introduction

Whenever my wife and I take our kids out for an undisclosed treat, I always tell them we're going to a broccoli farm. It's my way of creating a little suspense for our trip while keeping the expectations low. I mean, no kid wants to go pick broccoli or take a bunch home. Therefore, once we arrive at our actual destination, it's met with excitement and relief. *We avoided the broccoli farm again.* I come by this misdirection ploy honestly.

My dad did the same thing, only we lived just north of Baltimore City; broccoli farms weren't a plausible option. So my dad would pack us up for a trip to the grocery store, my aunt's house, or maybe the dentist's office. As we traveled down Loch Raven Boulevard, passing the grocery store and the dentist's and not turning left to my aunt's, I'd start looking out the passenger-side window. As soon as towering light poles loomed in the west, I'd celebrate because I then knew we were heading to Memorial Stadium to watch the great Orioles teams of the mid-1970s to the early 1980s. That was the ultimate treat for me. We attended a lot of games during those years. The stadium was close, the seats were cheap, and the baseball was thrilling.

Back then I had no idea where life would lead me. Now I consider those days as sort of an early internship. I ate peanuts in the bleachers with my father and mother or tagged along with my older sisters in the upper deck. (They'd hang out in raucous Section 34 while I was relegated to sit by myself a few sections over and not tell my mom and dad what I had heard, saw, or smelled.) It was definitely on-the-job training. Years later, I became a sportswriter. In 2001 I began covering the Orioles full time. In 2005 my hometown newspaper, *The Baltimore Sun*, hired me to keep writing about baseball. So when I was asked to do this book, it seemed like a natural fit. I'd been around the Orioles most of my life. I remember

Tito Landrum's homer, John Shelby's throw, and that make-your-skin-crawl Sister Sledge song. I figured I knew all I needed to know about the Orioles to write a book. I was completely wrong. As my research mounted and I talked to many of the men who shaped the franchise, I discovered stories I had never heard before, or had long forgotten, anyway. It was absolutely fascinating for me.

One thing I knew going in was that finding 100 interesting things to write about wouldn't be difficult. The Orioles have a deep, rich history of winning. And in the years they were bad, they were rarely boring. My biggest challenge became figuring out what to include and what to omit. Yes, the 1980 Orioles won 100 games and didn't make the playoffs, and that's intriguing. But Orioles reliever Alan Mills once had a poster of Darryl Strawberry in his college dorm room and years later famously punched Straw in the jaw. Sorry, 1980 team, you came up short again. There's plenty of room here for friendly debates—like the ordering of the chapters. How do you correctly put all these instrumental people and events into a one to 100 order? It really became tricky after about No. 25 or so and impossible by No. 50. For instance, should Gus Triandos be listed ahead of Mike Mussina? I thought yes—he was the club's first real star—but maybe not. That's what makes this whole concept so cool. Ultimately, I assembled the content in a way I thought would be both entertaining and informing.

On a personal note, I was honored that Hall of Famer Jim Palmer agreed to do the foreword. He was the perfect choice. The man won 268 games for the team, played in all six of the franchise's World Series, and has remained a visible part of the organization. Because I grew up watching him pitch and listened to him as a broadcaster for so long, I assumed I had heard most of his key stories. I hadn't. While interviewing him this year, he explained how attending one Baltimore Bullets basketball game in 1968 saved his career. In the middle of the interview, I stopped and said, "Wow. I never heard that one before." That's the reaction I am shooting for within these pages. I'm hoping even the most educated O's fan learns something here. But I'll settle for an enjoyable trip down memory lane together on our way to the broccoli farm or the dentist's office.

1 The Oriole Way

There could be 100 or more ways to start this book. So many different people had a hand in creating the tremendous history of the Baltimore Orioles, whether it's the incarnation that moved from St. Louis in 1954, the dominating teams in the late 1800s, or the minor league powerhouses that bridged the gap. But in crafting an overall assessment of the organization—the glories and the pratfalls—it's hard to ignore the foundation on which the modern-day success was built.

It had become somewhat cliché in Baltimore—the phrase being tossed around even when the club was in disarray. But the three familiar words were a source of pride for decades and may be experiencing a resurrection: "The Oriole Way." It's a phrase that was coined to describe a thorough and universal commitment to winning from the lowest level of the minors to the majors.

How important is the history of The Oriole Way to this franchise? Consider that one of the things Buck Showalter wanted to do when he took over managing the club in 2010 was to provide a tangible reminder of the previous triumphs for the club's current players. Not a competition, mind you, just a healthy blueprint of success. So Showalter had pictures of the club's Hall of Famers placed along the walkway from the Camden Yards home clubhouse to the dugout tunnel. Each poster contains a quote from the depicted Oriole great. The first one you see on the right when you turn the corner from the clubhouse is Jim Palmer, the best pitcher in club history. But his quote isn't about pitching. No, it's more encompassing. "The Oriole Way is no mystery," Palmer's quote reads. "Have an unparalleled work ethic, be a good teammate,

1

respect the game, have fun and an undying passion to be the best you can be."

The concept of The Oriole Way—though it wasn't coined at the time—can probably be traced to Paul Richards, the lanky Texan and former big leaguer who stressed pitching and defense and doing the little things correctly to win baseball games. From 1955 to 1958, Richards was the Orioles manager and general manager before being replaced as GM by Hall of Fame executive Lee MacPhail. Richards remained as the manager until 1961, when he eventually left to take over the expansion Houston Colt 45s. A renowned taskmaster and consummate teacher of baseball, Richards wanted instruction to be uniform throughout the system. For him nothing was too routine: bunt defense, proper positioning for relay throws, or the most efficient base-running techniques.

He put together an instructional manual for all of his managers and coaches. Full staffs would gather during spring training so they were—literally and figuratively—on the same page as the various seasons began. As the Orioles surged above mediocrity in the early 1960s—the 1960 team under Richards was the modern-day franchise's first to win more than it lost at 89–65—a consistent player development program was paramount.

Perhaps the two most influential disciples of The Oriole Way were minor league lifers with an unrivaled passion for the game: Hall of Fame manager Earl Weaver and former coach and manager Cal Ripken Sr. In 1961 Weaver was charged with directing the organization's minor league spring training camp at former military barracks in Thomasville, Georgia, which often included hundreds of players at a time. He built on that organizational instructional manual, which, in a sense became The Oriole Way handbook. Weaver continued that emphasis on fundamentals when he became the Orioles manager in 1968, kick-starting an amazing run of 18 straight seasons in which the club finished above .500.

Part of the fiber of the organization during that time was Ripken Sr., who spent 36 years in the organization, much of it as the no-nonsense professor of baseball for generations of minor leaguers. His mantra, "Practice doesn't make perfect. Perfect practice makes perfect," was an echoing theme throughout the 1960s, 1970s, and 1980s, when the Orioles went to six World Series and won three from 1966 to 1983.

"I don't think The Oriole Way phrase came along until later," said longtime Orioles slugger Boog Powell, who joined the organization in 1959. "But I played with Cal Sr. in Appleton, Wisconsin, in 1960. And he is the one who introduced me to The Oriole Way. The Oriole Way was just not making mistakes and practicing until you get it right. And that's pretty much what it boiled down to. And we did not beat ourselves."

The Oriole Way eventually took on new and often derisive meanings as the excellence of the glory years faded. There was the mid- to late-1990s, when it meant buying superstars and mixing them together with homegrown talent in hopes of a World Series title. Twice the club reached the American League Championship Series with outstanding players such as Roberto Alomar, Rafael Palmeiro, and Cal Ripken Jr. in 1996 and 1997. But that talented group never reached the World Series, and along the way, the organization's dedication to its farm system waned. By the 2000s the Orioles were stuck in an ugly spiral of rebuilding, acquiring stopgap free agents, and rebuilding again.

During a stretch of 14 losing seasons from 1998 to 2011, The Oriole Way represented a baseball form of Murphy's Law. Whatever could go wrong on the diamond—and throughout the organization—would go wrong. In what seemed like an act of desperation at the time, beleaguered owner Peter Angelos hearkened to the success of the old days in 2007 when he hired Andy MacPhail— the son of Lee—to be the club's president of baseball operations. Andy MacPhail thoroughly reassessed the organization, finding it lacking in talent from top to bottom. He orchestrated several trades that would ultimately point the Orioles back to respectability. Equally as important, in 2010 MacPhail hired Showalter, whose reputation was, like Richards, that of a taskmaster with a keen eye toward fundamentals.

In 2012 the Orioles made the playoffs for the first time since 1997. The following year they again were over .500 and boasted the best defense in the majors. In 2014 the club won its first division title in 17 years. That run gave the fan base hope that The Oriole Way could have meaning again—and not be just a catchy phrase on a poster.

2 A Human Vacuum Cleaner Named Brooks

It's difficult to overstate exactly what Brooks Calbert Robinson has meant to the Orioles as a player, as a broadcaster, and, most importantly, as the face of the franchise for so long.

The unassuming kid from Little Rock, Arkansas, debuted with the Orioles in 1955 at age 18 and spent parts of 23 seasons manning third base while becoming arguably the most popular player in club history. He won 16 consecutive Gold Gloves (from 1960 to 1975), made 15 American League All-Star teams, and won the 1964 AL MVP. He finished in the top five in MVP voting four other times. He was and is the standard bearer for third-base defense. Yet what made Robinson so endearing to scores of fans was the way he handled the spotlight: with a grace and dignity that made him seem like he had no idea just how rare his talent was. "He's an extraordinary human being, which is important, and the world's greatest third baseman of all time, which is incidental," the esteemed late sportswriter John Steadman once wrote.

Gold Glovers

Throughout modern franchise history, the Orioles have been known for their defense. Since the Gold Glove Award was created by the Rawlings Sporting Goods Company in 1957, Orioles have won 70 times, most in the American League and second overall to the St. Louis Cardinals.

Incredibly, the Orioles have had 16 multiple Gold Glove winners led by third baseman Brooks Robinson, who holds the club record with 16 Gold Gloves. He picked up the club's first one in 1960.

Here's a look at the players who have won multiple Gold Gloves for the Orioles.

16 Gold Gloves: 3B Brooks Robinson

8 Gold Gloves: OF Paul Blair, SS Mark Belanger

4 Gold Gloves: P Jim Palmer, P Mike Mussina, 2B Bobby Grich, OF/CF Adam Jones

3 Gold Gloves: 1B Eddie Murray, 2B Davey Johnson, SS J.J. Hardy

2 Gold Gloves: 2B Roberto Alomar, SS Luis Aparicio, 1B Rafael Palmeiro, SS Cal Ripken Jr., C Matt Wieters, RF Nick Markakis

Orioles great Boog Powell, a teammate of Robinson's for 14 seasons, remembers driving up to Miami from his home in Key West, Florida, for his first spring training in 1960. He was 18 years old, and his father made the trip with him. The first person the Powells met was a 22-year-old Robinson, who had established himself as a big leaguer but not yet a superstar. "I introduced myself, and he introduced himself to my father," Powell said. "And the last thing he said to my dad was, 'Don't worry, Mr. Powell, I will take care of him.' That's the person he was right there. And he was not BS-ing. He was always checking on me, seeing if I was okay. He's an incredible man. I've worshiped him since Day One, since I walked into spring training on the first day with my father."

Robinson inspired generations of people. If you grew up around Baltimore in the 1960s and 1970s, you wanted to play third base. And plenty of those who did were called Brooks. "Brooks never asked anyone to name a candy bar after him," late sportswriter Gordon Beard wrote. "In Baltimore people named their children after him."

And it wasn't just in Baltimore. Brooks Conrad, who was born in 1980 in Southern California and spent several seasons as a major league infielder, said his parents were huge baseball fans and loved watching Robinson. So they named their future big league son after him, even though the Gold Glover played on the other side of the country and had retired before their son was born. When Robinson began his professional baseball career for the York (Pennsylvania) White Roses of the Class B Piedmont League in 1955, he was far from a household name. The initial lineup card in his first game had him listed as "B. Robinson." No one knew who the kid was, so the public address announcer took a stab at the first name and introduced the teenaged second baseman as Bob Robinson. The mistake was quickly fixed at the stadium, though the local newspapers still referred to Robinson as Bob for a few more weeks.

Robinson's ascent to stardom began in 1960, which, not coincidentally, was also the first year the modern-day Orioles had a record over .500. (They were 89–65 in 1960 and finished second of eight teams in the AL; they had never before finished above fifth place.) Just 23, Robinson batted .294 with 14 homers and 88 RBIs and placed third in the MVP voting behind the New York Yankees' duo of Roger Maris and Mickey Mantle. Four seasons later, Robinson captured his only MVP Award, batting .317 with 28 homers and 118 RBIs, which would all represent career highs. Robinson received 18 of the 20 first place MVP votes in 1964; Mantle got the others.

Although Robinson was steady throughout his career with the bat—he had 268 career homers, 1,357 RBIs, and a lifetime .267 average—it was what he did at third base that made him a first-ballot Hall of Famer in 1983. Nicknamed the "Human Vacuum Cleaner," Robinson wasn't quick-footed. But he had tremendous

Though known for his prowess in the field, which led to 16 consecutive Gold Gloves, third baseman Brooks Robinson also totaled 1,357 RBIs.

reflexes, an unrelenting work ethic, and understood the game so well that he seemingly always had himself ready to make a play. "I'd just watch the way he went about his work. He would take 100 ground balls every single day before every game. The way he worked—no wonder he was so good," Powell said. "My first four years I stood behind him in left field, and he just amazed me. I never had to field any ground balls out there."

Robinson's defensive dominance was highlighted in the 1970 World Series, which will always be considered his ultimate defensive showcase, even though he was already 33. In the five-game series against the Cincinnati Reds, Robinson made several iconic plays, including spearing a liner by Johnny Bench and fielding a grounder to his right and throwing a one-hopper from foul territory to get Lee May by a step. May called Robinson "Mr. Hoover" after that display. Reds manager Sparky Anderson was even more effusive. "I'm beginning to see Brooks in my sleep," Anderson said in 1970. "If I dropped this paper plate, he'd pick it up on one hop and throw me out at first."

Like in his career, his defense in the 1970 World Series overshadowed his offensive performance, which was also outstanding. He was 9-for-21 (.429 average) with two homers and six RBIs while winning the World Series MVP Award. Robinson was a career .303 hitter in 39 postseason games. He seemed to have heightened focus as the stakes improved. "If I had one guy that I had to have drive in a big run in a clutch situation, Brooksie's my boy," Powell said. "He's the guy I'd choose. When it came to clutch time, he was special. He really was."

When his postseason heroics are mentioned, though, it's those indelible moments with Robinson's glove that take center stage. There are two statues of Robinson in downtown Baltimore, one on Washington Boulevard near Camden Yards and one inside the stadium complex that honors the modern-day franchise's six Hall of Famers. Both depict Robinson in the field—fitting for the greatest defensive third baseman of all time.

On Sunday September 18, 1977, the 40-year-old Robinson was honored with a sendoff billed, "Thanks, Brooks" Day, in which 51,798 fans jammed into Memorial Stadium. Although Robinson asked for no gifts, he was awarded a new car. There were two other presents that stood out. His successor, Doug DeCinces, ripped third base out of the ground and handed it to Robinson. And May, who was victimized by Robinson in the 1970 World Series but was an Oriole teammate in 1977, handed the retiring superstar a vacuum cleaner. It was the perfect end to an incomparable career. "I have seen all the clips. He was an actual vacuum cleaner," said

Orioles third baseman Manny Machado, who won a Gold Glove for the Orioles in 2013 at age 21. "Every time I see the clips, it just gives me goose bumps to see him play, just how he cared about the game and the way he played the game."

Junior from Aberdeen

It once seemed impossible that anyone would be able to knock Brooks Robinson off his perch as Mr. Oriole. That became at least an arguable reality in the early 1990s, when the greatest debate in Orioles history emerged: has Cal Ripken Jr. eclipsed Brooks Robinson as the most beloved, most important, and/or greatest player in franchise history?

It's an argument often waged over generational lines. If you grew up in the 1950s, '60s, and '70s, you champion Brooks; in the 1980s, 1990s and 2000s, you throw your support behind Cal. "If you ask people nowadays who was the ultimate Oriole, you get two answers: either Brooks or Cal," said former Orioles outfielder Ken Singleton. "And having played with both of them, I could see why. Brooks came from Arkansas, of course, but he was the first real star on the team, became MVP, and all that sort of thing. And Cal is more of the local hero because he came from Aberdeen, Maryland, and in that regard, you could say Cal trumps Brooksie. But I think you'd get both answers depending on how old the person is. One would say Brooks, and the other would say Cal."

This much is definite: if a Mount Rushmore of Orioles baseball were to be constructed, Hall of Famers Ripken and Robinson (in some order) would be the first faces sculpted. Although Robinson has called Ripken "Mr. Oriole" in the past, they truly are 1 and

1A in that distinction. If Ripken gets the edge, it's because he was an Oriole well before he ever played for the team. He grew up in Aberdeen, about 35 miles northeast of Baltimore. His father, Cal Sr., was a longtime minor league instructor and manager who became the big league club's third-base coach in 1977. "If you were to set out and write about the ideal situation, the ideal career for a baseball player, I think my story would have to be considered," Ripken said the year he was retiring. "I'm a hometown guy. My dad was with the Orioles. I can't tell you when the Orioles were [first] really, really important to me because I can't remember that far back."

Former Orioles catcher Rick Dempsey said he'll never forget watching a teenage Cal Ripken Jr. taking batting practice against Cal Sr. and hitting line drive after line drive into the Memorial Stadium bullpen. "That wasn't easy, even for a veteran who already wore a major league uniform," Dempsey said.

The Orioles selected Ripken—known in Orioles circles simply as "Junior"—out of Aberdeen High School in the second round of the 1978 amateur draft. There were 47 players picked ahead of Ripken, including 10 shortstops/third basemen. He was the Orioles' fourth pick in that draft and second high school third baseman. There was a faction that thought Ripken should concentrate on pitching—he was 7–2 with a 0.70 ERA and 100 strikeouts in 60 innings as a high school senior—but the Orioles kept him on the infield and off the mound. Let's just say it worked out for the club and for the 6'4" kid with the icy blue eyes and tremendous work ethic.

Early on, it wasn't Ripken's now legendary resolve that struck his teammates. It was his playfulness and boundless energy that set him apart. "The kid was like a brand new pup and a Great Dane at that," said Dempsey, who roomed with a young Ripken. "He was always bouncing around that apartment, always wanting to fight

Drafted Before Junior

The Orioles selected Aberdeen (Maryland) High School third baseman Cal Ripken Jr. with the 22nd pick in the second round of the 1978 amateur draft. There were 47 players who went before Ripken that year, including 10 who are listed by baseball-reference.com as primary shortstops or third basemen.

The Orioles eventually selected baseball's Iron Man, who practically grew up in the organization where his father was a longtime instructor and coach. But they actually grabbed three players in the first two rounds of that draft before taking Ripken: third baseman Robert Boyce (22nd overall), outfielder Larry Sheets (29th), and right-handed pitcher Eddie Hook (35th). Sheets was the only one of the three to make the majors.

Here are the shortstops and third basemen taken ahead of Ripken in that draft, which clubs selected them, and with what picks.

3B **Bob Horner**, Atlanta Braves (first overall)
SS **Glen Franklin**, Montreal Expos (9th)
SS **Phil Lansford**, Cleveland Indians (10th)
SS **Lenny Faedo**, Minnesota Twins (16th)
SS **Nick Esasky**, Cincinnati Reds (17th)
SS **Rex Hudler**, New York Yankees (18th)
3B **Robert Boyce**, Baltimore Orioles (22nd)
SS **Buddy Biancalana**, Kansas City Royals (25th)
3B **Dave White**, Chicago White Sox (31st)
SS **Clay Smith**, Los Angeles Dodgers (47th)

and to wrestle. I didn't have the energy to put up with him and catch every day myself."

Ripken has carried that limitless supply of energy into his 50s. His myriad job responsibilities after baseball have included minor league team owner, co-founder of the Cal Ripken Sr. Foundation, author, business owner, international baseball ambassador, and color commentator. In 2013 he was working as a TV analyst for a Washington Nationals game and walked onto the field pre-game to chat with his former Orioles teammate Tony Tarasco, who had landed a coaching job with the Nationals. Ripken was peppering Tarasco with questions about his team. But that's not all he was doing. "For the first 20 minutes, I am talking to him. I'm talking, and he is punching me," Tarasco said. "He is throwing me around, and Rip is no small guy. It just shows you the playful nature of him that's still there."

Ripken made his major league debut pinch-running for Singleton in the 12th inning of a 2–2 nail-biter on August 10, 1981 against the Kansas City Royals and scored the game-winner on a RBI single by John Lowenstein. In his first moment as a big leaguer, the fresh-faced 20-year-old from Aberdeen, who had dreamed of playing for his hometown club, touched home plate to secure a walk-off win. Maybe that was a sign that great things would follow this kid in his career. Or maybe it was the baseball gods setting him up with immediate success before making sure he was quickly humbled. Ripken played in 22 other games for the Orioles in 1981 and didn't score another run. He hit .128 with just five singles in 39 big league at-bats that year, walking once and striking out eight times.

Still, the next year, Hall of Fame manager Earl Weaver named Ripken his Opening Day starter at third base after the club had dealt incumbent Doug DeCinces to the California Angels for outfielder Dan Ford that January. In *The Evening Sun*'s 1982 baseball preview, Ripken's picture, along with shortstop Lenn Sakata's and Ford's, was featured on the front page with the headline, "The New Faces." In the accompanying story, Weaver said this about his 21-year-old infielder, "I've seen enough good things from Ripken to believe he can continue the improvement he made through the minor leagues and to think he might be like Eddie [Murray]. We don't know that, but it could happen."

It was an impressive prognostication by the Earl of Baltimore, considering Ripken won the American League Rookie of the Year Award in 1982 and then the AL Most Valuable Player Award in 1983, edging out Murray, also an eventual Hall of Famer. Whatever Weaver saw initially in Ripken took time to materialize for everyone else. The kid had three hits in his first game in 1982, including a two-run homer against Kansas City's Dennis Leonard in his first at-bat of the season. Reality then set in again. Ripken went 1-for-21 in his next seven games. Heading into May 2, he was batting .117 (7-for-60) with only four hits post-Opening Day. Yet Weaver kept putting him in the lineup. Every day.

On May 30, after Ripken sat in the second game of a double-header the previous day, Weaver started him at third base—certainly unaware at the time that Ripken would be in the Orioles' starting lineup for the next 16-plus years. Another huge development in Ripken's career occurred on June 22, 1982, when he started a game at shortstop instead of third base. He made seven more starts at third and then on July 1 started at short again—this time for an extended trial. "If we wait much longer, then we'll never find out how good he might be as a shortstop," Weaver said at the time.

It was an unconventional decision, considering Ripken's size. But Weaver felt Ripken had the arm strength and instincts to play the position. He was right. Shortstop is where Ripken would remain until officially switching back to third base in 1997, when the club signed free agent shortstop Mike Bordick. Ripken eventually won two Gold Gloves, two MVPs, and eight Silver Sluggers as a short-stop. He was selected to 19 consecutive All-Star Games, winning two All-Star MVP awards, including one in his final Midsummer Classic in 2001 when he homered against Chan Ho Park in his first at-bat. Ripken compiled 3,184 hits and 431 homers in a Hall of Fame career—and revolutionized the position, paving the way for bigger players such as Derek Jeter, Alex Rodriguez, and Troy Tulowitzki to thrive in the spot. He also set the tone for the Orioles in the clubhouse and off the field, making time for teammates and fans throughout his career. "Baseball-wise, everybody knows what he is. But he is a great person also," said former Orioles teammate and fellow native Marylander Harold Baines. "He is a very giving man. He gives of himself more than most major league players would. He has that great foundation that he still has here. He still lives in the area, so that shows how much he loves being here."

Yet for all the platitudes about the person and the player, Ripken's career was defined by—or at least will forever be remembered for—his incomparable consecutive games-played streak and the night in which the Iron Horse moved over to make room for the Iron Man.

4 The Streak

The record itself is expected to live on forever. The images from September 6, 1995, though, also appear frozen in time. There's Cal Ripken Jr. swinging at a Shawn Boskie pitch in the fourth inning and sending the ball hurtling into the night, a teaser for what would be a most magical evening. There's the iconic unfurling of the illuminated numbers—2,131—on the B&O Warehouse beyond right field at Oriole Park at Camden Yards in the middle of the fifth.

There's Ripken sharing an embrace with his wife and kids— heart-tugging and then funny when five-year-old Rachel wipes away her famous father's kiss for the world to see. There's the famous son pointing up to a skybox and his father, Cal Sr., clapping and gesturing back down. There's Rafael Palmeiro and Bobby Bonilla pushing Ripken out of the dugout to properly thank the frenzied crowd. And then there was "The Lap."

Like "The Streak," "The Lap" doesn't need further explanation in the minds of Orioles fans. Ripken's hand-slapping, tear-inducing victory lap around the edge of the stands that night contributed

Orioles announcer Jon Miller introduces Cal Ripken Jr. to the Camden Yards crowd in 1995 after the "Iron Man" tied Lou Gehrig's streak of consecutive games played.

to the most celebrated 22-minute, 15-second delay in team (and probably) baseball history. "It was more intimate," Ripken said hours after his impromptu and now iconic jog in the middle of the fifth inning. "Being there and seeing the enthusiasm was really meaningful." In a piece for *The Baltimore Sun* marking the 20th anniversary of Camden Yards in 2012, Ripken's lap was named the most memorable moment in the stadium's history. It likely will get top billing in 2042 and 2092 as well.

That day, that month, that year, everyone wanted a piece of Ripken, who had been moving toward Hall of Famer Lou Gehrig's seemingly unbreakable record of 2,130 consecutive games played, which started for Ripken in May 1982. He finally arrived there in September 1995. On the record-eclipsing night, Gehrig's New York Yankees teammate, Hall of Famer Joe DiMaggio, was in attendance, as was president Bill Clinton and vice president Al Gore—the first time the country's top two executives had ever attended a baseball game together outside of Washington D.C.

ESPN televised the game and broadcast the lap in almost complete silence—with the loquacious Chris Berman saying only, "A moment that will live for 2,131 years." The soundtrack was provided by unyielding cheers from the sold-out crowd of 46,272 and composer John Tesh's stirring "Day One." It was a celebration of work ethic and determination more than just athletic achievement. As Clinton told Berman during the ESPN telecast, "These stands tonight are full of people who never get recognized but show up every day. These are the people who make America. Cal Ripken, in a funny way, has made heroes of all of them."

The true irony of Cal Ripken Jr.'s Iron Man streak is that it was a lunch-pail accomplishment—what you're supposed to do in any profession. Showing up is not something that is usually feted. But baseball needed a celebration in 1995. Ripken's record-breaker happened roughly one year after Major League Baseball and its

Ripken's A through Z (Aase to Zito)

In his career, which spanned from 1981 to 2001, Orioles Hall of Famer Cal Ripken Jr. amassed 3,184 hits against 813 pitchers. Using the first letter of the surnames of the opposing pitchers, Ripken registered hits against every letter of the alphabet with the exception of X.

He got two against former teammate Don Aase and two hits against Barry Zito—with 811 pitchers, alphabetically, in the middle.

Technically he got all 26 letters if you include his four hits against Xavier Hernandez. But if we are only counting last names, then X is the lone escapee.

Ripken picked up hits against 79 pitchers whose last names ended in S, 77 that ended in M, and 75 that ended in B. He got hits against eight Joneses, seven Williamses, and six Johnsons, though he also got hits against a Johnstone, a Johns, and a John. He managed to victimize just three Smiths (and one Smithson).

Here is how many hits he recorded against the hard-to-get letters.

I
Mike Ignasiak (1 hit)
Hideki Irabu (2)
Daryl Irvine (3)

Q
Paul Quantrill (7)
Dan Quisenberry (6)

U
Jerry Ujdur (2)
Pat Underwood (1)
Tom Underwood (1)
Ugueth Urbina (1)

Y
Esteban Yan (2)
Rich Yett (2)
Curt Young (10)
Matt Young (10)

Z
Geoff Zahn (5)
Victor Zambrano (1)
Jeff Zimmerman (1)
Barry Zito (2)

commissioner, Bud Selig, canceled the 1994 World Series due to labor strife. It's often been proclaimed that Ripken helped save baseball, that he brought fans back to a sport that they felt had betrayed them over a money squabble between two well-heeled factions. Ripken has always been uncomfortable with the "saved baseball" talk, but there's no question his record—and the way he handled the accolades and pressure—was the first true olive branch offered by baseball to its fans. "A lot of people were just looking for something good in baseball," Ripken said. "People were upset and angry and mad about that, but at the same time, it's proven that you can come back to the game. But when people came back to the game they were looking for something they could relate to that was good. And it just so happened that the streak was first and foremost."

Selig, for one, won't downplay Ripken's major role in the sport's revitalization. "The night itself had so much significance," Selig said years later. "For historians who will review this, as people are always doing with baseball, the night of September 6, 1995, cannot be underestimated. People can read what they want to read into it, but it can never be underestimated."

The following year, on June 14, 1996, Ripken passed Japan's Sachio Kinugasa for the world record of 2,216 consecutive games played. Ripken continued his games-played streak until finally choosing to sit on September 20, 1998, the Orioles' home finale in a lost season. Ultimately, Ripken's Iron Man streak ended at 2,632 games—an unfathomable number that appears to be unbreakable. "He was the perfect guy," said Brady Anderson, Ripken's best friend and former teammate. "It was coming after the year we missed the World Series. And he is such an admirable person and player, a guy with a real, American, down-in-the-trenches work ethic. A superstar, still, but that work ethic and being well-spoken, he was the perfect representative for baseball."

Former Oriole Miguel Tejada got the closest of anyone after Ripken, ending his streak of 1,152 games played in June 2007 due to a fractured wrist. It was the fifth longest streak in MLB history. No one else has come within 2,000 games of Ripken's mark since Tejada. Texas Rangers first baseman Prince Fielder had been the active leader with 547 before neck surgery ended his season in May 2014. Fielder would have had to play nearly 13 more seasons without missing a game to catch The Iron Man. That further puts Ripken's streak in perspective. Yet it was the climate of baseball in 1995 and Ripken's reputation as the ultimate professional that make the streak so revered. "It wasn't me in particular. It was the timing. It was something good for baseball that people wanted to embrace," Ripken said. "If you get a little bit deeper, I think we all look back at baseball as a sport, not as a business. And because there was a connection to Lou Gehrig, there was sort of a feeling of nostalgia, when it was a sport, and there was a personal relationship between the fans and the players. And I think that had something to do with it, kind of taking you back [to those times]."

5 Frank Robinson

Frank Robinson has heard the same proclamation for roughly five decades—even from his close pal and former Orioles teammate, Brooks Robinson. And he still bristles every time it's mentioned because he won't subscribe to the common belief that the trade that brought him to Baltimore from the Cincinnati Reds in 1965 forever changed the Orioles franchise. "That's just Brooks being Brooks, being nice. No one person wins championships," Robinson said. "I was probably the missing ingredient for that team to put them over the top. That's the way I looked at it when I came here. I said, 'If I go over there and do my part, they are a pretty good ballclub now, [and] we have a good chance to win.' And that's the way I approached it."

The reality, of course, is that Robinson, the 1961 National League MVP and 1956 NL Rookie of the Year, joined the Orioles when he was supposedly on the downside of his career. And the Orioles, a franchise that had never made the playoffs, suddenly were in four of the next six World Series. Certainly, that's more than just coincidence and fortunate timing. "We were already a pretty good ballclub. It's just that Frank made everybody better. That's what Frank Robinsons do," Hall of Fame pitcher Jim Palmer said. "He was the barometer for where we wanted to go."

The 1965 Orioles won 94 games and finished third in the American League. They had six pitchers with both double-digit victories and ERAs under 3.40, but only one player, Rookie of the Year Curt Blefary, had hit more than 18 homers that season. Meanwhile, the 1965 Cincinnati Reds scored 100 more runs than any other club in the NL but had the league's second worst ERA. There was an obvious fit between the two clubs and they began working on a trade in the offseason. The talks continued after general manager Lee MacPhail left in November and Harry Dalton took over. In the first week of December, the Orioles made two fairly minor trades, acquiring outfielder Dick Simpson from the California Angels and reliever Jack Baldschun from the Philadelphia Phillies. Then, on December 9, 1965, the Orioles orchestrated their blockbuster, sending Simpson, Baldschun, and established, 26-year-old right-hander Milt Pappas to the Reds for Robinson, the 30-year-old All-Star. Robinson was coming off a season in which he hit .296 with 33 homers and 113 RBIs, but there were some questions about his take-no-prisoners attitude and prior off-the-field incidents. "When we got Frank, none of us really knew what to expect. We had heard all the stories about all the problems he had had over there in Cincinnati and all that," Orioles slugger Boog Powell said. "So we just didn't know what to expect."

They soon learned. On the first day of spring training, Powell said he and catcher Andy Etchebarren watched Robinson crush a ball into the trees that lined Miami Stadium. "He rattles one into the coconut trees there in Miami, and I looked over to Etch and I said, 'Etch, I think it's all over. I think we just won it,'" Powell said. "And we did."

The Kangaroo Court

The Orioles from the great 1960s and early 1970s teams like to talk about how much fun they had during those years. They hung out together, they played baseball together, and they won together. And after they won, they'd have even more fun.

The Orioles had a Kangaroo Court in those years led by Frank Robinson, who was the judge. He'd wear a mop on his head and preside over the various infractions and allegations presented by the club's players. Overthrow a cutoff man, miss a sign, or boast in the newspaper and you'd get fined—and have your day in court. "If a guy yawned, or if a guy wasn't out on the bench on time, or if a guy didn't do this or that or whatever, you could bring it up," Orioles Hall of Famer Jim Palmer said. "It kind of kept you in line, but it only happened when you won."

Palmer remembers a classic exchange between Curt Motton and Chico Salmon on opposite sides of the clubhouse. They were arguing over a proposed fine when Salmon accused Motton of collusion. "And Motton says, 'Don't accuse me of something you can't spell.' And here is Chico trying to spell it," Palmer recalled.

There were a lot of laughs. And lots of props, like a toilet seat painted red that was known as "The Don Buford Red Ass Award." "We had the Kangaroo Court every time we won. And we wanted to have Kangaroo Court every night," first baseman Boog Powell said. "When we didn't win and we didn't have Kangaroo Court we were really disappointed."

He was such a competitor that opposing managers and infielders implored their pitchers not to plunk Robinson. Because if they did, Robinson's resolve would strengthen, and he'd either homer in retaliation or slide spikes up into second the next time he was on base. Well, Bill DeWitt Sr., the owner and general manager of the Reds, threw the ultimate verbal beanball several months after dealing Robinson to the Orioles. To justify the move—which was criticized then and is now considered one of the most lopsided in baseball history—DeWitt said: "Frank Robinson is not a young 30." Over the years the quote has been simplified; basically DeWitt called Robinson an old 30-year-old. "Frank might have been 30, but he certainly wasn't an old 30. Bill DeWitt traded him, so what is he going to say?" Palmer said. "You end up trading a guy who hits 586 home runs and won the Triple Crown. Is he going to say, 'I misjudged him?' No."

In April of 1966, Robinson quipped: "It seems I suddenly got old last fall between the end of the season and December 9th." The bear had been poked. Robinson won the 1966 American League Triple Crown with 49 homers, 122 RBIs, and a .316 average. That season he became—and still remains—the only player to have won MVP awards in both leagues. He also led the Orioles to a sweep in the 1966 World Series and captured the World Series MVP Award. His 586 career home runs are ninth all time in baseball history. Pappas, in contrast, lasted two-plus years with the Reds (30–29, 4.04 ERA) before being traded away; the other players in the deal made no impact at all in Cincinnati. But as much as Robinson added on the field for the Orioles, it was his demeanor that caused a seismic shift. "Frank brought an air of nastiness with him," Powell said. "We all had friends on the other side, and everybody was hugging and things like that [before the game], and Frank goes, 'What the hell is this? Don't talk to those guys. You can talk to those guys after the game, take them out to dinner, do whatever you want to do. But before the game, don't talk to them. Let's just go out there and beat their ass.' And that's what we were all about."

What the Orioles received from the Reds was not only a superb athlete—he played high school basketball with NBA legend Bill Russell—but a supremely driven competitor who would run into stands for balls or go barreling into second base to break up a double play. In essence, the Orioles' most talented player was also their hardest worker. And that rubbed off on everyone. "That was a part of my personality. That was instilled in me when I was a youngster in Oakland, California, in the sandlots by my coach George Powles. He taught me the way to play the game," Robinson said. "Play it to win. Play it to do things to help your teammates and help your team in any way you possibly can. This is why, to me, when I got to first base, my job on a ground ball was to take the shortstop or the second baseman out...I didn't come in here and say, 'This is the way we are going to play.' I just went out there and played that way myself, and they picked it up."

Robinson spent only six of his 21 big league seasons with the Orioles—he played 10 with the Reds—but when he was inducted into the Hall of Fame in his first year of eligibility in 1982, he went in as an Oriole. He has a statue at Camden Yards and at Great American Ball Park in Cincinnati. Robinson made an impact beyond the playing field as well. He broke baseball's managerial color barrier in 1975 when he became a player-manager with the Cleveland Indians. He also was the first African American manager in the National League in 1981 with the San Francisco Giants and won the AL Manager of the Year Award in 1989 with the Orioles. He worked in Baltimore's front office as an assistant general manager and as a vice president for Major League Baseball. He also has been a resounding voice for civil rights, including exposing the then-segregated and bigoted real estate industry in Baltimore when he was a player.

His legacy is multi-faceted. But his impact on the Orioles' franchise is unmistakable, even if he downplays it. He turned a good club into a perennial powerhouse, starting with his seminal 1966 season. "Frank brought that extra ingredient along to us," Powell said. "And having 49 home runs and driving in 122 runs and winning the Triple Crown wasn't too shabby either."

Jim Palmer

During an Orioles' off day in 1978, left-hander Scott McGregor hosted a cookout at his new Cockeysville townhouse. Most of the players and their families attended, played wiffle ball, and ate burgers and hot dogs. Since it was a new property, McGregor's lawn was a work in progress. "You know how construction guys are, they'll sod over anything, dead bodies, pieces of wood," McGregor joked. "So my lawn was really uneven." That fact bothered Orioles star right-hander Jim Palmer—immensely. McGregor said Palmer spent much of the day complaining about McGregor's lawn. The next morning McGregor woke up to a strange sound. When he looked out his window, he was astonished to see Palmer, the three-time American League Cy Young Award winner, landscaping. "Palmer's got a rototiller in my front lawn and he's doing my whole lawn. There's a sod truck there, and he laid down a lawn for me. I go, 'Really?'" recalled McGregor. "He just has a big heart. He was something."

When reminded of the story, Palmer smiled sheepishly and explained that that's what happens when you obsess over details. Palmer's obsession for doing things the right way served him well.

He became an eight-time 20-game winner, a first-ballot Hall of Famer in 1990, and the franchise's greatest pitcher. "If I had one game to win, he was my guy," former first baseman Boog Powell said. "I'd pick Jim Palmer."

At 6'3" with a blazing fastball and a high leg kick that would be mimicked for a generation in Baltimore, Palmer embodied all that a starting pitcher should be: long, lean, athletic, smart, articulate, intense, driven, and confident. It was as if he were constructed in a starting pitching factory, though as a high schooler in Scottsdale, Arizona, he wanted to play college basketball and had a scholarship offer to UCLA, among other schools. Palmer had led the state in scoring his senior year and felt basketball presented more of a challenge. "I loved it, and it was hard to play. I had to work at basketball," said Palmer, who was all-state in baseball, basketball, and as a wide receiver in football. "Not that I didn't work at pitching, but it came naturally." In 1963 Palmer played in a college summer league in South Dakota on a team sponsored by the Orioles. In the league's finale, Orioles farm director Harry Dalton watched Palmer pitch an inning, picking up two strikeouts and a ground out, and gave the okay to be aggressive in signing him. After that game, however, disaster nearly struck. Two carloads of players from the league were driving back to Arizona, taking turns driving through the night. Palmer was sleeping in the backseat of his red Corvair when the driver fell asleep at the wheel, lost control of the car, and flipped it three times. The Corvair was demolished, but there were no serious injuries. Palmer banged his head and cut his knee, but otherwise, miraculously, was fine. Shortly after he finally arrived home, the 17-year-old agreed to a $50,000 signing bonus with the Orioles.

Within two years Palmer was in the big leagues, debuting at Boston's Fenway Park in relief of his first roommate, Hall of Famer Robin Roberts. The first batter he faced, future Hall of

Palmer's Lack of Grand Slams

In his 19-season career with the Orioles, Jim Palmer put up some phenomenal numbers. Four times he pitched at least 300 innings in a season. Eight times he made at least 30 starts and posted an ERA under 3.00. There are the three Cy Young Awards, the 2,212 strikeouts, and the eight 20-win campaigns.

But nothing is connected to Palmer's legacy quite like this number: 0. That's how many grand slams he allowed in 3,948 regular season innings and another 124⅓ postseason innings. Combined, Palmer pitched in 575 regular season and postseason games and never once served up a granny. "It's very impressive to me," said former Orioles catcher Andy Etchebarren. "How can you pitch that long and never throw a grand slam home run?"

In the regular season, Palmer faced bases-loaded situations 213 times. He allowed 30 singles, five doubles, one triple, and 13 walks while striking out 40. Opponents hit .196 against him with the bases loaded. "What is one of the keys to starting? Stay away from big innings," Palmer said. "I was pretty good at math. Four was not a good number—unless you were Earl Weaver, and it was on the back of your uniform."

Legend has it that Palmer never gave up a grand slam in his professional career. That's not entirely true. According to a story in *The Baltimore Sun* written when the right-hander went into the Hall of Fame in 1990, Palmer yielded two slams as a pro. One was in spring training, and it was hit by the most improbable of characters: 5'5" infielder Freddie Patek, who didn't have a regular-season grand slam in a 14-year career.

The other was at Triple A in 1967 when Palmer was trying to pitch through a right shoulder injury. He gave up a blast—Palmer estimated it went about 450 feet—to future Hall of Famer Johnny Bench. Palmer said giving up four runs on that one swing "left a very, very negative imprint."

So he vowed not to do it again. "He wasn't going to give one up. He said one is better than four. I'll walk him before I give one up," fellow Orioles starter Scott McGregor said. "But one thing about Jimmy and what made him so good is that whenever he got in trouble he would just throw a little bit harder to better spots."

> Orioles catcher Rick Dempsey said that Palmer was very
> cognizant of the accomplishment and that he'd pitch particularly
> carefully to renowned sluggers with the bases loaded.
>
> "He would never say it, but he would unintentionally walk the guy
> (with power) and go to the next guy," Dempsey said. "I can remember
> that for years before he retired he was always focused on never giving
> up a grand slam. It was something he thought about way ahead of
> time."
>
> Palmer said not giving up a grand slam wasn't a career goal; it's
> just that he didn't want to ever allow it to occur because of how it
> could affect the outcome of a game. That, he said, was his motivation.
>
> "Grand slams," Palmer said, "are like somebody just hit your
> whole team in the face with a door."

Famer Carl Yastrzemski, walked—typical of a young Palmer,
who worked for years to master his command. He allowed two
inherited runners to score (on a single by future Orioles executive Lee Thomas), but otherwise threw two scoreless innings.
Palmer pitched in 27 games and made six starts that season—all
at age 19. The next year Palmer started 30 regular season games,
going 15–10 with a 3.46 ERA. His welcome-to-stardom moment
was Game 2 of the 1966 World Series when he blanked the Los
Angeles Dodgers for nine innings, allowing just four hits, and
outpitched Sandy Koufax in the Hall of Fame lefty's final major
league outing. At 20 Palmer was the youngest pitcher in World
Series history to throw a shutout. "Jimmy could blow you away,
but he had a knack of taking on and putting off on his fastball,"
Powell said. "He could throw 95 or 91 or he could throw 89. And
he could paint the corners."

It was around that time when the superstitious Palmer picked
up his enduring nickname "Cakes" because he'd often eat pancakes
on the morning before he pitched. With his All-American good
looks, engaging personality, and abundant talent, Palmer was

primed for a splendid career; then it took a sudden detour. Arm injuries cost him most of 1967 and all of 1968. He tried to pitch through right shoulder pain and ultimately tore his rotator cuff—often a death knell for pitchers. Because of the injury, the Orioles left him unprotected for the expansion draft in October 1968, and the Kansas City Royals and Seattle Pilots passed.

The sense was that Palmer's promising career might be over at 23. With a fastball in the low 80s, he allowed 10 runs in his final instructional league game that fall. Pitching coach George Bamberger told Palmer to give pitching one more shot in winter ball in Puerto Rico. With a flight set for a Thursday morning, Palmer attended a Baltimore Bullets game on a Wednesday night. He sat with a group of friends, which included a pharmaceutical company representative. The friend suggested Palmer try Indocin, a non-steroidal, anti-inflammatory drug for his shoulder discomfort and gave him a bag of it at halftime. The next morning Palmer flew to Puerto Rico, taking an Indocin tablet with each meal that day. In his next throwing session, his fastball jumped back to the mid-90s. The inflammation was gone. "It was the most amazing thing in the world. It was like somebody gave me a whole new life," Palmer said. "I went 6–0 and threw a no-hitter [in winter ball], went to spring training, made the Orioles, and the rest is history." Palmer was 16–4 with a 2.34 ERA in 1969. The next year he threw 305 innings and started a run of 20 or more wins in eight of nine seasons. Ultimately, Palmer pitched 19 seasons, winning a franchise-record 268 games. He threw nearly 4,000 regular-season innings, posting a sparkling 2.86 career ERA. "Imagine if I don't go to that Bullets game," he said.

Palmer is the only Oriole to play in all six of the franchise's World Series and he's the only pitcher in history to record a World Series victory in three different decades. His thirst for winning was admired by teammates but also could be a source of conflict. He'd rankle some by stepping off the mound to position his defenders. A four-time Gold Glover, Palmer wasn't afraid to challenge teammates to play better defense. He did that in 1981 with third baseman Doug DeCinces, who was quoted by *The Baltimore Sun* as saying, "What gives him the right to downgrade everyone who plays behind him?" Palmer's most frequent sparring partner was manager Earl Weaver. They feuded even after they retired, though they played golf together and maintained professional respect. Palmer disliked Weaver's abrasive, unrelenting style, and Weaver questioned Palmer's willingness to pitch through discomfort. Both later admitted they wouldn't have been as successful without the other.

Although he could be demanding, Palmer also was generous with his time, money, and knowledge. Outfielder Gary Roenicke was a first-year Oriole in 1978 when Palmer approached him "with a brand new full-length leather coat. And he says, 'You are about my size. Here, take this.' And he gives me a $500 or whatever-it-was coat," Roenicke said, laughing. "Yeah, he always treated me well." Teammates that wanted to learn more about the game flocked to him. "Jim Palmer was probably the biggest influence on me of anybody in baseball," catcher Rick Dempsey said. "He was a teammate, but he was a teacher." McGregor, Mike Flanagan, and Dennis Martinez would constantly pick Palmer's brain. "He would teach us how to get through a game and what to do in certain situations and how to watch things," McGregor said. "He didn't try to make us pitch like him. He was a wealth. He still is."

After his playing career ended in 1984—an attempted comeback at age 45 in 1991 ended with a torn hamstring in spring training—Palmer became one of baseball's most highly regarded analysts with his keen observations and brutal honesty. He's appeared in movies, including the classic comedy, *Naked Gun,* and was a spokesman for various businesses. Most famous, of course, was his underwear modeling campaign for Jockey. "That was a guy that took advantage of what God gave him. That's all it was. He was a character in baseball in his own right," Dempsey said. "You become an icon for doing things like that. And he was literate, he could talk, he was funny, he was a really good looking guy. But above everything he was a great pitcher."

7 Visit Oriole Park at Camden Yards

The Orioles organization refers to its home—Oriole Park at Camden Yards—as "The Ballpark That Forever Changed Baseball." Pompous, perhaps, but it's hard to argue with the sentiment. If you are a baseball fan and if your city has a downtown, baseball-only stadium that has a retro vibe with modern amenities, then you might want to send a thank you card to the Orioles for thinking out of the box, for eschewing a larger, impersonal structure, and for creating an intimate ballpark that seems like the city was built around it.

If you are a baseball fan, you need to take in at least one game at Camden Yards. And you'll be struck by how it simultaneously feels new and old. "I love it. I still love every minute of going down there to this day," said former catcher Chris Hoiles, who played 10 seasons for the Orioles, including his final seven at Camden Yards. "Being able to call that home is still an honor years later. There have been some aesthetic changes, but it's still Camden Yards. It was a trendsetter in the game of baseball, and those that have been built since were built to model after that ballpark. It's a huge tribute to the Orioles and to the people that built it."

On May 2, 1988—as part of Fantastic Fans Night when the Orioles returned to Memorial Stadium after dropping a record 23 of their first 24 games of the season—Baltimore mayor William Donald Schaefer announced that club owner Edward Bennett Williams and the Maryland Stadium Authority had agreed to a long-term lease for a new downtown stadium just west of the Inner Harbor at the old Camden Yards rail station. It was bittersweet news. It meant that Baltimore's fans would keep their beloved Orioles, a legitimate fear because they had lost the NFL's Colts to Indianapolis four years earlier. But it also meant that Memorial Stadium, the iconic—albeit dingy—ballpark that had housed so many great sporting memories, would be no more.

What fans didn't realize at the time was just how tremendous the new park would be. Initially, the new stadium in Baltimore was going to be similar to the one the HOK Sports architects had created for the Chicago White Sox in 1991. But Orioles team president Larry Lucchino rejected that design. He wanted something distinctively Baltimore, a baseball-only stadium with the charm of yesteryear. With an assist from the vision of architect Janet Marie Smith, Lucchino got his wish: a brick facade that meshed perfectly with the B&O Warehouse wall that would loom over the right-field scoreboard, and green seats that seemed to be an extension of the impeccably green grass on the asymmetrical field. Odes to long-gone treasures such as the Polo Grounds and Ebbets Field were ever-present.

And, somehow, all of it came together in a construction period of 33 months. "I was wondering how they were ever going to get the place built. I thought there was no way they are going to get all this crap out of here. There was lumber and steel and stuff in the walkways. It was all over," said former Orioles slugger Boog Powell, who has run Boog's Barbecue at Camden Yards since the stadium opened. "And when Opening Day [1992] came, there wasn't anything left. How they did it, I'll never know. But it was beautiful. And I think it is just as beautiful today as it was when it opened."

The fans ate up the new stadium, drawing 3.57 million that first year, up more than a million from the final season at Memorial Stadium in 1991. From 1992 to 1993, the Orioles set a major league record with 65 straight sellouts. In 1997 the attendance peaked at 3.71 million. Over time with the franchise's continual losing, the attendance dropped, plummeting to 1.73 million in 2010. Yet despite the on-field product, the park is continually chosen as one of the best in baseball. And those that often receive higher marks, such as PNC Park in Pittsburgh and AT&T Park in San Francisco, were unquestionably influenced by Camden Yards. Since Baltimore's jewel opened on April 6, 1992, 20 other MLB ballparks have been built, and most have that retro classic feel. So, incredibly, Camden Yards is now the 10th oldest big league ballpark in the majors.

For Camden Yards' 20th anniversary in 2012, several improvements were made, including the addition of a rooftop bar above center field and the Hall of Fame statues beyond the batter's eye wall. Unfortunately, the magnificent view of the city's skyline—including the Bromo-Seltzer Tower on Eutaw Street—has been blocked by the Hilton Baltimore, which opened in 2008. Inside the park, however, it still looks like 1992—or earlier. The advertising is minimal and must fit in with the park's interior. Ownership has refused to sell naming rights despite the millions it would bring in. It's just old-fashioned Oriole Park at Camden Yards. "I marvel at its modern retro feel. You see green everywhere. When you come in here, you see green. You know how unusual that it is?" Orioles manager Buck Showalter said. "In the offseason when I'm here, I see all the improvements. They redo all the seats, they are constantly adding stuff. It's clean, it's safe, it's ahead of its time."

8 The Earl of Baltimore

Andy Etchebarren was a 19-year-old catcher for the Orioles' Eastern League affiliate in Elmira, New York, when 31-year-old manager Earl Weaver approached him on the mound one evening, loitering long enough to bait the umpire for his shaky strike zone and prompt an ejection. "Weaver threw up his arms and he fell on the mound like he had had a heart attack. And they made the paramedics come and get him. He just laid there," Etchebarren said. "I knew he didn't have a heart attack. I knew exactly what he was doing."

What he was doing was being Earl, years before he was a household name, decades before he was a YouTube sensation. Weaver took the Orioles to four World Series in 17 seasons—winning once in 1970. The most decorated manager in modern Orioles history, Weaver was always ticked at the umps, always believing they targeted his teams. He was ejected 94 times—third most all time—in the big leagues. His antics were legendary: expletive-spewing, dirt-kicking, hat-turning, rule-book-ripping craziness that exhilarated the home crowd. But he's also the only manager to post 100 or more wins in his first three full years, and his .583 winning percentage (1,480–1,060) is ninth highest all time and second best for those who managed after 1955. "If he wasn't the greatest manager ever, he was up there," said Steve Stone, the 1980 American League Cy Young Award winner under Weaver. "He wasn't the easiest guy to play for, but he was as good as they came. You could go into every game understanding you were never going to get out-managed."

Umpires weren't the only ones subjected to Weaver's constant criticism. He'd continually rip his players—often in front of the whole team. His veteran clubs did a solid job of ignoring Weaver's

rants, but younger players were more shell-shocked and more com-
bative. Bobby Grich once threw Weaver down the dugout steps
and didn't miss an at-bat. Doug DeCinces needed a police officer
to separate him from Weaver during the first game of a doubleheader. DeCinces started the nightcap. Catcher Rick Dempsey,
one of Weaver's most frequent whipping boys, lost count of the
times he was supposedly pulled from the lineup. "I never hated Earl
really. I hated the way he acted all the time. He would get really
belligerent. He would get mean and nasty," Dempsey said. "He'd
scream at you in front of everybody. He was miserable in that
respect. But playing for Earl was the best thing that really happened
to me in the game. I loved him because he never played favorites.
If you were supposed to be in the lineup, he never held a grudge.
You'd be in that lineup." Weaver's philosophy was winning. He
wanted his epitaph to read, "The sorest loser that ever lived."

Growing up in St. Louis, he had an odd, early connection to
the big leagues: his father's dry-cleaning business laundered the uniforms for the hometown Cardinals and Browns. As a 17-year-old in
1948, Weaver signed a deal with the Cardinals for a $1,500 bonus.
The 5'7", 180-pound second baseman played more than a decade
in the minors, never reaching the big leagues. A good fielder he
was a .267 career hitter primarily in Low A and Double A. Orioles
Hall of Fame pitcher Jim Palmer used to tweak Weaver by saying
the only thing he knew about pitching was that he couldn't hit it.
Weaver, though, knew early on which managerial buttons to push.
Orioles executive Harry Dalton recognized that. At age 26 Weaver
was hired to be the player/manager of the organization's Class D
affiliate in Fitzgerald, Georgia. After a rough first season at the
lowest rung, Weaver never again had a losing record in the minors,
plying his craft in Dublin, Georgia; Aberdeen, South Dakota;
Appleton, Wisconsin; and Elmira before eventually making it to
Triple A Rochester, New York. Dalton, then the organization's
farm director, told *The Baltimore Sun* in 1961 that Weaver was,

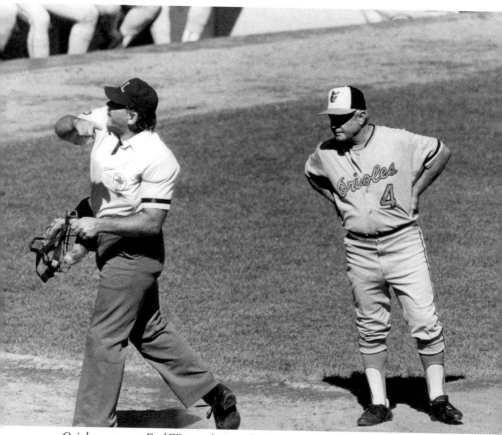

Orioles manager Earl Weaver, known for his arguments with umpires that led to 94 major league ejections, is thrown out of a game in 1980.

"colorful and aggressive. Once he charged an opponent's dugout with a flying tackle, hit a post, and wound up in the hospital with a shoulder separation. But he has mellowed some lately, and that is good." A year later Weaver faked a heart attack to make a point. Within a decade he was unleashed on the majors.

Dalton promoted Weaver to be the Orioles' first-base coach in 1968. The die was cast. After winning the World Series in 1966, the club fell to sixth place in 1967. When it finished the first half of 1968 with a 43–37 record, 10½ games behind first-place Detroit,

Dalton made a change. He fired Hank Bauer and replaced him with Weaver. The Orioles won their first six games under Weaver, finishing the season with a 48–34 record. It started a trend. Weaver didn't have a losing season from 1968 until he first retired in 1982 at age 52. When Orioles owner Edward Bennett Williams coaxed him out of retirement in the middle of 1985, Weaver's team posted a 53–52 record. In 1986 it dropped to 73–89—his only losing campaign—and he walked away for good at 56. He twice retired but was never fired.

Weaver was a pioneer in many ways. Known for his simple philosophy of pitching, defense, and the three-run homer, his teams also consistently drew walks and rarely ran into outs. He was a master at using his bench and pushed his starting pitching to last deep into games. Weaver wasn't afraid to defy convention like

Ejected in Doubleheaders

Fifteen times in baseball history a player or manager has been ejected in both ends of a doubleheader. Orioles manager Earl Weaver is the only one to have done it twice.

(07/21/1963), **Walter Alston**, Los Angeles Dodgers
(07/28/1915), **Jim Bluejacket**, player, Brooklyn Tip-Tops (Federal League)
(08/04/1897), **Jesse Burkett**, player, Cleveland Spiders
(06/14/1982), **Enos Cabell**, player, Detroit Tigers
(08/16/1906), **Mike Donlin**, player, New York Giants
(06/06/1954), **Jimmy Dykes**, Baltimore Orioles
(07/27/1946), **Frankie Frisch**, Pittsburgh Pirates
(07/14/1974), **Billy Martin**, Texas Rangers
(06/09/1946), **Mel Ott**, New York Giants
(08/07/1956), **Dave Philley**, player, Chicago White Sox
(08/03/1958), **Paul Richards**, Baltimore Orioles
(09/04/1911), **Fred Tenney**, Boston Rustlers
(08/04/1963), **Johnny Keane**, St. Louis Cardinals
(08/15/1975), **Earl Weaver**, Baltimore Orioles
(09/29/1985), **Earl Weaver**, Baltimore Orioles

putting eventual Hall of Famer Cal Ripken Jr. at shortstop, though the 6'4" player was considered too big for the position. Weaver continually mined the most out of veterans past their primes and youngsters deemed not quite ready. "Playing for Earl Weaver was the most important thing that could happen to me personally," said right-hander Dennis Martinez, who debuted at age 22 for Weaver in 1976 and ultimately won 245 big league games. "He took out of me what I didn't know I had. That man made me the player I was."

Weaver used statistics as a tool long before it was commonplace. He kept a stack of yellowing index cards that included batter vs. pitcher histories. He juggled lineups to focus on players' strengths. "You could be 10-for-10," Dempsey said. "But if you didn't have good numbers against the guy on the mound that day, you were sitting your butt on the bench."

No matter the successes, Weaver forever will be known for going nuts on umpires. Yes, he once got thrown out of a game in 1969 for smoking a cigarette in the dugout. The next day he delivered the lineup card to home plate with a candy cigarette dangling from his lips. Yes, he once ripped up a rulebook on the field. Yes, he was ejected from both ends of a doubleheader on two different occasions. Yes, he twice was given the thumb before the games even started. Yes, he pulled his team off the field and accepted a forfeit with the club just two-and-a-half games out of first place in September 1977 because he claimed there was a safety hazard in foul territory that the umpires wouldn't remove. Nothing, though, matches his Internet-preserved tirade in the first inning on September 17, 1980, thanks in part to umpire Bill Haller, who was wearing a hidden microphone. Haller called a balk on pitcher Mike Flanagan, and Weaver stormed to first base, accusing Haller of being there for one reason, "to f--- us." Weaver was immediately ejected, but the hilarious and profane discourse continued. Haller delivered the best line. When Weaver boasted that he'd end up in the Hall of Fame, Haller snapped, "Are you gonna be in the Hall of Fame for f----ing up World Series?" Flanagan later added a post-script to the scene that wasn't caught on camera. As Weaver walked off the field, he asked his pitcher if he had balked. Flanagan said he probably did, and Weaver cursed him out, too.

Weaver got the last laugh. He was inducted into the Hall of Fame in 1996, and his likeness was immortalized with a bronze statue—seven feet high—at Camden Yards in June 2012. Months later, on January 19, 2013, Weaver died while on a baseball-themed cruise in the Caribbean. He was 82. His death was announced that morning at the Orioles' annual winter FanFest. "Every time I look at an Oriole now," manager Buck Showalter said, "it's going to be missing a feather without Earl."

9 Steady Eddie

Former Oriole third baseman Doug DeCinces was with the California Angels in the early 1980s when his new team was battling with his old one in a tight contest. Young Orioles star Cal Ripken Jr. came to the plate, prompting a meeting at the mound. California's pitching coach told his hurler to be careful with Ripken and walk him if needed. DeCinces interrupted. "Don't do that," the veteran said. "Don't purposely bring up Eddie Murray with runners on." DeCinces was overruled. Ripken reached first. Then Murray quickly crushed a pitch for a homer to give the Orioles the lead. As Murray trotted toward third, DeCinces made his feelings known again. "I looked at Eddie and I said, 'I told them not to do that.'"

That's Eddie Clarence Murray in a snapshot. Those who don't know him, those who only observed him from afar, didn't get the complete picture. Despite being a future Hall of Famer, Murray was basically run out of Baltimore at age 32 after the club's disastrous 1988 season. There was a perception that he wasn't doing enough, wasn't working hard, wasn't getting his uniform dirty. He was openly criticized by owner Edward Bennett Williams, and as the negativity percolated, Murray dealt with growing overt racism from fans even at Memorial Stadium. When he was traded to the Los Angeles Dodgers for infielder Juan Bell and pitchers Brian Holton and Ken Howell (who was flipped to the Philadelphia Phillies for outfielder Phil Bradley) in December 1988, the 12-year relationship between Murray and Baltimore was officially severed. In his time with the Dodgers and later the New York Mets, Cleveland Indians, and Anaheim Angels, Murray just kept chugging along, steadily putting up Hall of Fame numbers in an easy, effortless way that was oft-criticized, oft-mischaracterized. "Eddie's work habits always looked sloppy. In his batting practices, he would just flip at the ball, hit a grounder to third base, or flip one over the infield. His last two or three swings he'd hit a couple of home runs, maybe, and have you wondering, *God, wasn't that a waste of time,*" said catcher Rick Dempsey. "Then with the game on the line, he'd take a nasty pitch and do that same line drive inside the bag or flick one over the guy's head at third base. And if you made a mistake, he would bomb you. Eddie Murray was amazing."

Murray is one of only four players in baseball history—and the only switch-hitter—to have at least 500 career home runs and 3,000 hits. Yet he never had more than 186 hits or 33 home runs in a season. He did, however, have 170 or more hits 12 times and 20 or more homers 16 times. He never won a Most Valuable Player award, but he finished in the top five in voting six times, including five straight years. "A quiet assassin is the best way to describe him," Dempsey said.

Murray grew up one of 12 children in an exceptionally close-knit and athletic family in Los Angeles. His brothers all played professional baseball. Murray's little league coach was a former minor leaguer; Murray shared a high school infield with future Hall of Famer Ozzie Smith. Murray seemed destined for baseball stardom. Yet when he made it to the majors in 1977, he was quiet and respectful, just looking to fit in. As a 21-year-old rookie, he hit 28 homers, batted .283, won the American League Rookie of the Year award, and played all but one game for a team that posted 97 wins. Almost immediately, Murray was looked at as a leader. "Initially, when that happened I didn't want to really believe it. We had people like Lee May on the club," Murray said. "You win people over by going out there every day. When they know that you're hurt and there's no bailing and you're out there fighting with them the next day, that does more than jumping up and saying anything in the locker room. But I was kind of amazed because I'm 21, 22, and you've got guys that were 30 looking up to you, and saying, 'No, Ed's running this team.'"

Murray was emerging into the national spotlight when the Orioles made the 1979 World Series. An incident that October would forever change how he dealt with his burgeoning profile. *New York Daily News* sportswriter Dick Young, known for his acerbic style and edgy copy, wrote a piece about Murray that included assertions that Murray's family harshly dismissed the scout who tried to sign him. There were allegations that one of his brothers attempted to hit the scout with his car. DeCinces, one of Murray's best friends on the 1979 team, remembers when Murray entered the clubhouse—with a World Series game to play that night—after the story ran. "He is upset and quiet. I said, 'Eddie, what's up?' And he flips over this article," DeCinces said. "This was a good family in L.A. that had all their kids going in the right direction. Were they a great family unit? Yes. Was it something like what Dick Young wrote? Absolutely not. But this was a national thing, what Dick Young wrote, and Eddie was so upset that he would never really talk to the press again. He'd say, 'You see the game, you write it. I'm not trusting you with anything in my life ever again.' And that's what it was."

Throughout the rest of his career, Murray's relationship with the media was practically non-existent. His common response to interview requests, "No, thank you, sir," became a running joke. It may have cost him as far as national prominence was concerned, but Murray preferred his privacy anyway. The writers, at least, didn't carry a grudge; Murray was named on 85.3 percent of the submitted Baseball Writers' Association of America (BBWAA) ballots in 2003, easily achieving the 75 percent needed for induction in his first year of Hall eligibility. Partially that was because his statistics were undeniable—504 homers, 3,255 hits, 1,917 RBIs, career .836 on-base plus slugging percentage (OPS)—but also because those who played with him continually testified to his ability, character, and clutch hitting. "Eddie was a fantastic teammate. I can't say anything bad about the guy," former Orioles outfielder Ken Singleton said. "I know he didn't get along with the press and that sort of thing, but as a teammate, he was wonderful."

When Tito Landrum was traded to the Orioles in 1983, he lived with Murray and would ride with him to Memorial Stadium every afternoon. They'd arrive early, Landrum said, because Murray dealt with an arthritic condition in his hands and would have to soak them in a balm hours before games. He kept that routine a secret because he wanted no excuses for his play. "He was one of those guys who was a team leader that you wanted to follow," Landrum said. "And he was hysterically funny with that little voice of his. I used to call him Darth Vader. He hated it. He used to chase me around the clubhouse. But he had a great sense of humor, great personality."

Between the time Brooks Robinson retired and Ripken Jr. emerged, Murray was the unquestioned fan favorite in Baltimore. Throughout area little leagues, there were countless kids mimicking Murray's distinctive batting stance—the front leg stretched, the upper body coiled in a crouch, the bat waving in slow circles. It sure worked for him. "I think it is very tough to hit standing straight up. I always thought a ball could beat me down low. And to me that's where the pitchers really throw the majority of their pitches—down low. And I felt like if I was in my crouch, I got to see more of that baseball." Then there was the chant every time he came to the plate: "Ed-Dee, Ed-Dee." At first it embarrassed him—too much attention for a young player. But that changed as he got older. He admitted to that during his Hall induction speech, which, of course, was punctuated with "Ed-Dee" cheers. "That Eddie chant, it took me a while to learn to deal with it. But I did. I loved it," he said.

Those chants went dormant in Baltimore from 1989 until July 1996, when the Orioles brought Murray back, primarily so he could hit his 500th homer in an Orioles uniform. He hit 10 home runs in two months, helped the club get to the playoffs for the first time in 13 years, and took it upon himself to bring the clubhouse together. Four days into his second tenure with the Orioles, Murray walked into manager Davey Johnson's office and said he would take care of cliques that had surfaced. "You had to break them up. You've got to play this game together," he said.

Perhaps the most important development that occurred in 1996 is that the fans embraced Murray again. The time apart healed the wounds. And when Murray was inducted into Cooperstown, thousands of Orioles fans made the trip. "A nice little sea of black and orange out there," Murray said during his induction speech. "It's a wonderful thing."

10 The New Beginning

After splitting a two-game series at Detroit in April 1954, the brand spanking new Orioles boarded an overnight train for Baltimore with the knowledge that they would meet their new fans the following morning. They didn't realize they'd soon be treated like kings of their new city. First, though, the kings had to assemble their regal vestments in rapidly moving dressing quarters. "We got in uniform on the train," said the modern-day franchise's first shortstop, Billy Hunter. "We got off right where [Oriole Park at Camden Yards] is now, the B&O train station. We got off with our clothes on hangers and [us] in our uniforms, got in convertibles and rode up the streets of Baltimore on the way to Memorial Stadium."

These new Orioles didn't know what to expect. But the city of Baltimore, which hadn't had a major league team since 1902, had been waiting breathlessly for this moment. The city had virtually shut down, schools were closed, and a parade route had been established in the 50-plus blocks from Camden Station to Memorial Stadium. Despite a cold drizzle, thousands of euphoric fans lined the streets on Thursday, April 15, 1954—baseball's new beginning in Baltimore. "They knew we weren't going to win the pennant, so they had the parade before the game rather than at the end of the season," Hunter joked.

That first day was some celebration. Richard Nixon, U.S. vice president at the time, threw out the first pitch. The crowd was announced at 46,994, which would be the largest at Memorial Stadium that year. And the fans left happy. The new club's ace, Bullet Bob Turley, threw a complete game, allowing just one run to the Chicago White Sox. Clint Courtney and Vern Stephens each hit solo homers against right-hander Virgil Trucks, a 20-game winner in the previous year, to hand the Orioles a 3–1 victory and give the fledgling franchise a 2–1 record and a tie for first place. It was the last time that this group of retreads and newbies would be over .500 in 1954. They ended up 54–100 on the season, including 10 straight losses in May, nine straight in June, and 14 in a row in August. They finished seventh of eight American League clubs, besting only the hapless Philadelphia Athletics. "It was a struggle," Hunter said matter-of-factly.

But the results were secondary. Big league baseball was back in Baltimore, and the fans responded. Those Orioles drew 1,060,910 fans in 67 home dates, averaging 15,384. That was the highest average attendance at Memorial Stadium until the Kiddie Corps club in 1960 battled with the vaunted New York Yankees for the pennant into late September.

The 1954 Orioles almost didn't happen. With the St. Louis Browns struggling on the field and at the gate, Baltimore mayor Tommy D'Alesandro and Maryland attorney Clarence Miles were in New York prior to the 1953 World Series expecting a vote that would send the Browns to Baltimore. This dance had occurred before. D'Alesandro thought he had a deal with Bill Veeck, the eccentric owner of the Browns, in March 1953 to move the club to Charm City, but the American League owners voted against the relocation. In September, D'Alesandro and crew were facing another challenge. Other cities were attempting to land the Browns, and the first vote for a move to Baltimore was a disappointing 4–4 deadlock. According to John Eisenberg's *From 33rd Street to Camden Yards*, the majority of the owners weren't actually against putting a team in Baltimore. They were opposed to continuing along with the boat-rocking Veeck, who owned 80 percent of the Browns' stock. Understanding this, the Baltimore contingent raised the money to buy out Veeck. And, in a key development, Jerold Hoffberger, president of Baltimore's

National Brewing Company, agreed to sponsor TV and radio broadcasts of the Washington Senators. That helped capture the support of Senators owner Clark Griffith, who had initially opposed the Orioles insertion into his region. Ultimately, at those meetings, the owners approved the sale and relocation of the Browns to Baltimore. And a giddy D'Alesandro proclaimed to reporters, "Right has prevailed."

That winter, Baltimore prepared for the new Orioles. And the Browns prepared for Baltimore. Hunter said he was playing winter ball in Mexico City and received a contract for the next season from Baltimore and not St. Louis. That's when he knew the franchise had moved. That was fine with him; Baltimore was closer to western Pennsylvania, where he grew up. Only Browns farm director Jim McLaughlin relocated as part of the Orioles' new front office. Baltimore native Art Ehlers was named general manager, and longtime manager Jimmy Dykes, who had just been fired by the 1953 Athletics after a 95-loss season, inherited an even worse team in the 100-loss Browns. Within a year, things had changed dramatically with the fledgling franchise. Paul Richards, who was the manager of the White Sox when they lost the Orioles' franchise opener at Memorial Stadium in April 1954, was hired to be the Orioles GM and field manager for 1955. That winter he agreed to a 17-player deal with the Yankees that sent Hunter and Turley, among others, to New York. With the move, Richards began setting the groundwork for an Orioles organization that eventually became the majors' top franchise.

11 Sweeping the 1966 World Series

The team that won the 1966 World Series in just the 13th year of the modern franchise's existence is probably the most important Orioles club ever fielded. It may have not been the best, but it established a level all others would follow. The Orioles had posted seasons of 97 wins in 1964 and 94 in 1965, so it's not as if they weren't good before 1966. What changed that year is that the Orioles added future Hall of Famer Frank Robinson and his win-first attitude. "Frank was a tough guy. He was a tough guy off the field and especially on the field. He made everybody better," said Hall of Famer Jim Palmer. "Not only did he play, but it was the way he played. There was just an edge to Frank, and if you were on his team, it was a good edge." Led by Robinson's Triple Crown and American League MVP season, the Orioles cruised to their first league title and then to a country-shocking, four-game sweep of the defending World Series champion Los Angeles Dodgers.

The season: The Orioles won 97 games, the lowest total for any of the franchise's six World Series entrants. And because the league wasn't broken into divisions until 1969, the Orioles didn't have to worry about surviving an additional round of the playoffs as they did in their other postseasons. But they were a tremendous team from the start of the season. They began the year 12–1 and never fell further back than four-and-a-half games in the league race. They had to endure a 17-game, five-city road trip and ended up 12–5 in that span. They won their next five at home and never were challenged again. Robinson led the AL in home runs (49), RBIs (122), and batting average (.316) while Brooks Robinson and Boog Powell each drove in 100 runs. Palmer, who was just 20, went 15–10 with a 3.46 ERA in 30 starts and led the team in wins and complete games (six). In the World Series, the Orioles were without Steve Barber, who was 10–5 with a 2.30 ERA but missed a chunk of the season with an ailing left elbow.

The playoff opponent: The defending champion Dodgers were heavy favorites thanks to a four-man rotation that included future Hall of Famers Sandy Koufax, Don Drysdale, Don Sutton, and 17-game winner Claude Osteen. As the Orioles approached Dodger Stadium before Game 1, there was a billboard on the road that read, "How About Four Straight?" Great pitching breeds that kind of confidence, and for the Orioles to orchestrate their own sweep, they needed to beat Drysdale twice and Koufax once.

The key moment: It came in the first inning of the first game against Drysdale, though it was technically two moments. With one out and one on in the first, Frank Robinson homered to give the Orioles a 2–0 lead. Brooks Robinson, in his first career World Series at-bat, made it back-to-back jacks. Not only were those three runs good enough to win Game 1, but they also were more than the Dodgers scored in the entire four-game series.

The top performances: Frank Robinson won the series MVP with four hits, including two home runs. His homer in Game 4 and Paul Blair's homer in Game 3 were the only runs scored in 1–0 affairs. But it was the Orioles' pitching that was the star. The Orioles held the Dodgers scoreless for their final 33 innings, including three straight complete-game shutouts by Palmer, Wally Bunker, and Dave McNally. In Game 2 Palmer became the youngest pitcher to accomplish that feat in a World Series with a four-hitter to outduel Koufax, who never pitched again due to an arthritic left elbow. Three errors by Dodgers center fielder Willie Davis aided the Orioles' cause. The unsung hero was reliever Moe Drabowsky, who turned in six and two-thirds scoreless innings in Game 1 in relief of McNally. Drabowsky allowed one hit and two walks while striking out 11 in one of the greatest relief outings in World Series history.

The quote: "The Los Angeles papers and around the country said we didn't belong on the field with the mighty Dodgers. And there was no way we had a chance to win," Frank Robinson said. "The scouting report was read to us in the clubhouse the day before the game, and after that I told our team that we could score runs off of their pitchers. And our pitchers could shut their offense down. And if we played the defense we were capable of playing and played all year long that we had a real good chance of winning the series. No one mentioned, I don't think, about sweeping the Dodgers. But I certainly felt confident that we could beat the Dodgers."

12 Scream the "Ohhhhh"

There's a public address announcer at a spring training ballpark in Florida whose face tenses and jaw clenches every time the national anthem is set to begin for a game against the Orioles. It's as if he is hoping that it won't happen, that the visiting Orioles fans in his ballpark will change their ways and spare the cherished "Star-Spangled Banner" just this once. Then the 61st word of the anthem is sung, the first word of the seventh line. And Orioles fans scream it with gusto.

"'Ohhhhh' say does that star-spangled banner yet wave."

The Florida announcer sneers, shakes his head, and curses under his breath about the disrespect heaped on this great country's national anthem by those barbarians from Baltimore. He's not the only one, of course. National pundits have complained about the "Ohhhhh" for years. The typical response from Orioles fans? It hurts no one. It's a fun, quirky Baltimore tradition. So get over it.

In fact, try it the next time you're at Camden Yards. You certainly won't be alone.

Marylanders feel they have a natural birthright to accentuate the anthem. After all, it was written by Maryland amateur poet and lawyer Francis Scott Key while in a ship watching the bombing of Baltimore's Fort McHenry during the War of 1812. Screaming the "Ohhhhh" at Orioles games—and at Ravens games and University of Maryland games and high school games in the Baltimore area— has become a time-honored tradition. It makes most people from Baltimore smile and it surprises most visitors. And that makes people from Baltimore smile more.

Although it's tough to pinpoint exactly when the "Ohhhhh" started, superfan "Wild Bill" Hagy and his band of crazies in Section 34 at Memorial Stadium are credited with originating it at some point in the 1970s. By the early 1980s, it had become a constant at sporting events in Maryland. And wherever the Orioles are on the road, there will be pockets of "Ohhhhhs" heard from the crowd when the seventh line of the anthem rolls around. "I'm kind of proud of that because it began when Oriole Magic was [in the 1970s], and it just got bigger and bigger and louder and louder all the time," former Orioles catcher Rick Dempsey said. "Every time you hear it now, it is getting louder and louder all the time. It really brings joy to your heart."

It's such a part of Camden Yards now that anthem singers are warned about it before they perform. The best advice is to hold the note a little longer than normal and eventually the crowd's "Ohhhhh" will pass. The seasoned pros can do it without incident. Leading American operatic tenor Richard Troxell, a Thurmont, Maryland, native who often performs the Opening Day anthem at Camden Yards, actually encourages the "Ohhhhh." He'll hold his arms wide above his head and prompt the fans to belt it out when he approaches that point in the song. Others, though, aren't as successful. Some have laughed while performing, and others have lost their place entirely when the scream occurs.

That's okay. It just adds to the quirkiness of the "Ohhhhh."

13 The Best Orioles Team Ever

It may have been a different story if the Orioles had been champions in either 1969 or 1971, but they weren't. So this 108-win club is considered the best in franchise history. *The Baltimore Sun* proclaimed it as such in 2014. *Sports Illustrated* senior baseball writer Tom Verducci named the 1970 Orioles the seventh best team in the history of the sport. That's what happens when a club doesn't relinquish first place after April 26. These Orioles won 19 of their final 22 and swept the Minnesota Twins in the American League Championship Series. They were determined to erase the sour taste from the previous World Series in which they lost to the underdog New York Mets. In the 1970 World Series, which highlighted the greatness of third baseman Brooks Robinson, the Orioles beat the mighty Cincinnati Reds in five games. "In all of the years I played baseball, I never had a five-game stretch like that. Not anywhere," Robinson once told *The Sun*. "And there's no doubt having them in the World Series gave me exposure I never could have gotten."

The season: It was about as complete of a season as a club could have. The Orioles started the year with five wins and ended the regular season with 11 straight—including five in extra innings. They were 40–15 in one-run games and 25–5 in games that were decided by five runs or more. Eight Orioles had 10 or more homers, led by first baseman Boog Powell, who hit 35 homers, 114 RBIs, and a .297 average to claim his only American League MVP

Award. Brooks Robinson finished seventh in MVP voting, Frank Robinson was 10th, lefty Mike Cuellar was 11th, and fellow lefty Dave McNally was 16th. McNally, who was 24–9 with a 3.22 ERA, finished second in the AL Cy Young Award balloting with Cuellar (24–8, 3.48 ERA) finishing fourth and Jim Palmer (20–10, 2.71 ERA) finishing fifth.

The playoff opponents: The Twins were the only team that had had a winning record against the Orioles in the regular season, but the Orioles dismissed them in three ALCS games. In the first the Orioles crushed Cy Young Award winner Jim Perry for eight runs and two homers, including one by Cuellar. The Reds won 102 regular season games and swept the Pittsburgh Pirates in the three-game National League Championship Series, triggering the ascent of "The Big Red Machine." Hall of Fame catcher Johnny Bench, just 22, was named NL MVP after bashing 45 homers and driving in 148 runs. Hall of Famer Tony Perez hit 40 homers and finished third in the MVP voting. Their pitching was paced by 20-game winner Jim Merritt and 18-game winner Gary Nolan.

The key moments: Most had to do with Robinson, the "Human Vacuum Cleaner," who seemingly gobbled up every ball hit anywhere near him during the series. The first throw he made in the second inning of Game 1 was an error. After that he was spectacular. In the sixth inning of Game 1, Lee May hit a hard bouncer down the third-base line that appeared to be a double, but Robinson backhanded it and made a one-hop throw from foul territory. (May later admitted he was beginning to prepare for a hard turn to second when he saw the ball arriving out of the corner of his eye.) In Game 2 Robinson backhanded another May shot and started a double play. In Game 3 he turned a high hopper by Perez into another double play. Robinson also speared two liners by Bench in the series, one to his left and one to his right. Another memorable moment occurred in the sixth inning of Game 1—and didn't involve Robinson. Catcher Elrod Hendricks fielded a chopper in front of home plate and tagged Bernie Carbo, who was running in from third. But Hendricks tagged Carbo with his mitt and had the ball in his bare hand. Umpire Ken Burkhart was knocked to the ground on the play. When he turned and saw Hendricks with the ball, he called Carbo out. The Reds argued, but the ruling remained.

The top performances: As good as World Series MVP Brooks Robinson was with the glove, he hit, too. He was 9-for-21 (.429 average) with two doubles, two homers—including the game-winner in the seventh inning of Game 1—and six RBIs. If it weren't for Robinson, center fielder Paul Blair probably would have been MVP. He was 9-for-19 with two walks and five runs scored in the series, posting a .524 on-base percentage. McNally threw a complete-game victory in Game 3 and hit a sixth-inning grand slam against Reds reliever Wayne Granger. It was the first grand slam by a pitcher in the October Classic.

The quote: "It was one of the most amazing things I've ever seen in baseball," the late Earl Weaver said of Robinson's play in the 1970 World Series. "And the only guy that could have done it was Brooks."

14 Four 20-Game Winners

When Hall of Famer Jim Palmer is asked if the 1971 rotation was the best he has ever been with, he answers quickly—but with a qualifier: "Well, yeah, but I didn't pitch on too many bad staffs." Palmer spent parts of 19 seasons with the Orioles, winning 20 or more games eight times. And, yes, he was part of some sublime rotations, but 1971 will always be considered—locally and nationally—the greatest. Palmer, Dave McNally, Mike Cuellar, and Pat Dobson became the second quartet of teammates to each win at least 20 games in a season, matching the 1920 Chicago White Sox.

In a 13-season stretch from 1968 until 1980, the club had at least one 20-game winner, a major league record. Before that only one Oriole had reached 20 wins: Steve Barber in 1963. After 1980 they've had one do it: Mike Boddicker in 1984. Despite the 30-year drought, the Orioles boast the most 20-game winners in baseball since 1968 with 24. The Oakland A's are next at 17. To put it in further perspective, in 2013 and 2014 combined, there were only four 20-game winners in the majors. With the advent of five-man rotations and the reliance on bullpens after the sixth inning, the 20-win season is now a rarity; four on one team is a virtual impossibility. "It will never happen again, no one allows pitchers to come close to that," said former Orioles catcher Andy Etchebarren. "That record will never get broken. One hundred years from now, they are going to say the '71 Orioles are the last one."

In 1970 the Orioles won the World Series with a formidable rotation of McNally, Palmer, Cuellar, and a combination of Tom Phoebus and Jim Hardin. General manager Harry Dalton decided to further bolster his staff that offseason, dealing hometown boy Phoebus and three others to the San Diego Padres for reliever Tom Dukes and Dobson, a 28-year-old right-hander who had 25 career wins. A groundball-inducing pitcher, Dobson was 14–15 with a 3.76 ERA for the Padres in 1970. He wasn't, however, playing in front of a Gold Glove defense. "That was the difference," first baseman Boog Powell said. "Dobber comes over from San Diego. And he won an extra six games just because of our defense. He was a helluva pitcher, too."

The two-time defending American League champions started solidly in 1971 with a 27–19 record through May, then caught fire, winning at a .661 clip (74–38), including their last 11 to finish the season. During that final streak, all four starters picked up wins No. 20, all in complete games. Three were shutouts.

McNally, who led the staff with 21 wins, was the first to the milestone. His record was 6–4 on May 28, but he won his next 13 decisions. He lost at Detroit on September 17 to snap his streak but threw a complete-game, five-hit, 5–0 shutout at Yankee Stadium

Part of a rotation that impressively featured four 20-game winners in 1971, pitcher Jim Palmer went 20–9 with a 2.68 ERA that season.

on September 21. It was the fourth straight season that McNally (21–5) had won at least 20 games. It was also the last time he'd do it. Three days later the Orioles had a Friday, twi-night doubleheader in Cleveland, and two more joined the 20-win club. Cuellar (20–9) allowed just two runs in a complete-game, 9–2 victory in the first contest. Technically, the Orioles had clinched their third straight division crown the day before on an off day, but it wasn't until after Cuellar's gem that they could have celebrated. Dobson, however, joked that he hid the champagne until he could pitch the nightcap, which he won with a 7–0 shutout to end up 20–8. The only member of the rotation without 20 wins was the 25-year-old Palmer.

There was plenty of motivation for Palmer to reach 20. He had seen McNally get a $20,000 raise in the 1968 offseason after the first time the lefty won 20 games. Palmer, who made a $15,000 salary after his breakout 1966 season, was forced to take a pay cut after sitting out a year and a half due to arm trouble heading into 1969. "And then Dave won the 20 games and got a $20,000 raise, and all of the sudden, it was like a big neon sign saying this is what you have to do," said Palmer, who first won 20 games in 1970. "And it was $17,500 or $20,000 [extra] every time you did that. That was a great incentive." His final 1971 chance came on Sunday, September 26 before an announced crowd of 2,967. (The Indians were 40½ games out of first place.) Palmer pitched brilliantly, allowing three hits, two walks, and striking out nine in a 5–0 shutout.

It wasn't, however, a breeze.

Cleveland right-hander Alan Foster also took a shutout into the seventh. In Palmer's first two at-bats, he reached base on errors and was stranded. In the seventh inning, the Orioles broke the scoreless tie on a bases-loaded, sacrifice fly by Mark Belanger. Then Palmer came to the plate again and doubled to score Elrod Hendricks, giving himself a 2–0 cushion. "Finally, I doubled down the line," Palmer said. "I was pretty desperate. I mean, 20 [wins] had cachet—19, no." Foster uncorked a wild pitch to allow a third run to score in the seventh. The Orioles tacked on two in the eighth to thrust its rotation into legendary status.

More Than Just Wins

Over the years the win statistic has been devalued. The argument is that a win is a matter of circumstance, that there are so many variables beyond a starting pitcher's control that determine the outcome of the game, including the defense behind a starting pitcher and the run support that's generated by his offense. Certainly, there is merit to that; Pat Dobson's ascent from 14 wins in 1970 with San Diego to 20 wins with Baltimore in 1971 supports the argument. He played on a better team with a better defense in Baltimore.

But take away the win totals—which made the Orioles' 1971 rotation legendary—and the numbers still indicate an incredible quartet of performances. For only the second time in baseball history, and surely the last, four teammates won 20 games in one season. All four made at least 30 starts and pitched more than 220 innings. Lefty Dave McNally (21–5) posted a 2.89 ERA in 224 1/3 innings and finished fourth in the AL Cy Young voting. He was the only Oriole to get a vote. Lefty Mike Cuellar (20–9) led the staff with 38 starts and 292 1/3 innings pitched. His 3.08 ERA was the highest of the four, but he also threw a team best 21 complete games. Palmer (20–9) posted the lowest ERA at 2.68 while making 37 starts and throwing 282 innings. Dobson (20–8) had a 2.90 ERA in 282 1/3 innings over 38 games. He made 37 starts; in his lone relief appearance, he picked up the save to secure McNally's 21st win.

Perhaps the most impressive statistic from that rotation is that the quartet combined to complete 70 of the team's 158 games. Add in a complete game from spot starter Dave Leonhard, and the Orioles' starters went the distance in 45 percent of their contests that year. For perspective, the Orioles' 71 complete games in 1971 were more than the 61 recorded by the entire American League's 15 teams in 2014. "Today guys would die if they had to pitch as much as our guys did," said former Orioles catcher Andy Etchebarren. "They would just die."

The group stayed together for another season, winning a combined 68 games. Each of the four won at least 13 in 1972, but Palmer, with 21 victories, was the only one to reach 20. Dobson was traded away after that season; McNally was traded two years later. In a sad postscript, Palmer is the only surviving member of the greatest rotation in club history. McNally died from lung cancer at age 60 in 2002, Dobson died from leukemia at age 64 in 2006, and Cuellar died from stomach cancer at age 72 in 2010. "We played golf together. We rooted for each other," Palmer said. "McNally and Cuellar and Dobson made me better. It goes back to having passion, having pride. You want to be as good as the other three guys."

Boog Powell

The first thing you need to know about Boog Powell, one of the greatest sluggers in Orioles history, is that you've been mispronouncing and mis-chanting his nickname all this time. Pretty much everyone else has, too, except for Hall of Famer Brooks Robinson, who nails it perfectly with his smooth Arkansas drawl.

Powell's moniker was given to him as a baby by an aunt for no discernible reason except that she liked a radio show that had a character with a similar nickname. It was never intended to be pronounced with the hard "OOs" in boo or food. It's supposed to be more like the O sound in good. But Powell doesn't mind if the original has been replaced with the mispronunciation. He believes "Booooog" is more for fun to chant. "It's not that big of a deal. The 'Booooog' thing is cooler than 'Buuuug' because you couldn't do 'Buuuug' at the ballpark I don't think," Powell said.

"They could be booing me with 'Booooog,' and I can say, 'They are saying my name, isn't that sweet?' And a lot of them were booing me, and that's okay. The more they booed me, the more I liked it, especially on the road."

His given name is John Wesley Powell, but no one calls him that, though legendary Yankee Stadium public address announcer Bob Sheppard would always introduce him as John. Powell was once told by Hall of Famer Dizzy Dean that Boog "was the worst name I ever heard." Powell, a green big leaguer at the time, respectfully said he was sticking with the moniker, "But what I should have said is, 'You are Dizzy Dean and you had a brother named Daffy? So what's worse, Boog or Dizzy or Daffy?'" Powell said he considered introducing himself as an adult as Wes or J.W., which is what his grandfather and namesake used. "But the Boog thing just kept coming back no matter what. And I just said the heck with it."

Good thing because Powell became America's most famous and quintessential "Boog," which conjures up an image of a big man with a big laugh and a huge appetite for life. Powell possessed all of that as well as the most powerful left-handed swing in club history, smashing 339 homers in 17 major league seasons, including 303 for the Orioles from 1961 to 1974. He's still third on the franchise's all-time list—behind Hall of Famers Cal Ripken Jr. and Eddie Murray—and is tops for left-handed hitters (though Powell threw right-handed). He did most of his damage in Memorial Stadium, which wasn't as friendly as the club's current park, Camden Yards. "Add another 100 home runs to my total if I played [at Camden]. No doubt in my mind," Powell said. "And not necessarily down either line, but in the alleys in right center and left center. I hit a lot of 390-foot fly ball [outs], 380-foot fly balls."

He also hit a lot of balls over the wall, recording 25 or more dingers six times. Powell hit a career-best 39 homers in 1964 when his teammate Brooks Robinson won the American League MVP. He homered 34 times in 1966 when his teammate Frank

Robinson won the MVP. In 1969 he homered 37 times, drove in a career-high 121 runs, and turned in his best average (.304.) And he finished second to Minnesota's Harmon Killebrew in the MVP race. Powell finally landed his elusive MVP award the following season, when he batted .297 with 35 homers, 114 RBIs, and a career-high 104 walks while striking out just 80 times.

Many observers argue that 1969, though, was actually Powell's best season. He believes that, too. "I thought '69 was. I think that the writers had already made their minds up to vote for Killer, and Killer had a hell of a year," Powell said about Killebrew. "Harmon came up to me in the start of the '70 season and says, 'You should have won it.' And I said, 'Nah, I think the right guy won it.' And he said, 'Nope, you should have won it and you know you should have won it.' And I said, 'Well, why don't you just give it to me then?' And we just laughed about it."

Like most people Powell encounters, he and Killebrew became good friends. Listed at 6'4" and 230 pounds in his playing days, Powell was a gentle giant who wanted to win at all costs on the field. But he was approachable and affable off of it, making him an enduring fan favorite. After his playing days, he utilized that big buddy persona as a spokesman for Miller beer and then as greeter/expert grillmaster with his Boog's BBQ stand at Camden Yards. For a few more $1,000 or a more aggressive push by the St. Louis Cardinals or Detroit Tigers, Powell may never have been an Oriole.

As a kid growing up in Lakeland, Florida—his team played in the 1954 Little League World Series tournament in Williamsport, Pennsylvania, and lost in the first round—Powell was a fan of the Tigers, who trained each spring in Lakeland. As a high schooler and hitting prospect in Key West, Florida, he wanted to sign with the Tigers, but they showed little interest. The two clubs that presented concrete offers were the fledgling Orioles and the Cardinals. Powell had a football scholarship from the University of Florida as a fall-back option, but he really wanted to play pro baseball. "St. Louis came in and offered me $20,000, the Orioles came right behind and offered me $25,000, and St. Louis wouldn't go any higher," Powell said. "So I signed for $25,000, and then it was off to the races."

Powell made his major league debut in September 1961, shortly after his 20th birthday. By the next year, he was the club's primary left fielder; first base was blocked by slugger Jim Gentile. The Orioles sent Gentile to the Kansas City Athletics after the 1963 season for first baseman Norm Siebern, who was traded in December of 1965 in preparation for the landmark Frank Robinson deal. In 1966 Robinson became the Orioles right fielder, Curt Blefary moved to left, and Powell went to first, where he would stay for the next nine seasons until his at-bats began to dwindle. He was dealt to the Cleveland Indians (managed by his buddy Robinson) before the 1975 season. Powell spent two seasons with the Indians, including a 27-homer year in 1975, before retiring with the Los Angeles Dodgers in 1977. But Powell will always be an Oriole—and a favorite of his teammates and the organization's fans. "We had a good time as a team," Powell said. "We just enjoyed the game a lot and we enjoyed each other a lot."

16 Ain't the Beer Cold

Chuck Thompson couldn't help himself. The man, whose rich baritone was invited warmly into the homes of Orioles and Baltimore Colts fans for decades via radio or television, was about to deliver his speech after receiving the National Hall of Fame Ford C. Frick Award in 1993. As the hour approached for Thompson to speak, he decided to trim his speech. It was brutally hot that day in Cooperstown, New York, and the majority of people were there to see outfielder Reggie Jackson be inducted into the Hall and not Thompson accept the Ford C. Frick Award. So, as Thompson always did, he considered the audience and decided to self-edit. But as he approached the dais, he changed his speech one last time. He added four words to the beginning: "Ain't the Beer Cold."

"I was suddenly aware of my extreme good fortune and reacted the way I would have for a Frank Robinson grand slam or a Johnny Unitas touchdown pass," Thompson wrote in his autobiography. "So I started my speech with a phrase out of the past, one that I could no longer resist: 'Ain't the Beer Cold.'"

"Ain't the Beer Cold"—also the name of Thompson's autobiography—was used for moments of elation, when things were going right for his teams. Thompson said he borrowed it from Bob Robertson, who worked with him in the broadcast booth during Colts games as a spotter, assisting Thompson by pointing out which players had entered the game or contributed on a tackle. It was one of two catchphrases for which Thompson, who announced Orioles games in parts of seven decades, was known. The other was "Go To War Miss Agnes," which was his version of, "How about that?" or "Can you believe it?" Thompson said he picked that one up from Bob Sharman, a golfing buddy who would mutter the phrase after missing a putt.

The two catchphrases became an essential part of Baltimore's baseball lexicon, even though Thompson retired them long before he stepped away from the booth. He said he phased out "Miss Agnes" as the Vietnam War continued and casualties mounted. A World War II Army Sergeant who participated in the Battle of the Bulge, Thompson said he just couldn't justify using the war reference with so many Americans losing loved ones. At some point in the 1970s, he also stopped referring to icy brew. He said he received letters of complaint from listeners in North Carolina and "the Bible Belt," who felt like they shouldn't be subjected to alcohol references both in the game and during commercial breaks from sponsors. "I thought they had a legitimate beef," Thompson wrote. So that was it for "Ain't the Beer Cold." Yet his phrases endured far after he stopped using them. That's the kind of impact Thompson made on his listening community.

Weaver's Risqué Radio Rant That Wasn't

Hall of Fame manager Earl Weaver was known as direct and profane throughout his career. So it came as no surprise that Weaver might snap while doing a radio segment and rapidly spit out curse words like they were sunflower seed casings in the dugout. I was a high schooler when I first heard the tape of Weaver losing it and cursing a blue streak during his "Manager's Corner" segment. For me, it was teenage gold. Weaver ripped former reliever Don Stanhouse and pinch-hitter extraordinaire Terry Crowley and speed demons who couldn't hit his beloved three-run homer. And what Weaver suggested that listener Alice Sweet from Norfolk should do instead of plant tomatoes made my teenage self blush a little. It was incredible, amazing, just too good to be true. And that's because it was a fake, a lark between longtime radio broadcaster Tom Marr and Weaver. An audio urban legend, if you will.

Marr, who had been an Orioles broadcaster for WFBR, the Orioles' flagship station, once explained to *The Baltimore Sun* how it all occurred. Marr and Weaver had started a "Manager's Corner" segment in 1982 before a game in Seattle. They messed it up, started laughing, and decided to do a fake segment. Marr asked Weaver questions from fans, and Weaver ran with it, using just about every expletive in his arsenal. It was hilarious and crude, and Marr sent it back to his engineer as a joke. They then recorded the real segment, and that's the one that aired. The fake one was never intended to be broadcast and it wasn't. It was just two guys messing around in the middle of another long baseball season. The tape, though, was never destroyed. Copies of it bounced around Baltimore for years—often with the fabrication that it once aired. Eventually, the audio made it to the Internet and it can still be found by a quick Google search. It's still funny and profane today. It's just not real.

Born in Massachusetts, Thompson spent most of his formative years in Reading, Pennsylvania, and after high school messed around as a vocalist in a dance band before landing a radio gig at WRAW for $14 a week. In 1949 he came to Baltimore to announce International League Orioles games. Because of contractual obligations, he missed out on broadcasting the Orioles' first year in the majors in 1954. But he joined Hall of Famer Ernie Harwell in 1955 and 1956 before spending a few seasons announcing Washington Senators games. He returned to the Orioles by 1962 and remained the most trusted voice of Orioles baseball for the next 26 years. He had a litany of tremendous partners on radio and TV, including Bill O'Donnell, Jon Miller, and Hall of Fame third baseman Brooks Robinson, who said he always was in awe of the way Thompson had the perfect words for unique situations. "I remember when we played the game in New York right after [Thurman] Munson died, and Chuck gave a little eulogy before the game," Robinson said. "And I sat there and I was just amazed at what came out of his mouth, the words, and how wonderful it was."

Thompson continued to broadcast on a part-time basis in the 1990s but eventually was forced to give it up completely in 2000 due to macular degeneration, which robbed him of his sight. It was the great irony of his life. His voice remained the sound of summer, but his eyes no longer allowed him to set the scene. Thompson died in March 2005 at age 83 after suffering a stroke.

He left behind an unmistakable legacy. "To think about baseball and to think about baseball in Baltimore, you hear Chuck Thompson on Sunday afternoons while you're sitting out on your deck in your backyard eating crabs," said former Oriole first baseman Boog Powell. "That's what life is all about. You can't have anything better than that."

17 The 1983 World Series

By the time 1983 rolled around, the Orioles had dealt with their share of heartbreak. Many of the players had experienced the collapse of 1979, when they were up three games to one to the Pittsburgh Pirates in the World Series and dropped three straight. Those who weren't around in 1979, such as emerging star Cal Ripken Jr., had just suffered through the pain of 1982. The Orioles were down three games to the Milwaukee Brewers with four remaining. They beat the Brewers three straight to set up a winner-take-all battle at Memorial Stadium on the last day of the season. They lost 10–2 to the Brewers that Sunday afternoon, which was supposed to be Weaver's last day managing. (He came out of retirement three years later.)

In 1983 the Orioles had nearly the same roster as 1982, but it was hungrier and more experienced. Veteran baseball man Joe Altobelli took over as manager, and his team cruised, ending up in the same position as in 1979, though this time it was against the Philadelphia Phillies. "When we got in that same situation—up three games to one—every one of us remembered what happened four years prior," said outfielder Gary Roenicke. "Scotty McGregor pitched a great, great game, and Eddie Murray came up with some big hits. And it was a great relief to get that monkey off our backs."

The season: The Orioles won 98 games in 1983, needing a strong run in mid-August through late September to separate from the pack. After dropping their seventh in a row on August 12, they fell to 62–49, one game behind the Detroit Tigers and Milwaukee Brewers and into a tie with the New York Yankees. The Orioles won 15 of their next 18 to end August and take control of the division. Ripken and Murray carried the club's offense. The

23-year-old Ripken, who hit .318 with 27 homers and 102 RBIs, won his first American League MVP the year after capturing the AL Rookie of the Year Award. Murray, who batted .306 with 33 homers and 111 RBIs, finished a close second in the MVP race. McGregor was sixth in Cy Young voting, and right-hander Mike Boddicker finished third for Rookie of the Year.

The playoff opponents: The Orioles reached their first World Series in four years in dramatic fashion. They beat the Chicago White Sox in four games in the American League Championship Series with reserve outfielder Tito Landrum hitting a homer to snap a scoreless tie in the 10th inning of Game 4, which the Orioles ultimately won 3–0 at Comiskey Park. The Phillies, known as the "Wheeze Kids" for their veteran lineup, won 90 games in the regular season and then beat the Los Angeles Dodgers in four games to advance to their second World Series in four seasons. Mike Schmidt, the club's 34-year-old third baseman, slugged 40 homers, drove in 109 runs, and finished third in the National League MVP balloting. Starter John Denny won the NL Cy Young Award by going 19–6 with a 2.37 ERA. The Phillies had four future Hall of Famers; Schmidt was the youngest by several years.

The key moments: Murray, who was 6-for-42 in his previous 11 World Series games, gave the Orioles a 1–0 lead in the second inning of Game 5 with a home run against Charles Hudson. Murray then put the game out of reach and a championship in sight with a two-run homer in the fourth. He had three hits in the game and just two in his previous four games. Relegated to pinch-hitting duties, Ken Singleton drew a bases-loaded walk to tie Game 4 in the sixth inning, and John Shelby followed with a sacrifice fly to give the Orioles the lead.

The top performances: Catcher Rick Dempsey batted .385 with four doubles and a homer to win series MVP honors. McGregor pitched a complete-game shutout in Game 5. Boddicker, in his first World Series appearance, picked up a complete-game victory in

Game 2. Jim Palmer entered in relief in Game 3 and recorded the win. He is the only player to win World Series games in three different decades. He also appeared in each of the Orioles' six World Series. Country singer John Denver performed the national anthem for Game 1 as well as "Thank God I'm A Country Boy," a seventh-inning-stretch staple in Baltimore.

The quote: "Earl left one little statement to Joe, basically told him, 'Don't F it up, that these guys were going to win,'" Murray said. "And it was just that simple. We knew we were going to win."

18 Memorial Stadium

The Orioles' first shortstop, Billy Hunter, remembers breaking to his left for a ground ball hit up the middle in a game against the Washington Senators at Memorial Stadium in 1954. It was the first year that the majors had returned to Baltimore and it's fair to say that not everything was big league at that point—like the stadium's infield. The dirt would bake under the hot summer sun, and by the time the Orioles took the field, it was, as Hunter said, "like playing on concrete." He found that out the hard way in trying to snag that grounder against the Senators. It took a bad hop right at him. "It hit me in the forehead and went right to Bobby Young at second who turned a double play. I never touched it with my hands," Hunter said while laughing.

A longtime Orioles coach, Hunter said the infield eventually became better manicured. And other improvements at Memorial Stadium changed things, too—like having a fence all the way around the playing field. In the early years, there was no fence in center—just a hedge—so players could crush a ball only to have it caught 450 or more feet away. Hunter said outfielder Vic Wertz was victimized multiple times in 1954 by long outs during his two months with the Orioles before being dealt away in June. "He was very pleased to be traded to Cleveland," Hunter said. (The irony, of course, is that Wertz, while with the Indians, was on the wrong end of the most famous tracked down fly ball in baseball history, when the New York Giants' Willie Mays made an over-the-shoulder basket catch against Wertz in Game 1 of the 1954 World Series at the Polo Grounds.)

Old Memorial Stadium will forever glisten in the mind's eye of Baltimore sports romantics as the "Old Gray Lady of 33rd Street." In reality, the horseshoe-shaped structure was far from perfect. Large concrete columns—which held up the upper seating bowl—obstructed spectators' views throughout parts of the lower area. The gold bleachers sizzled in the summer heat. The player amenities were antiquated by the 1970s, and the rats that roamed the bowels of the structure were rumored to have the size and speed to hold their own in the Preakness Stakes. What made Memorial Stadium special were the people who played there, the fans that cheered there, and the memories that were created in northeastern Baltimore. The place, maybe because it was located in the middle of a neighborhood, fostered a certain camaraderie between the athletes and the fans. It was dubbed "The World's Largest Outdoor Insane Asylum" for how loud it would get—especially for Baltimore Colts' games. And section 34 in the upper deck became its own community of rowdy fans celebrating Orioles games in the late 1970s and 1980s. "I loved Memorial Stadium and all the memories there like being able to park my car behind home plate outside of the stadium," said former Orioles closer Gregg Olson. "So you'd park right behind there, and a couple months into my rookie year, people figured out which one was my car was and what time I'd get out. So I'd have a bunch of people standing around my car, and we'd talk for 30 minutes and sign autographs after the game. That was Memorial Stadium. You knew all the faces."

The first stadium on those grounds was built in 1922 and was called Baltimore Stadium (and also Municipal Stadium and Venable Park Stadium). It was used mainly for football but also was reconfigured for baseball (sort of) in 1944 after the International League Orioles' all-wood facility burned down July 4. More than 50,000 people attended then-Municipal Stadium for Game 1 of the 1944 Junior World Series, which triggered major league baseball's interest in returning to Baltimore. With that in mind, a deconstruction/reconstruction of Municipal Stadium began a few years later.

Memorial Stadium was initially constructed between 1949 and 1950, and the upper deck was added in 1953–54, as the Orioles re-entered the big leagues. The stadium had already housed the Colts, who won the NFL championship on those hallowed grounds in December 1959. The Orioles clinched their first World Series there in 1966's Game 4 against the heavily favored Los Angeles Dodgers. There were also some difficult moments in the stadium's history. In May 1964, as part of "Safety Patrol Day" in which 20,000 students received free admission to the Orioles game, an escalator was partially blocked by a metal gate at the top, causing children to topple onto each other. One 14-year-old girl was killed, and more than 40 others suffered injuries. In December 1976 a small private airplane crashed into the upper deck minutes after the completion of a Colts game. No one was seriously injured.

The Orioles were the lone, primary tenants from 1984 until they moved to Camden Yards for the 1992 season. Memorial Stadium then served as a temporary home for various franchises, including the Canadian Football League's Colts/Stallions, the NFL's Ravens—before they moved to their new home across from Camden Yards—and one year of the Double A Bowie Baysox. Demolition of Memorial Stadium began in 2001. The site now houses a YMCA, senior-citizen apartments, and a youth sports park and baseball field built by the Cal Ripken Sr. Foundation.

Parts of Memorial Stadium, however, live on. Both foul poles at Camden Yards were originally used at Memorial Stadium. Also, at the south end of the B&O Warehouse is an 11-foot granite wall that is a tribute to Memorial Stadium and the veterans of U.S. wars for whom the old stadium was dedicated. An urn with soil from American military cemeteries throughout the world—which was displayed at 33rd Street—is now at Camden Yards, as is a plaque explaining the significance of the old stadium. On the granite wall is the quote about U.S. war veterans from former General John J. Pershing that was famously featured on the outer facade of Memorial Stadium behind home plate. The quote reads: "Time will not dim the glory of their deeds." It also seems an appropriate remembrance of those who starred on 33rd Street.

19 How the Orioles Became the Yankees

There are plenty of reasons why Orioles fans don't like the New York Yankees. The Bronx Bombers have consistently been the most successful club in baseball; they also have the deepest pockets. During the Orioles' down periods, Yankees fans have descended on Camden Yards and taken over. And in years when the Orioles were competitive and made the playoffs, they had to battle with the Yankees to get there. Well, here's another reason to wag your finger at those Yankees fans, a deep-rooted one that has become a trivia question of sorts. The Yankees once were the Orioles but left Baltimore for New York—sort of.

In the late 1890s, the Orioles were the best team in the National League, but Baltimore lost its club in 1899 to Brooklyn, New York. Baltimore then had an American League team for two seasons, but it collapsed in 1902. The next year a new AL club, the New York Highlanders, was formed with a handful of the same players as the previous year's Orioles. In 1913, the Highlanders became the New York Yankees. And Baltimore went from 1902 to 1954 without a traditional major league squad until the Browns moved from St. Louis.

Baltimore's deep baseball history started in 1859 with a club named the Baltimore Excelsiors, according to Ted Patterson's book, *The Baltimore Orioles*. In the second half of the 19th century, there were various baseball teams playing in Baltimore in myriad leagues, such as the Pastimes, the Canaries, the Marylands, the Lord Baltimores, and the Monumentals. In 1882, Baltimore formed a team in the American Association, and that club, the Orioles, remained there until becoming an expansion member of the National League in 1892. They lost 101 games in their first NL season, finishing in last place.

But that May, Ed "Ned" Hanlon was brought in to be captain and manager. Just 34 at the time, the eventual Hall of Famer quickly turned the Orioles into a force. Considered one of the game's greatest innovators and talent evaluators, "Foxy Ned" acquired several future Hall of Famers, including Joe Kelley, Hughie Jennings, Wee Willie Keeler, and Dan Brouthers while getting the most out of some existing Orioles such as Wilbert Robinson and John McGraw. With an in-your-face style and future Hall of Famers at six positions, the Orioles won the National League in 1894, 1895, and 1896 and finished second in 1897 and 1898. Hanlon is credited with inventing the hit-and-run play and the Baltimore chop, among other tactics that are now referred to as "small ball." He utilized double steals and sacrifice bunts and just about anything else that could score his team runs. Hanlon, and several of his best players, left Baltimore after the 1898 season when ownership merged with the Brooklyn Bridegrooms.

Hall of Famers from Yesteryear

When fans think of the Orioles' Hall of Famers, they undoubtedly concentrate on the six men who have statues outside of Camden Yards. They are the ones most responsible for the great teams in the 1960s, 1970s, and 1980s. But before any of those players were born, the Orioles made a name for themselves with players who also ended up in the Hall of Fame. Here's a list of those men:

Baltimore Orioles, American Association (1882–1891)/ National League (1892–1899)
- Wilbert Robinson (played for and managed Orioles, elected to HOF as a manager)
- John McGraw (played for and managed Orioles, elected to HOF as a manager)
- Joe Kelley
- Hughie Jennings
- Ned Hanlon (played for and managed Orioles, elected to HOF as a manager)
- Dan Brouthers
- Willie Keeler
- Joe McGinnity

Baltimore Orioles, American League (1901–1902)
- Roger Bresnahan
- Joe McGinnity
- McGraw
- Robinson
- Kelley

Baltimore Terrapins, Federal League (1914–1915):
- Chief Bender

Baltimore was without a team in 1900, but the next year the Orioles re-emerged in the fledgling American League with McGraw leading the way at third base and as manager. It didn't last long. In 1902 McGraw was indefinitely suspended for refusing to leave the field after an altercation with an umpire. He asked for his release from the Orioles. The board of directors owed him $7,000 and agreed to forgive the debt on condition of obtaining his release. He then returned to the National League, where he managed the New York Giants for the next 30 years. The Orioles limped through the rest of that year, using some players on loan from other teams. Before the 1903 season, a new AL franchise, replacing the Orioles, was sold to New York investors, laying the groundwork for the current-day Yankees.

Baltimore had a team—the Terrapins—for two seasons in the upstart Federal League, a third major league that lasted from 1914 to 1915. But the city didn't have a true big league team until 1954. When it was announced that the Browns were moving to Baltimore, renowned American poet and Baltimore resident Ogden Nash wrote an ode to those 1890s teams in his poem celebrating the Orioles return, "You Can't Kill an Oriole."

20 Paul Richards, the Wizard of Waxahachie

He spent seven seasons in Baltimore, never won a pennant, and only had two years in which his clubs were better than .500. Yet the argument can be made that no one had more of an impact on shaping the Orioles into a perennial contender than Paul Richards, the "Wizard of Waxahachie."

Born in the small town of Waxahachie, Texas, Richards gained fame as a high schooler when he won both ends of a doubleheader while pitching one right-handed and the other left-handed. Richards was a major league catcher for eight seasons in the 1930s and 1940s, playing on the Detroit Tigers' 1945 World Series championship team. He was already an accomplished manager with the Chicago White Sox when the fledgling Orioles hired him away in September 1954 to be their new skipper for 1955, the organization's second year of existence.

Richards, though, didn't just want to manage the Orioles. He wanted full control to shape the roster and the minor league organization. He was given it, becoming the first simultaneous general manager and field manager since Hall of Famer John McGraw with the New York Giants decades before. There was no question that Richards was in charge of the Orioles. "He had the knack of being everywhere at once. I'll never forget that," said former Oriole Boog Powell. "In spring training if you thought you might take a little break and relax, you'd look up, and he would be standing right next to you. 'What are you doing son?' he'd say. 'Nothing, Mr. Richards.' And you'd just get going again."

Richards was known for his baseball intellect and his innovations. He is thought to be the first person to regularly compute on-base percentage. He put an emphasis on pitching and defense and stressed that all his pitchers attempt to learn a version of the change-up. He was a boxing fan and admired the way those athletes trained, so he brought in a pro boxer to work out with the Orioles in spring training and show them some exercise techniques. Richards required the same instruction from the minors to the majors, which became the blueprint for "The Oriole Way."

As a personnel man, he built from within and he immediately blew up the roster, agreeing to a 17-player trade with the New York Yankees in November/December 1954 that is still the largest in the sport's history. Catcher Gus Triandos, one of the Orioles' first stars, came in that deal. But Richards made the Yankees better by giving up two good starting pitchers, Bob Turley, who would win a Cy Young with the Yankees, and Don Larsen, who threw the only perfect game in World Series history. When questioned why he would orchestrate a trade that could help the Yankees win the American League, the quick-witted Richards reportedly quipped, "What concern is it of mine who wins the pennant? I need to get the Orioles out of seventh place."

Richards' Orioles finished seventh in 1955—and never again under his reign. In 1957 the club reached .500 for the first time, and in 1960 the Orioles won 89 games and finished second in the division while battling the Yankees for first place into September. Richards didn't have a particularly great relationship with his players—he didn't talk much to them—but most respected him. "He walked through the clubhouse on his way in and through the clubhouse on the way out and never said a word," first baseman Jim Gentile said. "If you were gonna pinch hit, he wouldn't say, 'Jim get a bat.' He would tell [coach] Luman Harris, 'Tell Gentile to get a bat.' If you made a mistake, he'd tell you about it. And if you'd go out and do it again, you'd be in Rochester. He was great, but he didn't say a lot. But you knew he knew what he was doing."

Richards, a religious man who could curse a blue streak, was always looking for an edge. Because his catchers had trouble handling Hoyt Wilhelm's knuckleball, Richards designed an oversized catcher's mitt that, in the words of Gentile, was "the size of a damn pizza pan. He told the catchers to just knock [the pitches] down." Eventually, the size of the mitt was reduced, and the "pizza pans" were banned.

One of the ways Richards attempted to build the Orioles was through signing as many highly regarded amateur players as possible. It was under Richards' leadership that the Orioles landed Hall of Famer Brooks Robinson, a teenaged infielder from Little Rock, Arkansas, for $4,000. But many of Richards' bonus babies didn't pan out, which likely led to the Orioles taking away his front office duties before the 1959 season when they hired Lee MacPhail to be general manager. One of Richards' biggest bonus baby success stories was right-hander Milt Pappas, whom the organization had scouted for years and signed for $4,000 out of a Detroit high school in 1957. By that August the 18-year-old had been promoted to the majors. Pappas pitched twice that month and then came up with a mysterious arm ailment. Call it Richards-itis. About 10 days into Pappas' big league career, Richards told Pappas he thought the kid might have a sore arm. Pappas said he felt great, but Richards pressed on. "Finally, in a real nasty voice, he said, 'You've got a sore arm, don't you?' And I said, 'Well, I guess I've got a sore arm,' which meant he could put me on the disabled list and bring somebody else up that could help the team at that particular moment," Pappas said.

The injury didn't last long. A few days later, Pappas was throwing batting practice to his teammates while the Detroit Tigers were in town. The Tigers were still miffed that the hometown kid signed elsewhere and they weren't amused that he was hidden on the DL despite throwing low-90s fastballs in batting practice. They called the commissioner's office, and the Orioles had to remove Pappas from the disabled list. "Paul was very shrewd," Pappas laughed. "He was something else, I tell you. I loved the man."

Not all of Richards' players felt the same way, especially when his innovations backfired. Joe Durham, the club's first African American position player, hated playing for Richards. He felt like the manager played favorites, didn't treat blacks equally, never gave him a shot to prove himself, and only kept him on the roster in 1957 because Richards would have been criticized in the media for cutting him. Richards told Durham that he didn't like the way he lunged over the plate when he swung, even though Durham batted nearly .400 in the minors that year. To attempt to break him of the habit, Richards tied a rope around Durham's waist and tugged at it each time Durham swung during a batting practice session. Not only was it humiliating, but Durham felt it messed up his mechanics. "They say he was a genius," Durham said. "No, everybody in Baltimore was just afraid of the man."

Richards' tenure with the Orioles ended in 1961, when he left with 27 games to play to become the new general manager of the start-up Houston Colt .45s, the first big league team in Richards' home state of Texas. Fifteen years later in 1976, Richards would manage one more season with the White Sox. Richards posted a 923–901 managerial record in parts of 12 seasons, never once making the postseason. He was 517–539 with the Orioles and is still second on the organization's all-time list for games managed, wins, and losses—behind only Hall of Famer Weaver. In 1986 at age 77, Richards suffered a heart attack and died in Waxahachie.

21 Motormouth

Hall of Fame right fielder Frank Robinson spent six seasons playing next to eight-time Gold Glove center fielder Paul Blair. He saw Blair start shallow and dash to deep center to track down fly balls that seemingly were over his head. He saw Blair glide to his left—like he was walking on air—for a ball that Robinson initially thought was his. He saw Blair scale the center-field fence to take away a sure homer.

Robinson saw Blair accomplish incredible feats in the outfield at Memorial Stadium, but there's one thing Robinson said he never once witnessed. "I never saw Paul Blair run into a wall," Robinson said. "He'd go back to the wall full speed, jump, come down with the ball straight down, and he would never run into the wall. He knew where the wall was at all times."

Considered one of the greatest defensive center fielders in baseball history, Blair won seven consecutive Gold Gloves for the Orioles from 1969 to 1975. He could handle the bat, too. His best season was in 1969 when he set career highs in home runs (26), RBIs (76), and runs scored (102) while batting .285 and stealing 20 bases. It was one of two times in his career that he made an All-Star Game.

Blair was known for something else in addition to his stellar fielding. "He loved to talk. I think he probably tried to talk when he was sleeping," said Robinson of the man nicknamed "Motormouth." "On and off the field, he'd be yakking, yakking in the dugout. He'd keep you loose all the time."

In center field, though, he let his glove do most of the talking and at the most important times. Blair played prominent roles in the four World Series in which he appeared for the Orioles in the 1960s and '70s. He hit a solo homer in 1966's Game 3 against the heavily favored Los Angeles Dodgers in the Orioles' 1–0 victory. He also had a homer-robbing grab and caught the final out in Game 4 of the Orioles' upset sweep. In 1969, when the Orioles were stunned by the upstart New York Mets, Blair was victimized on a tremendous diving catch by Mets center fielder Tommie Agee with the bases loaded in Game 3. Blair also broke up Jerry Koosman's potential no-hitter and shutout in the seventh inning of Game 2 with a single, stolen base, and run scored. In 1970 he batted .474 and scored five runs in the Orioles' five-game victory over the Cincinnati Reds. And in 1971 he was the first batter in the first night game in World Series history. He singled to lead off Game 4 in Pittsburgh.

Offensively, Blair could be a spark plug for the Orioles, but his production at the plate never reached 1969 levels—possibly because he wasn't as aggressive after being beaned by a pitch from California Angels right-hander Ken Tatum in May 1970. Blair always contended what really damaged his offensive production occurred in the 1971 offseason when the Orioles traded away Robinson, who batted behind Blair and offered the ultimate protection. But Blair's defense never faltered. Ken Singleton, who became the Orioles' regular right fielder a few seasons after Robinson left, remembers one day in Cleveland when he was standing next to Blair during batting practice, and a loud fan in the near-empty stadium screamed at the duo. "Singleton, you are the luckiest right fielder in this league. There are two center fielders in the American League, and Blair is both of them," Singleton remembers the guy yelling. "Blair got a big kick out of it, and I did, too. I thought about it. The guy was right. Blair was the best."

A sportsman through and through, Blair collapsed and died at age 69 in a Baltimore bowling alley in December 2013 hours after he had played a round of golf. Generations later, people still know how loudly Motormouth's glove spoke. "His defense was unbelievable," said Orioles Gold Glove center fielder Adam Jones, who was born about five years after Blair retired. "Eight Gold Gloves? That's pretty impressive, doesn't matter how and when you get them."

22 Oriole Magic and Doug DeCinces

Third baseman Doug DeCinces sensed something special was happening; he just couldn't explain how or why he knew. It was a Friday night in late June, the Orioles had drawn their third largest crowd so far that season, and the fans weren't leaving Memorial Stadium despite the Orioles' two-run deficit heading into the ninth inning. "It was such a rare moment," said DeCinces, who played for the Orioles from 1973 to 1981. "I distinctly remember the reaction of the fans."

What he didn't know at the time was that his game-ending home run against Detroit Tigers reliever Dave Tobik on June 22, 1979, would kick off "Oriole Magic," the years-long catchphrase/ movement that encapsulated the club's penchant for comeback victories. It even had its own theme song—"Something magic happens, every time you go. You make the magic happen, the magic of Orioles baseball"—which is still played on occasion at Camden Yards decades later.

The Orioles were already a first-place team in late June 1979 and had begun to increase their lead over the Boston Red Sox. They had won seven of eight on a road trip, including six straight, when they returned to Baltimore for a 12-game homestand that began with the Tigers on June 22. The Orioles were losing 5–3 in the bottom of the ninth when Ken Singleton hit a one-out, solo home run against Tobik. Eddie Murray then singled, and Gary Roenicke followed with a fly ball for the second out. DeCinces was the Orioles' last chance, and on a 1–1 count, he lifted a Tobik pitch over the left field wall for a two-run, game-winner. His teammates gathered joyfully to greet and mob him, and DeCinces jumped on home plate while holding his hands high above his head to form an O. The announced 35,456 in attendance went crazy. That's where it could have ended. But it didn't. "When I was in the clubhouse, I got pulled back out. It was about maybe 10 minutes after the game was over," DeCinces said about his now famous curtain call. "They said the fans are still here. They are chanting your name. So when I walked out there, I was blown away because I don't think many people left. To walk back out there and hear that and feel that sensation was a very unique thing for an athlete to have."

What was eerie about the start of Oriole Magic was that DeCinces believes nearly everyone in the stadium sensed the Orioles were going to win. "When I walked up to home plate that night, the fans were totally expecting me to do something. It was two outs, the bottom of the ninth. The people could all have left.

"Orioles Magic" Lyrics

"Orioles Magic" was initially a promo jingle for WFBR's Orioles coverage in 1979. The lyrics were altered slightly, and the familiar, longer version was produced in 1980 by Perfect Pitch, the year after "Oriole Magic" became the catchphrase describing the club's late-season heroics. The song became a staple at Orioles games throughout the next few decades. In 2008 a group of Orioles recorded a video of the song at Camden Yards. The "lead singer" was veteran infielder Kevin Millar, and then-first-year Oriole Adam Jones "played" the drums. Here are the lyrics:

Something magic happens, every time you go.
You make the magic happen, the magic of Orioles baseball.

When the game is close, and the O's are hot,
There's a thundering roar from 34 to give it all they've got.

And you never know who's gonna hear the call.
Every game there's a different star.
That's the magic of Orioles' Baseball.

Orioles Magic! Feel it happen!
Orioles Magic! Feel it happen!

O-R-I-O-L-E-S !

Magic! Magic! Magic! Magic!

Something magic happens, every time you go.
You make the magic happen, the magic of Orioles baseball.

When Weaver moves and we score the runs.
Nothing could be more exciting.
Nothing could be more fun.

There's a love affair between you and the team.
You're the reason we win when we win.
And you know what the magic means.

Orioles Magic! Feel it happen!
Orioles Magic! Feel it happen!
Orioles Magic! Feel it happen!
Orioles Magic! Feel it happen!

O-R-I-O-L-E-S !

Magic! Magic! Magic! Magic!

Orioles Magic! Feel it happen!

Magic! Magic! Magic! Magic!

Something magic happens.

But no one was leaving," DeCinces said. "There was a certain air that night. The fans were cheering. They believed in it. They were expecting something. It was the fact that I accomplished it, and they were so blown away. It was just that magical moment. I mean, everybody hits game-winning home runs. It happens daily. It was just the energy between the team and the fans, and that's what made it so special."

That feeling didn't really subside all year. The next night the Orioles and Tigers played a doubleheader. In the first game, the Orioles trailed 6–5 in the bottom of the ninth when Murray hit a one-out, walk-off, three-run homer. The Orioles also staged a comeback in the nightcap with Singleton hitting a two-run single in the seventh to tie the game at 5 and Terry Crowley adding a two-out, pinch-hit RBI single in the bottom of the eighth for the eventual game-winner. The Orioles lost the next day to the Tigers, snapping their nine-game winning streak. But they won the next three—all by one or two runs—and eventually ended up in their first World Series in eight years. Those types of wins defined those excellent Orioles teams for the next few years.

It's fitting that DeCinces served as the hero on the night that Oriole Magic was born. There was probably no one who deserved more love from the Baltimore fan base than the lanky Californian. The Orioles drafted DeCinces in 1970, and he was groomed as the organization's next great third baseman. The problem was the Orioles' current great third baseman was practically the only third baseman the Orioles' fans ever knew. Replacing Hall of Famer and all-time franchise favorite Brooks Robinson seemingly would be daunting for a guy in his mid-20s. "It was a blessing," DeCinces says in retrospect. "It made me a better clutch player. My intensity, if anything, [increased] in the field. I had to be right on everything."

The transition from Robinson to DeCinces wasn't easy or quick. In 1975, when Robinson won his 16th and final Gold Glove, he started 134 games at third base while DeCinces started 25.

The next year Robinson started 59 games at the hot corner, and DeCinces started 103. In 1977 Robinson, then 40, played in just 15 games and made 10 starts at third before retiring. DeCinces started 146 games at third base and made 20 errors, the most he ever committed at one position in one season as an Oriole. "It was a difficult time, I've got to tell you. There were some times where I used to get hate mail. Some guys get fan mail; I was getting hate mail," DeCinces said. "I'm sure some of my teammates can remember what it was like in some of those games where [the fans] were chanting 'We want Brooks. We want Brooks.' There was nothing I could do about that. I had to just overcome that. I honestly look back and believe it made me a better player."

With Robinson gone in 1978, manager Earl Weaver attempted to take some pressure off DeCinces while getting his most potent hitters into the lineup simultaneously. His grand experiment was to move DeCinces to second base, switch unflappable future Hall of Famer Eddie Murray from first to third base, and reinstate veteran and primary designated hitter Lee May at first. It lasted the initial three games of the season—all losses in Milwaukee—before it was scrapped. DeCinces started nine more games at second base in 1978 but, for the most part, was the Orioles' everyday third baseman from Robinson's retirement until before the 1982 season when DeCinces was traded to the California Angels for outfielder Dan Ford. DeCinces played 15 seasons in the majors, made an All-Star team, and placed third in the American League Most Valuable Player voting in his first year with the Angels.

Although he's often remembered as the guy who succeeded Brooks Robinson at third base, he'll never be forgotten as the man who began Oriole Magic with one dramatic swing in 1979. That, for Orioles fans, is DeCinces' primary legacy. "They didn't want Brooks that night, did they?" Singleton joked.

Losing to the Pirates, Part I

It was the Orioles' third straight American League championship team and fourth in six seasons. It would be their last for eight years. It may have been the biggest disappointment for the club led by Brooks and Frank Robinson, Boog Powell, and Paul Blair—an offensive nucleus that would never play together again. (Frank Robinson was traded to the Los Angeles Dodgers in December of 1971.) For the third straight year, the Orioles won more than 100 games (101 in 1971) to capture their third consecutive American League East crown under manager Earl Weaver. For the third straight year, they swept their opponent in the American League Championship Series—the Oakland Athletics this time. The Orioles then won the first two games of the World Series and took a 2–0 lead to Three Rivers Stadium in Pittsburgh. Win two of the next five, and they'd be repeat champions. "We won the first two games and we won them pretty easily, and I guess we figured we had them. And we didn't," first baseman Boog Powell said. "We just sort of went flat again, and there really was no reason for it."

The season: It was typical Orioles of that era. They won seven of eight to begin the season and finished it with 11 consecutive regular-season victories. The offense produced seven hitters with double-digit home runs, and for the second time in three years, the same quartet—infielders Brooks Robinson, Mark Belanger, and Davey Johnson and center fielder Blair—won Gold Gloves. But it was another Orioles quartet that made history. The Orioles had four starting pitchers—Jim Palmer, Dave McNally, Mike Cuellar, and Pat Dobson—win at least 20 games, becoming the only staff in baseball history besides the 1920 Chicago White Sox to accomplish that.

The playoff opponents: The A's were about to start their own dynasty but were no match for the 1971 Orioles. The Pirates won 97 regular season games and defeated the San Francisco Giants 3–1 in the National League Championship Series. Offensively, Pittsburgh was led by Willie Stargell, who had the best season of his Hall of Fame career in 1971. Stargell belted 48 homers and drove in 125 RBIs and was second in the NL MVP race to Joe Torre of the St. Louis Cardinals. Right fielder Roberto Clemente batted .341 and finished fifth for MVP, and catcher Manny Sanguillen placed eighth after hitting .319.

The key moments: With the Pirates clinging to a 2–1 lead in the bottom of the seventh in crucial Game 3, they put runners on first and second with no outs against Orioles lefty Mike Cuellar. Pirates manager Danny Murtaugh called for slugger Bob Robertson to attempt a sacrifice bunt. Robertson didn't see the sign, and Clemente, who was on second, tried to call timeout, but Cuellar was in his windup. Robertson hit the pitch over the right-center wall for a 5–1 lead, guaranteeing that the Pirates wouldn't fall into an 0–3 series hole. Clemente's fourth-inning solo homer in Game 7 against Cuellar broke a scoreless tie, and the Pirates ultimately won 2–1.

The top performances: Clemente, who was 37, had hits in every game and batted .414 with two homers, two doubles, and a triple and was named series MVP. A little over a year later, he was killed in a plane crash while on a mission trip. Right-hander Steve Blass pitched two complete games, allowing one run in each, and was the winning pitcher in Games 3 and 7. Spot starter Nelson Briles allowed just two hits and two walks in a complete-game shutout in Game 5. Pittsburgh reliever Bruce Kison hit three batters in one outing, a series record, but otherwise allowed one hit in six and one-third scoreless innings to win Game 4, which was the first night game in World Series history.

The quote: "Frank said something that really hit home with me," Brooks Robinson said. "If we had won the '69 and '71 World Series, we would be known as one of the greatest teams ever. And I seriously believe that. But the problem was you've got to win."

24 Losing to the Pirates, Part II

After making the World Series four times in six seasons from 1966 until 1971, the Orioles didn't get back again until 1979. It was almost a completely different cast of characters. Only starter Jim Palmer and shortstop Mark Belanger played in both the 1971 and 1979 World Series against the Pittsburgh Pirates. Hall of Famer Earl Weaver was around for each and surely was still bitter in 1979 about his team's seven-game loss to the Pirates in 1971. (The Orioles were up 2–0 in that one before losing four of the next five.) There'd be more hand-wringing in Baltimore after the 1979 World Series, one in which the Orioles were up 3–1 and dropped three straight, including the final two at Memorial Stadium. "Unbelievable disappointment. The momentum shifted after that fourth game, and we never got it back. There were so many crazy things that happened," said Orioles catcher Rick Dempsey. "That was a heartbreaker because once we lost that momentum, everything went against us."

The season: The Orioles won 102 games, their most since 1970 and the first time they reached triple digits in victories since 1971. The offense was paced by right fielder Ken Singleton, who set career highs with 35 homers and 111 RBIs and finished second in the American League MVP voting to former Oriole Don Baylor. Left-hander Mike Flanagan, who went 23–9 with a 3.08 ERA, won the AL Cy Young Award and finished sixth in MVP voting. Future Hall of Famer Eddie Murray had a fairly typical Murray season: 25 home runs, 99 RBIs, and a .295 average. The Orioles were phenomenal at home, winning nearly 70 percent of their games (55–24) at Memorial Stadium. The club had nine walk-off wins, including Doug DeCinces' two-run homer on June 22, 1979 that kick-started Oriole Magic.

The playoff opponents: The Orioles faced the California Angels in the American League Championship Series and won the first game in dramatic fashion with a two-out, pinch-hit, three-run home run by John Lowenstein in the bottom of the 10th. They won the series in four games with lefty Scott McGregor pitching a complete-game shutout. The Pirates won 98 in the regular season and swept the Cincinnati Reds on the back of Willie "Pops" Stargell, the leader of a tight-knit club that used Sister Sledge's "We Are Family" as a theme song for the year. Stargell, a future Hall of Famer who batted .281 with 32 homers in the regular season, shared the National League MVP honors with Keith Hernandez of the St. Louis Cardinals. Pirates closer Kent Tekulve finished eighth in MVP voting and fifth for the Cy Young. Game 1 of the World Series was postponed a day due to a freezing rain. Snow fell overnight, and there were still flakes at noon on October 10, the earliest recorded snow in Baltimore history. The game was played that night, but it was a bitter 41 degrees at first pitch.

The key moments: In a tense series filled with big moments, the two most indelible occurred in Game 7. With one on and one out in the sixth and the Orioles leading 1–0, Stargell ruined McGregor's shutout bid with a two-run homer to right. It was Stargell's third home run of the series. The Orioles had a chance to take the lead in the bottom of the eighth against Tekulve. With runners on second and third and two outs, Pirates manager Chuck Tanner decided to intentionally walk Singleton with first base open to face Murray, who ultimately became one of the best clutch hitters in baseball history. But Murray, then 23, was hitless in his previous 20 at-bats. The future Hall of Famer hit a fly ball off Tekulve to deep right, but Dave Parker caught it to end the threat.

The top performances: Stargell capped an amazing year by going 12-for-30 (.400) with four doubles and three homers, winning the World Series MVP. He had four hits in the final game. Tekulve saved three games, which initially set a series record. Manny Sanguillen, who also was in the 1971 World Series, had a pinch-hit, ninth-inning single to win Game 2. Orioles shortstop Kiko Garcia had four hits, including a bases-loaded triple, to help the Orioles win Game 3. In Game 4 reliever Tim Stoddard had a RBI single during a six-run eighth inning that erased a 6–3 deficit in the only postseason at-bat of his career.

The quote: "As I look back on it, I know what happened. We got too over-confident, especially the way we picked up our third victory, rallying in Pittsburgh to take the lead," Singleton said. "I remember coming into the clubhouse. Everybody was really happy, and it seemed as though we thought we had the World Series won."

The Great Demper

If you take the Orioles' six Hall of Famers out of the discussion, an argument can be made that the most popular player in club history is a catcher who spent more than two decades in the big leagues and never once made an All-Star team.

Other more celebrated players in the conversation for all-time favorite Oriole not in Cooperstown: Boog Powell, Mike Flanagan, and Brady Anderson—to name a few. That trio of All-Stars also stayed close to the organization after their playing days ended.

But for Orioles fans, no non-superstar embodied the spirit of the club more than Rick Dempsey, the quirky catcher who played 24 seasons in the majors, half with the Orioles. You obviously need talent and a strong knowledge of the game to last that long in the big leagues. And Dempsey's excellent performance in the 1983 World Series won him MVP honors and further cemented his place in franchise history.

But what made the career .233 hitter into a Baltimore sports icon was his personality. No one had more fun playing baseball—or being a baseball player—than Dempsey. "I was the guy that made the most outs. I knew that; that's why I hit ninth. But I wasn't afraid to be outspoken and try to get everybody fired up because I wanted to win," Dempsey said. "That was the most important part of the game, and so I'd be yelling and screaming and doing whatever it took to get everybody into the game."

The blue-collar fans who came out to Memorial Stadium in the magical summers of the late 1970s and early 1980s appreciated the lengths that Dempsey would go to rally the troops. Whether it was waving a towel from the bullpen to pump up the fans, sliding on the tarp during rain delays, chanting the O-R-I-O-L-E-S cheer with superfan Wild Bill Hagy, or making music videos with his "Invisible Orioles Magic Band,"—somehow he convinced recalcitrant Hall-of-Famer Eddie Murray to sit in on drums—Dempsey is Baltimore baseball's Good Time Charlie. "I never ate glass or swallowed goldfish or any of that kind of stuff. I wasn't that wacky. But we did have the Invisible Orioles Magic Band and we pulled pranks," Dempsey said. "We just had good times together—good, clean good times."

It would do Dempsey an injustice, though, to dismiss him simply as a clown prince. He was one of the more competitive players to ever don an Orioles uniform. Case in point: a game in Milwaukee, in which Dempsey was involved in two unavoidable miscues and subsequently was benched by Hall of Fame manager and renowned hothead Earl Weaver. The crusty manager had threatened to take Dempsey out of games so often in their careers that normally the catcher ignored his skipper, put on his equipment, and went back behind the plate without incident. But this time Weaver was so angry that he summoned reserve catcher Dave Skaggs from the bullpen and told the umpiring crew that if Dempsey stepped onto the field, Weaver would purposely forfeit

Catcher and defensive whiz Rick Dempsey performs his famous rain delay theatrics on June 29, 1980. (AP Images)

the game. An enraged Dempsey remained in the dugout, tossing his equipment at Weaver. "Every piece of equipment I had I threw at him. My shin guards kind of boomeranged away, my chest protector I threw. Then I got to my mask and I knew I could have hurt him with that, so I threw it down in front of him, and it hit a helmet, and the helmet bounced up and hit him. He got madder and picked the helmet up and threw it back at me, and now we are throwing helmets and everything at each other in the dugout."

Coach Frank Robinson grabbed Dempsey and told him to go the shower before things worsened. Dempsey listened, but as he trotted out of the dugout tunnel he ripped off his uniform, walking into the shower in his underwear, socks, and spikes. Weaver followed him. "He walks right into the shower and started yelling at me, 'I'm the boss. You've got to do what I tell you to do. When I say you've got to leave the game, you've got to undress and leave the game,'" Dempsey recalled. "While he was doing that, it was a cold day in Milwaukee, I turned the hot water off and I took the nozzle above my head and aimed the stream at him and hit him right in the chest. All cold water. For about three or four seconds he took it, and then it was so cold that he had to get out. As he was leaving, he was yelling 'I am the boss.' And I yelled, 'That's right you are the boss—spelled backward it's 'Double SOB.' He walked out, and that was it. I played the next day."

Dempsey's calling card was his defense—he threw out 40 percent of would-be basestealers in his career—and the proficient way he handled pitchers. But he also had some important offensive moments, hitting .303 in 66 postseason at-bats, including batting .385 with a homer in the 1983 World Series against the Philadelphia Phillies. After playing with the Orioles from 1976 to 1986, Dempsey returned to Baltimore in 1992 and appeared in eight more games before retiring. At age 43 he became the oldest player to suit up for the modern-day Orioles.

He has maintained his connection to the Orioles throughout the years, coaching in the big leagues, working as a television announcer for the club-owned Mid Atlantic Sports Network, and operating Dempsey's restaurant in the warehouse at Camden Yards. He's seemingly always at the center of Baltimore baseball, laughing and joking with anyone who will play along—no matter how famous or important. After the Game 5 clincher in 1983, U.S. president Ronald Reagan called the visiting clubhouse to congratulate the new world champions. Dempsey was given the phone and, in his playful way, joked with the leader of the free world during the height of the Cold War: "Mr. President, you go tell the Russians that we're having a good time over here playing baseball."

Hit Me If You Can

It looms over Oriole Park at Camden Yards just daring left-handed hitters to smack it. Officially, it is listed as 439 feet from home plate—which is a serious poke on the fly but, theoretically, far from impossible. Yet that distance seems much farther when a baseball is hurtling toward it.

The eight-story B&O Warehouse, which sits approximately 60 feet beyond the right field wall, was supposed to be a magnet for home runs when Camden Yards opened in 1992. It's about as impressive a structure you'll see near a ballpark. The brick warehouse, built between 1898 and 1905, is more than 1,000 feet long. The Orioles list it as 1,016 feet and claim it's the longest building on the East Coast. It was initially used as storage for the Baltimore and Ohio Railroad, reportedly once able to hold 1,000 carloads of freight.

Now it serves as home to the Orioles' administrative offices and the unofficial bull's-eye for left-handed sluggers. Former Oriole Mickey Tettleton was the first to have a homer land on Eutaw Street, the walkway that separates the warehouse from the right-field flag court. At the time the Detroit Tigers catcher, with his python arms, was the clear favorite to hit a ball off the warehouse. Another behemoth left-handed hitter, the Orioles' Sam Horn, vowed to do it in a game in 1992. It didn't happen then. And—by 2014—it still hadn't. Those 63 shatter-proof windows on the bottom four floors of the warehouse seem like unnecessary accoutrements now.

The official 439-foot measurement from home plate to the warehouse constitutes the closest section of wall just beyond the right-field foul pole. But given that a ball must clear the 20-plus-foot, out-of-town scoreboard in right, a homer probably would have to travel roughly 460 feet to guarantee hitting warehouse brick. Although it has never happened in a game, some players such as Horn, Jay Gibbons, Jason Giambi, David Ortiz, and Chris Davis have done it during batting practice. And Ken Griffey Jr. reached the warehouse with a 465-foot blast on July 12, 1993 as part of the All-Star Game's Home Run Derby.

There's a bronze marker on the warehouse to show where Griffey's ball landed. There are baseball-shaped markers all along Eutaw Street to commemorate each home run that has come close to the wall. Technically, the longest clout to that part of the stadium was 443 feet by the Montreal Expos' Henry Rodriguez in 1997. But it was more toward right-center field, where the wall tails away from the stadium. The homer that landed closest to the wall was by the Houston Astros' Lance Berkman; it was estimated at 430 feet.

In September of 2009, Orioles designated hitter Luke Scott hit one against A.J. Burnett that caused a mini-controversy in Baltimore when several fans at the game thought it hit the wall. But replays showed it clearly bounced once before striking the facade.

Scott, who initially set the Camden Yards record with six Eutaw Street homers, said he thinks someday the wall will be hit on the fly in a game. It, though, has to be the perfect storm. "The conditions would have to be right," Scott said. "It'd have to be the right pitch, and the air would have to be right. Warm climate, a fastball or slider. A hanging slider about 86 to 88 [miles per hour] with a good, tight spin because with a tight spin, the ball will jump off the bat much better."

Ortiz, the Boston Red Sox slugger, said visiting players make a point of aiming for the warehouse during batting practice, but that's never an objective during games. Boog Powell, arguably the best left-handed slugger in Orioles history, said he wishes he had had a shot at the warehouse during his prime. Powell left the Orioles nearly 18 years before Camden Yards opened. "It would be my mission. I would never be happy until I hit the warehouse," Powell said. "By God, I would have hit this son of a [gun] if I had to go get golf balls and throw them up."

27 Cal Ripken Sr.

Attempting to write a short piece about Cal Ripken Sr., arguably the Orioles' most influential character, creates a dilemma. Do you focus on the instructor who made an entire franchise fundamentally sound by using an undeterred work ethic to inspire generations of ballplayers? Or do you just tell stories about how nails tough this son-of-a-gun was? Maybe a little bit of both, but you start with the tough guy stories—like the tractor crank yarn. Whenever there was a bad snowstorm in the Ripkens' hometown of Aberdeen, Maryland, Ripken Sr. would plow the neighborhood with an old borrowed tractor and a box drag he made out of wood. During one snowfall the tractor's battery died. So Ripken attempted to use a hand crank to start it, showing his 16-year-old son, Cal Jr., how to do it properly by pushing the crank safely away from his body. It wasn't working, so he changed methods, the crank slipped, and it hit the elder Ripken in the head, causing an immediate gushing wound. "He took an oily rag out of his pocket and stuck it up to his head to stop the bleeding," Ripken Jr. said. The son tried to take his dad to the hospital, but instead Ripken Sr. asked to stop at their house. There he found an old butterfly bandage, affixed it to his head, and had his son drive him back to the barn, where he started the tractor and plowed the neighborhood. "He never even went to the doctor," Ripken Jr. said.

In the late '70s, the three teenaged Ripken boys, Cal Jr., Fred, and Bill, played soccer in a winter league, and their father coached his kids' two teams. In his 40s Ripken Sr. would play along, running, kicking, getting stepped on, and then coming home with aching feet. Blood would pocket under his toenails, causing discoloration and immense pressure. So he'd grab his power drill, put in a small drill bit, place his foot on the edge of the toilet seat, and drill into the affected nail. "When you drill through stuff that's hard, there's that moment where it goes through. Well, blood would come squirting out, and that was instant relief to him," Bill Ripken said. "And it stopped the problem right away. He would put a Band-Aid on it and go about his daily business." Ripken Jr. chuckles at the memory of his dad's Black & Decker pain relief: "It seems a little bit insane, looking back on it."

Many of Ripken's tough guy stories doubled as teaching moments. Former Orioles pitcher Ben McDonald remembers a conversation when the 6'7" McDonald dropped his gaze and looked away momentarily from the wiry, 5'11" Ripken. "He was talking to me face to face, and I kind of glanced down. And he slapped me across my face like my dad would," McDonald said.

All in the Family

The Orioles have the only set of brothers to be managed by their father in baseball history: Billy and Cal Ripken Jr. played for Cal Sr. in 1987 and for six games in 1988.

The Ripkens (Cal Jr. from 1981–2001 and Billy from 1987–1992, 1996) and the Browns (Dick from 1963–65 and Larry from 1973) are the only sets of brothers to play for the Orioles; the Browns, however, didn't play on the same team.

The only father-son combination to play together as Orioles was Tim Raines and his son, Tim Jr., at the end of 2001. They were the second in baseball history to do that behind only Ken Griffey Sr. and Ken Griffey Jr. for the Seattle Mariners in 1990–91.

Six father-son combos have played for the modern-day Orioles at some point. They are: Bob Kennedy (1954–55) and Terry Kennedy (1987–88); Don Buford (1968–72) and Damon Buford (1993–95); John O'Donoghue Sr. (1968) and John O'Donoghue Jr. (1993); Dave May (1967–70) and Derrick May (1999); Dave Johnson (1989–91) and Steve Johnson (2012–13); and Tim Raines and his son.

"He said, 'Son, when I'm talking to you, you're going to listen to me and you're going to give me that eye contact that I deserve.' I really respected him for that." McDonald said he'd often seek out Ripken Sr. on the back of the team plane, "as he smoked those cigarettes and drank Schlitz beer on those long road trips. And I used to sit back there with him as a 21-year-old kid."

Ripken Sr. spent six years in the minors as a strong defensive catcher whose playing career ended due to arm woes. The versatile backstop also drove the team bus, a necessity once his minor league manager, Earl Weaver, fired the bus driver. Ripken, whose father died when he was 10, forcing him to be particularly resourceful, could learn to do pretty much anything. "He knew how to fix lawn mowers and cars because he had worked in gas stations. He worked on a contracting team so he knew how to build a house and how to renovate rooms. He worked on a farm so he knows how to grow [vegetables]. He had a great garden," Ripken Jr. said. "So it was almost like there wasn't anything he wasn't exposed to, and I think that's where the work ethic started for him."

More than anything, Ripken knew baseball and how to teach it. He stressed fundamentals, doing things uniformly and correctly and practicing concepts until they were perfect. Those were the tenets of The Oriole Way, which was preached throughout the system and led to success at the major league level. Ripken Sr. didn't take shortcuts, and that included his own career. He spent more than a decade managing in the minors in towns such as Aberdeen, South Dakota; Elmira, New York; and Asheville, North Carolina. Once school was out, his wife, Vi, and the family's four children would pack up the white Buick Electra 225—or a blue Buick station wagon before that—hitch a trailer to it, and trek to wherever the patriarch was managing that season. In 1976 Weaver promoted him to bullpen coach, and in 1977 he took over as third-base coach, a post he held until replacing Weaver in 1987. "Cal Sr. was the hardest working coach I have ever been around," said former Orioles outfielder Ken Singleton. "If you would tell him, 'I want to take batting practice at 3:00 in the morning,' he'd be there to throw it for you. When he would run the drills in spring train-ing—the base-running drills, the sliding drills—he would do them first. Everybody would say, 'If this old guy can do it, we can do it.'"

Ripken Sr. became the only person to manage two sons simul-taneously in the majors in July 1987, with Cal Jr. playing shortstop and Bill at second base. That opportunity didn't last long. He was fired six losses into the 1988 season, an exceptionally quick hook for an organizational lifer. "I remember being very upset, confused, angry, you name it," said Ripken Jr., who was the club's biggest star. "I had every one of those emotions going on." His father, though, used it as another teaching moment for 23-year-old Bill, who was in his first full season. When Bill Ripken arrived at the stadium on the day of the firing, his dad had left. Athletic trainer

Ralph Salvon met the kid at the door. "His message to me through Ralph was, 'He's a big boy. He can handle himself. These things happen,'" Bill Ripken recalled. "You've got to worry about yourself. Go out there and do your job because that is what you are supposed to do."

Ripken Sr. rejoined the Orioles organization later that summer as a scout and regained his third-base coaching job in 1989. He was fired again after the 1992 season and didn't return to the ballpark until Ripken Jr. broke Lou Gehrig's consecutive-games played record in 1995. Ripken Sr. died of cancer in March 1999 at 63. The Cal Ripken Sr. Foundation was established in 2001 to provide life lessons for underprivileged youth through baseball and softball. "He developed kids. Dad had a link that went all the way down to some kids that didn't have certain advantages and so he would speak to them through clinics," Ripken Jr. said. "Professionally, he was a father figure. He was always there looking out for people."

28 Losin' to the Amazin' Mets

Three years after they had pulled off a shocking upset of the Los Angeles Dodgers, the Orioles were caught in the opposite scenario. They were—by far—the best team in baseball, winning 109 regular season games, still the most in club history. They won the newly created American League East by 19 games over the Detroit Tigers and then won three straight in the first AL Championship Series against the Minnesota Twins. Meanwhile, the New York Mets had been a National League punching bag since their inception in 1962. But the Amazin' Mets put everything together in 1969. To this day, the Orioles say they didn't take the Mets lightly; they were just a good team with tremendous momentum. The Orioles were warned.

Former Oriole Milt Pappas was still living in Baltimore in 1969 after his Atlanta Braves were swept by the Mets in the NL Championship Series. Orioles first baseman Boog Powell says he clearly remembers Pappas telling him that the Mets were for real. Pappas said he was even more direct with Orioles third baseman Brooks Robinson: "I said, 'Brooksie, I hate to tell you this, my friend, but you're gonna get your ass kicked. Mark my words.' And they got beat four out of five. It was just one of those years where everything went right for the Mets."

The season: The Orioles pummeled the opposition with a run differential of +262. (In comparison, the Mets' run differential was +91.) The Orioles won 30 games by five runs or more. They had four hitters with 23 or more home runs, including Powell, who had 37 homers, 121 RBIs, and a .304 average to finish second in the AL MVP race to Minnesota's Harmon Killebrew. Veteran lefty Mike Cuellar was 23–11 with a 2.38 ERA and shared AL Cy Young Award honors with Detroit's Denny McLain.

The playoff opponents: The Orioles outscored the Twins 16–5, including an 11–2 blowout in Game 3, to advance to the World Series. The Mets swept the Braves, outslugging them 27–15 and scoring at least seven runs in each game. Their 100-win season was paced by 24-year-old ace and eventual Hall of Famer Tom Seaver and accomplished 26-year-old lefty Jerry Koosman. Seaver was 25–7 with a 2.21 ERA to easily win the Cy Young Award. He finished second in the MVP race, and Mets outfielders Tommie Agee and Cleon Jones placed sixth and seventh, respectively.

The key moments: The one that's forever smudged into baseball's consciousness occurred in the sixth inning of the decisive Game 5 with the Orioles leading 3–0. Dave McNally threw a pitch in the dirt. The ball bounced into the Mets dugout and manager Gil Hodges emerged with a ball that had a black smudge—presumably shoe polish from Jones' cleat—to prove his player had been hit. Jones was awarded first base. The next batter, first baseman Donn Clendenon, homered to reduce the deficit to 3–2. The Mets eventually scored three more runs to win their first title. Years later, Koosman claimed that he rubbed the baseball against his own cleat, at the direction of Hodges, to produce the smudge. It was one of several explanations given. Outfielder Ron Swoboda said, years later, that the game ball hit a bag of practice balls, and several poured out. And Hodges selected the one that was smudged.

There was also a memorable umpire's decision in Game 4 that ultimately allowed the winning run to score. In a tied game in the 10th, pinch-hitter J.C. Martin dropped a sacrifice bunt that was

Orioles manager Earl Weaver celebrates his team's American League East title, though Baltimore would later fall to the New York Mets in the 1969 World Series.

fielded by Orioles reliever Pete Richert, who threw to first. His throw struck Martin, the ball bounced down the right-field line, and pinch-runner Rod Gaspar scored the winning run. Replays showed that Martin was out of the base line—blocking Richert's path to throw the ball—but interference wasn't called.

The top performances: Clendenon, who had 16 homers in 110 regular season games, had three in 14 at-bats in the only post-season series of his 12-season career. He was named the MVP. Led by tremendous catches from Agee and Swoboda, the Mets' defense stole the show. Koosman threw six innings of no-hit ball in Game 2 and fell one out shy of a one-run complete game. He allowed three runs in a complete-game victory in the clincher.

The quote: "One of the most moving times that I ever had in baseball was when we came back from Shea Stadium after losing that last game. We landed at the airport, and there were, I don't know, 5,000 people or so waiting for us at the airport, and they were crying and we were crying," Powell said. "We went out, and they were behind the big fence and we tried to shake hands with them. We put our hands through the fence. We were trying to touch as many people as we could, and most of us had tears in our eyes, too. Not of sadness, but joy that people in Baltimore cared that much about us to come out."

29 Dave McNally

Earl Weaver didn't cry often, certainly not when he was jawing at one of his championship players during his managerial reign. He was a blusterer, not a blubberer. That's why the occurrence on September 20, 1969 against the New York Yankees in Memorial

Stadium was so surprising. Weaver broke down in tears after one of his players screamed at him—but it wasn't just any player. It was Mac, left-hander Dave McNally, whom teammates, fans, and Weaver admired for his steely nerve and work ethic.

By 1969 McNally had emerged as one of the franchise's greatest pitchers. He became only the second modern-day Oriole with 20 wins when he notched 22 and posted a 1.95 ERA in 1968. After winning his final two decisions that season, he began the next year 15–0, a streak of 17 straight victories without a loss. "McNally once told me, 'I don't care how many runs I give up just as long as I pitch better than the guy across from me,'" catcher Andy Etchebarren said. "He felt like whenever he went to the mound, he was going to win."

On that fall Saturday afternoon in 1969, McNally was going for his 20th victory of the season, which would have made him the first Oriole to reach the mark in consecutive years. Weaver, in his first full season managing the club, had his own milestone in sight. The Orioles, at 105–47, had already wrapped up the division title but needed seven victories in their final 10 contests to break the 1954 Cleveland Indians' American League record of 111 victories. McNally threw five innings against the Yankees, giving up four runs (three earned). In the bottom of the fifth and with the Orioles trailing 4–1, McNally was due up second. He had his helmet and jacket on and a bat in his hand when Weaver told him that Merv Rettenmund would be pinch-hitting for him. It meant McNally couldn't get the win; he'd have just two more chances for 20 that season. McNally, as his rotation-mate Jim Palmer describes it, was livid. "There goes the bat, the helmet, the jacket. He walks up on the warning track [in front of the dugout] and heaves those things," Palmer said. "Mac goes all the way to the other steps, walks down the three steps, up the three steps, and goes into the clubhouse. And Earl runs after him."

The ensuing spat between the feisty, diminutive Weaver and one of his players was different than the hundreds of others. When Weaver demanded to know what the pitcher's problem was, the highly respected McNally unloaded. "Mac says, 'You've got to stop thinking about yourself and winning more games than anybody else. Here I am, I'm going for my 20th win, and it would have been nice for you to give me the opportunity to do it,'" Palmer recalled. "'We have one of the best teams. And you are pinch-hitting for me? All you do is think about yourself.' Earl really started tearing up because he knew Mac was right, but Earl got lost in the moment." Etchebarren remembers Weaver returning to the bench after the altercation. "Here comes Earl and he's crying. I guess McNally said some things he shouldn't have said," Etchebarren said. "We had the pennant won, and McNally wanted to win 20. He thought he should have stayed in the game." (Incidentally, the Orioles, indeed, came back to win that one 8–7.)

McNally was known for his unrelenting drive on the mound—Weaver once described him as having "a lot of stomach"—but having a friendly, reserved demeanor away from it. A Montana native signed by the Orioles out of high school in 1960, McNally spent 13 of his 14 seasons in Baltimore. He picked up 181 of his 184 career victories with the Orioles and is No. 2 on the franchise's all-time wins list and tops for left-handers. Only Palmer had more wins, shutouts, starts, and innings pitched. McNally won 20 games each season from 1968 to 1971. In 1969 he recorded No. 20 with a complete-game victory in the next start after Weaver pulled him. During a nine season-stretch, he posted an ERA of 3.22 or lower eight times. Etchebarren, McNally's old roommate, to this day refers to McNally as, "the best pitcher I ever caught." He was good from the beginning, making his debut at 19 in September of 1962 and pitching a complete-game, two-hit shutout against the Kansas City Athletics. Often labeled a finesse pitcher, McNally could throw his fastball in the low 90s, had an excellent curveball, and had great command of his pitches. "He could go a whole game and not throw a ball in the middle of the plate," Palmer said.

McNally was part of some of the franchise's biggest moments, posting a 2.49 ERA in 14 postseason appearances, including four wins and a 2.34 ERA in 50 World Series innings. At age 23 he started the club's first World Series game against the Los Angeles Dodgers and Don Drysdale in 1966. McNally recorded just seven outs, yielding to reliever Moe Drabowsky, who threw six and two-third shutout innings for the victory. McNally bounced back in Game 4 with a complete-game, four-hit shutout to finish the surprising sweep of the Dodgers. The photo of third baseman Brooks Robinson leaping high into the air on his way to McNally's arms that day is the most iconic snapshot in club history. McNally's most memorable accomplishment in a World Series, however, came with the bat. His grand slam in the sixth inning of Game 3 of the 1970 World Series is the only one ever hit by a pitcher in the October Classic.

After the 1974 season, the Orioles traded McNally and outfielder Rich Coggins to the Montreal Expos for pitcher Mike Torrez and outfielder Ken Singleton, a cornerstone in the Orioles' next pennant run. With his left arm aching, McNally made just 12 starts with the Expos, never pitching again after age 32. But the battler had a few more important fights left. Although he never expected to pitch in 1976, he and Los Angeles Dodgers right-hander Andy Messersmith challenged baseball's reserve clause rule that allowed teams to maintain a player's rights even after his contract expired. McNally's and Messersmith's appeal was upheld, paving the way for free agency in baseball. McNally's final battle was with lung cancer and it lasted five valiant years before he died in 2002 at age 60.

30 The Kiddie Corps

For their first few years of existence, the modern-day Orioles were, in a word—awful. They lost 100 games in their first season and 97 in their second. With respected manager Paul Richards, there was some gradual improvement, but they didn't finish higher than fifth or have a winning record in their first six seasons. About halfway through 1959, another losing campaign, Richards and general manager Lee MacPhail made a decision. The next season would be all about playing their youngsters, including several of the bonus babies that Richards had collected.

Jerry Walker, a 21-year-old right-hander who had made his professional debut in 1957 as an 18-year-old and won 11 games in 1959, was the Opening Day starter in 1960 against the Washington Senators. He pitched into the sixth and allowed two runs before turning the game over to another 21-year-old righty, Jack Fisher, who finished the game and received credit for the win. The infield was comprised of third baseman Brooks Robinson, a 23-year-old who would soon become a household name; 22-year-old shortstop Ron Hansen, who had appeared in 14 big league games before 1960; 26-year-old second baseman Marv Breeding, who was making his big league debut; and 26-year-old Jim Gentile, who was practically on loan from the Los Angeles Dodgers and had just 16 games of major league experience.

The Orioles won the opener 3–2 on a RBI double in the seventh by the club's offensive Methuselah, 37-year-old outfielder Gene Woodling. The Orioles then lost five in a row, including a sweep at Yankee Stadium, and the "Kiddie Corps" looked over-matched. Something quickly changed, though. The Orioles won seven of their next eight, including two of three from the mighty

New York Yankees at Memorial Stadium. By the end of that little run, the Orioles had gone over .500. And they never fell under that mark again—for their first winning season in the fledgling franchise's history. "We had a great club," Gentile said. "And we knew there was something to look forward to as the year went on."

Under Richards, who was named the 1960 Manager of the Year by the Associated Press and United Press International, the Orioles had finally risen above mediocrity. And then they kept ascending that season led by five pitchers age 22 or younger who made at least 18 starts each. Right-hander Chuck Estrada had never pitched in the majors before and paced the team with 18 wins. Flame-throwing lefty Steve Barber, a Takoma Park, Maryland, native, went from Class D ball to the Orioles and won 10 games with a 3.22 ERA as a 22-year-old. Milt Pappas, who was in his fourth big league season at 21, posted 15 wins and a 3.22 ERA. Walker and Fisher combined to pitch in 69 games, including 38 starts. That Kiddie quintet picked up 58 wins, completed 38 games and threw eight shutouts. "Looking at it now, it was a big deal," Pappas said. "But when it happened, you had five young guys in the starting rotation all pulling for each other. It didn't mean much at the time. After the fact you look back and say, 'Wow, what we did was phenomenal.'"

The Kiddie Corps received some help from key veterans. Future Hall of Famer Hoyt Wilhelm, at age 37, won 11 games. With his knuckleball dancing between the rotation and the bullpen, he started 11 games and finished 24. And 35-year-old Hal "Skinny" Brown turned in the best season of his 14-year career, going 12–5 with a 3.06 ERA in 30 games (20 starts). But it was the kids in the rotation who stole the show. "We just knew how to reach back and throw. We didn't have any trick pitches. We just went out there with our best stuff every day," Pappas said. "Steve Barber could throw the ball through a brick wall. Estrada had a good, live fastball, and I had tremendous control. Fisher relied mainly on his other stuff—sliders and curveballs—and Jerry Walker had a good curveball and slider and had good control."

As Gentile put it, "My goodness, I'm glad I didn't have to face them. They were just good young pitchers. With Steve Barber, it was like hitting a rock. They were just good pitchers and they had a good pitching coach in Harry Brecheen."

Robinson had his first breakout season in a Hall of Fame career, hitting .294 with 14 homers and 88 RBIs. He won the first of his 16 consecutive Gold Gloves, made the first of his 15 consecutive All-Star Games, and finished third in the American League MVP voting. Hansen led the Orioles with 22 home runs and won American League Rookie of the Year honors with 22 of 24 possible first-place votes. Gentile drove in a team-leading 98 runs and finished tied for second in AL Rookie of the Year voting with Estrada, who recorded 18 wins. Estrada and Gentile each picked up one first-place vote. That's how good and young that team was. No other AL player received a single vote for Rookie of the Year.

But seasons aren't judged by individual awards. And the Kiddie Corps fell short of their goal: winning their first AL crown. The Orioles were in first place by themselves for seven days from September 3rd to 9th—spurred by a three-game sweep of the Yankees at Memorial Stadium—and became the talk of baseball. But they just couldn't finish off the juggernaut Bronx Bombers. With the teams tied for first on September 16, they clashed for a four-game series in New York. The Yankees won them all—three of them by two runs each. The Kiddie Corps fell four back and ultimately ended up in second place, eight games behind the Yankees despite a franchise-best 89 wins. The next season the Orioles won a then-record 95 games and placed third while the Yankees won 109 games. "The only problem we had was the damn New York Yankees," Pappas said. "It was like everybody was fighting for second. The Yankees were so dominant it was pathetic."

31 Hang with the Immortals

It'd be nit-picking to say something was missing at Camden Yards in its first 20 years of existence. It remains one of the best places in the country to see a ballgame. But there really wasn't a true destination spot if you wanted to stroll around the Yards. Sure, you could check out the plaques of the 52 Orioles Hall of Famers on a wall along Eutaw Street. You could stop by the team store or go to Babe Ruth Plaza to the see the metallic, retired numbers of the club's six Hall of Famers and Jackie Robinson's 42. While out there you could visit "Babe's Dream," the statue of Baltimore-born baseball star Babe Ruth.

But how cool is it to get your picture taken in front of a number? Or in front of a Yankees great? Exactly. The Orioles rectified that situation in 2012, unveiling, one-by-one, larger-than-life bronze statues of their six Hall of Famers in the picnic grove behind the batter's eye wall in center field.

There's third baseman Brooks Robinson, glove in his left hand, knees bent, waiting for a pitch to be delivered so he can create another highlight. There's shortstop Cal Ripken Jr., ranging to his right, glove prepared in back-handed fashion. There's first baseman Eddie Murray at the plate, staring fiercely at the pitcher, bat straight up, mutton chop sideburns down his cheeks. There's right fielder Frank Robinson, who appears to have already crushed a pitch, with the knob of his bat dangling in his left hand. There's pitcher Jim Palmer about to uncork a fastball with his left leg kicked waist-high, glove hand outstretched. And there's manager Earl Weaver, staring ahead and taking it all in, hands behind him, mouth slightly agape as if he's about to make a blustery point.

The statues were created by Maryland sculptor Antonio Tobias "Toby" Mendez, who also has sculpted statues of former U.S. Supreme Court Justice Thurgood Marshall and NFL coaching legend Don Shula, among others. The six Orioles statues, which are between seven and eight feet in height and weigh between 600 and 1,500 pounds each, were bronzed by New Arts Foundry in Baltimore. The hope was that people would come to see the statues, get their pictures taken, and reflect on the greats of yesteryear. That was never more evident than January 19, 2013, the day of the club's annual FanFest celebration and the morning after Weaver had died. There was a steady stream of fans all day who walked out to the picnic grove and left Orioles hats and flower arrangements at the statue, paying their respects as if it were a grave site.

In its infancy the area has already become a cherished part of Camden Yards. A place Orioles fans can flock to and Orioles players can use as inspiration. "All those statues out there have one thing in common: they were on championship clubs," Orioles manager Buck Showalter said he's told his players multiple times. "And if you want to get a statue out there, that's what we are going to have to do."

32 0–21

Rene Gonzales still has a puzzled look on his face decades later when he's asked about 1988. That spring training Gonzales said the team believed it would at least compete in the American League East. They had future Hall of Famers Cal Ripken Jr. and Eddie Murray anchoring a lineup that also included nine-time All-Star outfielder Fred Lynn, four-time All-Star catcher Terry Kennedy, and outfielder Larry Sheets, who was coming off a monster year with 31 homers and a .316 average. Mike Boddicker led a rotation that featured several young pitchers and former World Series hero Scott McGregor. Those 1988 Orioles figured they'd be better than the 1987 version that lost 95 games and finished second-to-last in the division. "Yeah, we might have been a little bit older," Gonzales said. "But, God, the experience we had, of course, we thought we had a chance."

The Orioles opened the season at Memorial Stadium with a 12–0 loss to the Milwaukee Brewers. Boddicker, who allowed four runs in five and one-third innings on Opening Day, said after the start that the team couldn't be judged on one game. It wasn't. It was judged by 21—all defeats—to set a major league record for futility to begin a season. The previous mark had been 13 set by the 1904 Washington Senators and tied by the 1920 Detroit Tigers. The Orioles crushed that and kept going. The 21 straight losses stands as the second most consecutive defeats—at any point in the season—since the modern baseball era began in 1900; the Philadelphia Phillies lost 23 straight in July/August 1961. "It was embarrassing. We had ambulance chasers following us, so many reporters and people in the clubhouse," Gonzales said. "Your season is over after the first month. At the end of April, you know you are out of it. That sucked."

Six losses into April, new general manager Roland Hemond and owner Edward Bennett Williams decided a change was needed. So they fired manager Cal Ripken Sr., the longtime backbone of the organization as a coach and minor league skipper. It was the quickest hook to start a year in baseball history. The team, including Ripken's sons, shortstop Cal Jr. and second baseman Bill, was gut-punched. "It was very hard to look [Ripken Sr.] in the eye. It was almost in an apologetic way," Gonzales said. "What else could he have done?"

Ripken was replaced with Hall of Famer Frank Robinson, who had been in the front office. Things didn't get any better under new leadership. The club kept failing in horrific ways. Outfielder Jeff Stone lost a fly ball in the lights in the ninth inning that cost them a win in Baltimore's ninth game, the first of three straight one-run defeats. In their 11th game, the Orioles and Cleveland Indians took a 0–0 tie into the 11th inning. The Indians scored once in the top of the inning, and then Murray nearly hit a two-run homer in the bottom of the 11th, but it missed clearing the wall by a few inches. Jim Traber failed to score from first on Murray's double, and then Kennedy fanned with the bases loaded for a 1–0 heartbreaker. Ten times during the streak the Orioles lost by two runs or fewer; seven times they lost by five or more. "It was like Murphy's Law. Any way we could lose, we would lose," McGregor said. "Obviously we were a bad team, but we weren't that bad to lose that many. It was one of those freak things. How do you hit in 56 straight games? They are both miracles. One's a good, one's a bad."

The *Sports Illustrated* issue dated May 2, 1988 featured "The Agony of the Orioles" on the cover with "0–18" in bold. The picture was of Bill Ripken sitting in the dugout with his eyes closed and his forehead leaning against the bat in his hands. It was, literally, the picture of frustration. "You could have gotten everybody's picture on there," McGregor said. "We were all feeling the same way."

Bill Ripken said, as perfect as it may have looked, that pose wasn't exclusive to the 1988 start. "I might have been sitting there collecting my thoughts, sitting my head against the bat. I was like that many times," Ripken said. "I don't think that's the way you want to be on the cover of *Sports Illustrated*, when you go through a season like that."

It, however, proved to be the *SI* Jinx in reverse. The Orioles streak actually ended before the cover date. On April 29, a cool Friday evening at Comiskey Park in Chicago, Murray hit a two-run homer in the first, Cal Ripken had four hits including a ninth-inning homer, and Mark Williamson and Dave Schmidt combined for a shutout in the Orioles' 9–0 victory against the White Sox. Cases of champagne bottles were at the ready, but there wasn't much celebrating.

Hemond, however, smelled like champagne. Or at least his suit did. In an attempt to channel some good luck, Hemond, who had previously been the GM of the White Sox, was actually wearing the same suit he had on when Chicago clinched the AL West in 1983 and he was doused in champagne and beer. The suit had been behind a glass display at Comiskey Park for several years, but it was sent to Hemond while the Orioles were playing in Minnesota earlier in the week. He took it with him back to Chicago and wore it that Friday night. "It didn't smell too good, but it worked," Hemond told John Eisenberg in the book *From 33rd Street to Camden Yards*.

When the 1–23 Orioles returned home fresh off a 1–11 road trip, they were greeted in an incredible way. The May 2 game, billed as "Fantastic Fans Night," drew 50,402 to Memorial Stadium. Hall of Fame announcer Jon Miller said it may have been the most memorable night of his career. "Fifty thousand people showed up, and the first pitch of the game was a called strike, and the crowd went nuts like it was the World Series," Miller said. "It was one of the most exciting nights of baseball I have ever seen. And the Orioles, who couldn't beat anybody, took a 9–1 lead into the ninth inning that night as if they had been doing it all along. Just the pure emotion of that night stood out when the team expected none."

The Orioles won 9–4 that night behind the pitching of right-hander Jay Tibbs, a 26-year-old who was making his club debut. Williams announced that night that he had signed a long-term deal with the city for a new stadium that would become Oriole Park at Camden Yards. Morganna Roberts, an exotic dancer known as "the Kissing Bandit," ran onto the field and planted a smooch on Ripken Jr.'s cheek before being taken away. It was a bizarre night and surely the highlight of a 54–107 season—the worst record in Orioles modern franchise history.

Even Fantastic Fans Night had its downside. To make room for Tibbs, the Orioles released the 34-year-old McGregor, one of the most popular players in club history. He was 0–3 with an 8.83 ERA in four starts, and his left shoulder was shot. McGregor said he'll never forget what Kennedy, the veteran catcher, said to him as he prepared for his farewell press conference. "He goes, 'You are one lucky blankety-blank. You get to go home. You don't have to stay here and watch this anymore,'" McGregor said, laughing at the memory. "It was pretty ugly."

That kind of disastrous start has not happened since—to any team. And Ripken says he hopes it doesn't again. "Every baseball season I want every team to start out of the gate 1–1," Ripken said. "Because as soon as somebody goes 0–5 or 0–6 or 0–7, everybody wants to start talking about that 0–18 on the cover and 0-for-21 on the start. And it's something I don't wish on anybody."

33 Gregg Olson and the Why Not? Season

Gregg Olson left Auburn University as one of the greatest relievers in college baseball history. When the June 1988 draft occurred, he was hoping he'd be taken fifth by the Los Angeles Dodgers. Instead, he was selected fourth by the laughingstock of baseball: the Orioles, a club in the middle of a 107-loss season that had set a record by losing 21 straight to begin that year. "It was the elation of being drafted because I had never been drafted before and all my dreams had just come true," Olson said he remembered thinking. "And then it was a little bit of, 'Oh, I've been drafted by the worst team in baseball, and the next team was the best team in baseball.'" Olson signed at the end of June and by September he was playing for that worst team in baseball. He joined several other players age 25 or younger—Pete Harnisch, Bob Milacki, Jeff Ballard, Craig Worthington, and Brady Anderson, among others—who would form the nucleus for the magical season that would follow. "The guys that had been there a while, had been on a 54–107 team, I'm sure it was a miserable last two months. But for me and the other couple rookies, I couldn't get to the ballpark soon enough," Olson said. "I was having the time of my life."

The 1989 Orioles began as the consensus pick for last place in the American League East. But no one told the players that they had to stink again. On Opening Day at Memorial Stadium, the Orioles beat the defending AL East champions, the Boston Red Sox, 5–4 in 11 innings. Cal Ripken Jr. smashed a three-run homer against Boston ace Roger Clemens, and Worthington delivered a game-ending single. Emotions always run high on Opening Day; in reality, it's just the first of 162 games. But this time it meant something. The Orioles carried forward that momentum. By mid-June they were in first place, an unfathomable position for a club that was basically eliminated before Memorial Day the previous year. "Just about everybody had less than one year experience, and I don't think we knew any better. We didn't know we were not supposed to compete in the AL East with the Yankees and the Red Sox and the Tigers," Olson said. "All we knew is that we were there. And why can't we be good here? Why Not?"

There were several moments throughout the "Why Not?" season that served notice that something special was happening. Olson entered an April 26 game in the eighth inning with the Orioles up 2–1 in Oakland. He pitched a scoreless frame and was given the ball again in the ninth for what would be his first traditional save opportunity. (He had one previous career save in a blowout.) Olson struck out Dave Parker, Dave Henderson, and

Mark McGwire on 14 pitches, setting the tone for his 27-save Rookie of the Year season. On Saturday, July 15, the Orioles rallied for four runs in the bottom of the ninth to beat the California Angels 11–9. The final play is one of the most controversial in club history. With the score tied at 9–9, center fielder Mike Devereaux hit the third pitch from Bob McClure deep to left, and the hooking ball was called fair by umpire Jim Joyce, setting off a walk-off home run celebration in front of 47,393 fans at Memorial Stadium and sparking the ire of the Angels. The next day Angels manager Doug Rader took the lineup card to home plate, said some choice words, and was immediately ejected by umpire Ken Kaiser before the first pitch. "I don't know if it was fair or foul to this day, I swear," Milacki said. "It's so close you can't tell on video."

On September 5, Cal Ripken Jr. hit his 20th homer of the season, taking the ball and the center fielder over the wall. Cleveland's Brad Komminsk, who played for the Orioles the following year, caught Ripken's blast against pitcher John Farrell, but Komminsk flipped over the wall and dropped the ball. It became a staple on baseball blooper reels for decades.

Still, the weirdness of the season may not have prepared the Orioles and their fan base for the final weekend in Toronto. The Orioles were one game behind the Blue Jays with three to play, so they needed to win at least two to force a first-place tie to end the season and a sweep to complete the worst-to-first turnaround. On the first pitch of the series, Phil Bradley homered against Toronto's Todd Stottlemyre, something he had told teammate Rene Gonzales he would do if Stottlemyre threw a first-pitch fastball. "It was a huge series and, *bam*, he hit this ball out to left field and he came in. And I'm going, 'You called it, dude,'" Gonzales said. "We were so pumped up." The first-pitch run nearly stood up. Ballard carried a shutout into the eighth before being replaced with one on and one out by Olson. With two outs and pinch-runner Tom Lawless on third, Olson eventually struck out the dangerous Kelly Gruber. But on a 1–2 pitch, the rookie uncorked a curveball that skipped to the backstop and allowed Lawless to tie the game. Olson said he was trying to add a little extra "tilt" on his devastating curve. "In the grand scheme of life, if you had a do-over moment, that would probably be in my top couple," Olson said. "I made a stupid decision, tried to do something I didn't work on, felt like I needed to do something special." Lloyd Moseby then smacked a game-winning hit off the wall in the bottom of the 11th inning against Mark Williamson to score Nelson Liriano from second. The Orioles were two back with two games to play.

Then the season got even weirder. On his way back to the hotel that Friday evening, Saturday's scheduled starter Pete Harnisch stepped on a nail that punctured his foot. He couldn't pitch Saturday, so the Orioles turned to 29-year-old rookie and Baltimore native Dave Johnson. A former truck driver who had been the embodiment of the unexpected 1989 season, Johnson didn't get called up until August and then pitched great in his first month with the Orioles. "They were taking guys up left and right," Johnson said. "Mickey Weston, Mike 'Texas' Smith, Mike 'Mississippi' Smith, and I'm sitting there in Rochester with a bad elbow. So then I got healthy and started pitching well and then I came up."

Johnson, however, had lost his last five decisions when he received the emergency start and he gave up a walk and a RBI single in the first. He then settled down and allowed just one more hit through the next six innings. The Orioles were up 3–1 in the eighth when Johnson walked a batter, and then Williamson allowed two RBI singles and a sacrifice fly to George Bell that gave the Blue Jays the win and the AL East title. Even with that heartbreak, it will go down as one of the Orioles' most memorable seasons. "Harnisch steps on a nail. It goes through his shoe. He can't pitch. And in spite of that, Dave Johnson steps in and throws an unbelievable game," Gonzales said. "That was the kind of year it was. I wish we could have kept it going. That really was a great team."

34 Frank Robinson Homers out of Memorial Stadium

In terms of importance to the team, the home run Frank Robinson hit on May 8, 1966 was insignificant: a two-run shot in the first inning of a game the Orioles eventually won 8–3. It was No. 331 in a Hall of Fame career that included 586 longballs in 21 seasons. Robinson hit 179 regular-season home runs for the Orioles and nine more for them in the postseason. (Perhaps none was bigger than his two-run, first-inning shot in the first game of the 1966 World Series against Don Drysdale that set the tone for the Orioles' improbable, four-game sweep against the Los Angeles Dodgers.) So going deep in the first inning against Luis Tiant in the second game of a Sunday doubleheader against the Cleveland Indians in May probably should have been a footnote in Robinson's stellar career. Except the ball disappeared—vanished from sight.

"I knew we were facing Luis Tiant in the [second] game there, and he had thrown three straight shutouts. I had never seen him before," Robinson said. "The first pitch was a fastball down and in, and I hit it."

Oh, did he hit it. Robinson became the only player to hit a fair ball completely out of Memorial Stadium, which hosted the Orioles from 1954 to 1991. The ball cleared 50 rows of left-field bleachers and was estimated at traveling at least 465 feet, according to the Orioles. It ended up under a car in a stadium parking lot, reportedly 540 feet from home plate. "With a home run, you know when you get one. You don't know how far it's going, but you know you got it," Robinson said. "I knew I hit it good and I went around the bases. And I came into the dugout, and the guys were saying the ball went completely out of the ballpark. And I said, 'Get out of my face. No way.' They said, 'Yes, it did.' And I did not believe them."

After the inning Robinson jogged out to right field to take his defensive position. And something strange was happening. "The fans gave me a standing ovation. Everybody was up, and I said,

On May 8, 1966, Frank Robinson launches a home run, which landed under a car in a stadium parking lot reportedly located 540 feet from home plate.

'Well, maybe it did go out,'" Robinson said. "And that was the first time I realized that it did go out."

Orioles first baseman Boog Powell, who was batting two spots behind Robinson that day, said he couldn't believe his eyes as the ball kept soaring. "It was a pretty good pitch. It was down a little bit," Powell said. "He hit it good. Then I thought, *Wow, he smoked that one.* And then I said, 'Hey, that thing went out of here.' Frank just acted like, 'No big deal.'"

Powell, one of the most prodigious sluggers in Orioles history, said he once hit a ball out of Memorial Stadium during batting practice in 1962 or 1963. He said he smacked line drives in games that may have had the distance but didn't have the height. So he, maybe more than anyone, understood just how difficult it was to send a ball completely out of Memorial Stadium. "That was a blast by Frank," Powell said. "He got all of it. He really did."

What makes the homer even more impressive is that it came off Tiant, who was making his fourth start of the season and hadn't allowed a run. He had thrown three straight complete-game shutouts, giving up just 14 hits in 27 innings before facing the Orioles. In that first inning, he allowed a leadoff single to future Hall of Famer Luis Aparacio, who moved to second on a wild pitch. After Russ Snyder grounded out, Robinson hit his legendary homer. The Orioles ended up scoring five runs (four earned) against Tiant and chased him from the game with two outs in the third inning. Tiant didn't give Robinson another chance that day. He walked Robinson to lead off the third.

The Orioles commemorated Robinson's blast by flying an orange flag with the block letters "HERE" at the spot at which Robinson's ball left the park. It flew until 1991, when the Orioles closed Memorial Stadium. A fan won the flag in a giveaway at the end of that season.

The 1997 Season

Although they'll be remembered for failing to reach the World Series, the 1997 Orioles were one of the best teams in franchise history. They were in first place from Opening Day to season's end, outpacing the defending World Series champion New York Yankees for the division crown. They won 98 in the regular season and toppled the Seattle Mariners in the American League Division Series, twice defeating all-world lefty Randy Johnson in his prime. Led by stars such as Hall of Famers Cal Ripken Jr. and Roberto Alomar, the Orioles set a franchise attendance record, drawing 3.71 million. "That was a great year. The Yankees had a good ballclub," manager Davey Johnson said. "When you can go wire-to-wire and beat the Yankees, you've had a hell of a year."

It just didn't end well.

The motivation started the previous October when the Orioles lost in five games to the Yankees in the American League Championship Series, including dropping the opener in extra innings in a game that will forever be remembered for 12-year-old Yankees fan Jeffrey Maier's redirection of a likely fly-out into a score-tying homer in the eighth. That series stuck with the Orioles all winter, and they wanted a chance at redemption. "With what had happened before, with that little kid in right field, we kind of had our eyes set on getting back to the playoffs and having the rematch against the Yankees," said reliever Alan Mills.

The Orioles made some roster upgrades to improve in 1997. They bolstered their rotation by picking up two Yankees, Jimmy Key and Scott Kamieniecki. Instead of buying a third baseman, the club moved Ripken, their eventual Hall of Famer, a few steps to his right and signed shortstop Mike Bordick. Ripken had been hesitant to switch positions previously but gave his blessing to add the steady Bordick. "From the onset he made me feel comfortable," Bordick said. "I'm sure inside he was probably upset about having to go over to third base, but he understood, I think, like everybody on that team what kind of team they had."

The Orioles won Opening Day against the Kansas City Royals at Camden Yards with Key getting the victory and another newcomer, outfielder Eric Davis, delivering the go-ahead RBI. A three-run rally in the next game gave the Orioles first place by themselves. They never handed it back, winning nine of their first 11, posting a 20–8 record in May, and cruising to a first-half, 55–30 record. They had five players named All-Stars—their most since 1972. Closer Randy Myers was automatic, recording a then-franchise record 45 saves while blowing just one attempt. Eight different Orioles hit 10 or more homers, including 38 by Rafael Palmeiro.

They, however, dealt with some adversity. In May, Davis learned he had a cancerous mass in his colon. It required surgery, and he was out until mid-September. Serving as an inspiration, Davis, who was still undergoing treatment, returned for eight games in September. In Game 5 of the ALCS, he delivered a pinch-hit homer in the ninth that helped return the series to Camden Yards. "Here's a guy that's going through all that, and he's still going out and playing at a high level. I think that made everybody elevate their game," catcher Chris Hoiles said. "It was unbelievable. I don't know how many of us in that clubhouse would've been able to do what he did."

Aside from Davis' return, perhaps the highlight of 1997 was Game 4 of the ALDS versus Seattle's Randy Johnson. Davey Johnson stacked his lineup with right-handers against the fierce, 6'10" lefty. Utility infielder Jeff Reboulet, who had 20 homers in his 12-season career, took Johnson deep in the first. Geronimo Berroa also homered against Johnson, who lost 3–1 despite striking out 13. It was the second time in the ALDS the Orioles had beaten Johnson, who was 0–4 in five starts against the Orioles that year and 20–2 against everyone else. Everything set up for the Orioles to knock off the Yankees and advance to the World Series for the first time in 14 years. But the Indians beat the Yankees in five games. They were the ones looking for redemption after being ousted from the postseason by the Orioles in 1996. "When we got to the ALCS, we faced Cleveland instead of the Yankees, and it was almost like a letdown for us," Mills said. "And Cleveland came out and beat us."

That series was filled with bizarre twists. After winning Game 1, the Orioles lost Game 2 when reliever Armando Benitez served up a three-run homer to Marquis Grissom. Mike Mussina struck out 15 Indians in Game 3, but the Orioles lost in the 12th inning when Grissom dashed home on a pitch that catcher Lenny Webster thought was fouled off. The Indians won Game 4 in the ninth on a Sandy Alomar single. Earlier in the game, the Tribe scored twice on one wild pitch because Webster's view of the ball was screened by umpire Durwood Merrill. After Davis' homer in Game 5, the clubs were knotted in a scoreless tie at Camden Yards in Game 6 until the 11th, when Benitez faced Tony Fernandez with two outs. Fernandez, 35, started the game only because his pregame liner struck Bip Roberts' thumb, forcing Roberts to be scratched. When the fireballing Benitez threw a head-scratching slider to Fernandez, the veteran ripped it over the right-field wall. The Orioles lost the game 1–0 and the series 4–2. "Tony at that time was getting up in age," Hoiles said. "And I just thought with a fastball, especially Armando's fastball, we could beat him. But Armando chose to differ and threw the slider, and the end result is what it was."

In the offseason, Davey Johnson resigned in a dispute with owner Peter Angelos, the core of the club began to crack, and the franchise didn't return to the ALCS for another 17 years. "I still think we were the best team in baseball that year," Hoiles said. "Unfortunately, in the end, we didn't get to where we wanted to, and it was a huge disappointment."

 **Flanny**

On an off day in the early 1980s, Orioles outfielder Gary Roenicke and catcher Rick Dempsey went fishing and caught some crappies. As Roenicke was filleting the small fish in his kitchen, his phone rang. It was Orioles pitcher Mike Flanagan, who lived on the same block as Roenicke in Cockeysville. Flanagan, an avid angler, also had gone fishing that day and he asked Roenicke if he would mind cleaning the fish he had caught. "Mike walks in the door, and this fish is so big he had to turn sideways," Roenicke recalled. "And he sees me with these little bitty fillets and he looked down at his great big fish. So he throws it down on my counter and says, 'Feed your family' and walked out the door. He never came back for it. That was Mike."

For parts of 18 major league seasons, including 15 with the Orioles, the left-hander from New Hampshire mixed a sharp wit, a steely nerve, and a deep compassion in becoming one of the most popular figures in team history. Blessed with a heavy sinker and several other quality pitches, he won 167 games and posted a career 3.90 ERA in 2,770 innings. His best season was 1979, when he went 23–9 with a 3.08 ERA and won the American League Cy Young Award. In one eight-season span, Flanagan never posted an ERA over 4.20, never lost more games than he won, and threw 225 or more innings six times. He is in the franchise's top five in wins, strikeouts, innings, and games pitched. "He was the bulldog;

that nickname fits him better than anyone. He wasn't coming out of a game, no matter what," Dempsey said. "He would throw 150 pitches in a game and he'd tell the manager, 'You aren't taking me out.' He was as gritty as anyone I've ever seen out on the mound." Fellow Orioles lefty Scott McGregor said he learned how tough Flanagan was in 1979. "He had a pain in his ankle every time he threw a pitch in the second half," McGregor said. "And he won the Cy Young. He'd just grind it out."

Away from the mound, Flanagan's understated, self-deprecating sense of humor and keen observational skills took over. He nicknamed eccentric reliever Don Stanhouse "Stan the Man Unusual" and created a nickname/translation for Dominican-born right-hander Jose Mesa: Joe Table. Flanagan played freshman basketball at the University of Massachusetts and remembered a scrimmage in which he took a jumper and a varsity forward came out of nowhere to block the shot. That player was future NBA Hall of Famer Julius "Dr. J" Erving. Flanagan told the *Toronto Sun* what he was thinking at that moment of basketball rejection: "Better work on my slider." Closer Gregg Olson remembers Flanagan passing time in the Orioles' bullpen in the early 1990s by changing the words to songs on the public address system to be more baseball appropriate. The Monkees' "I'm a Believer," became "I'm a Reliever," and Steve Winwood's lyrics, "Bring me a higher love," were Flanny-ized into, "Bring me a bigger glove."

Dempsey's favorite Flanagan line came at the expense of manager Earl Weaver, who would harp on Flanagan for not holding runners closely enough. During one Flanagan side session, "Earl came out and stood next to him. In the middle of Mike's windup, Earl started running down the left-field line. Everybody was like, 'What is Earl doing?'" Dempsey said. "And then Earl came up to Flanny and said, 'I just stole second on you.' And Mike said, 'How the hell did you get on first base?' We just all started laughing. It was one of the all-time great baseball lines." McGregor remembers sitting next to Flanagan on the Orioles' bench trying to make each other laugh for nine innings. If the Orioles were losing, Weaver would shoot McGregor a dirty look. "I'd say, 'Hey, I'm sitting next to *this* guy. I'm sorry I shouldn't be laughing, but I can't help it.'" Outfielder Ken Singleton said he'd stay far away from Flanagan when Weaver was rampaging. "I didn't want to be laughing in the middle of one of Earl's tirades. So I made sure I didn't look at Flanny."

The Orioles traded Flanagan to the Toronto Blue Jays in August 1987 for Oswaldo Peraza and a player to be named later, which ended up being Joe Table. Flanagan returned in 1991, reinvented himself as a 39-year-old reliever, and posted a 2.38 ERA in 64 games. He also became the last Oriole to pitch in Memorial Stadium, striking out both Detroit Tigers he faced in the top of the ninth inning. Flanagan pitched one more season as a reliever, ushering in the Camden Yards Era, before retiring at age 40. He remained omnipresent with the club, whether it was as big league pitching coach, Orioles TV analyst, team vice president, or executive vice president of baseball operations. The Orioles never posted a winning record during his six seasons as a front office decision-maker. His biggest impact occurred in his handling of the spring training death of 23-year-old pitcher Steve Bechler, who collapsed during conditioning drills in February 2003 and died the next day. Flanagan kept vigil in the hospital with Bechler's pregnant wife, who publicly lauded Flanagan for his compassion and sincerity. Later, Flanagan advocated successfully for the ban of ephedra-based diet pills, which were implicated as contributing factors in Bechler's heatstroke. "I don't think I ever will—or will ever want to—go through something like that again," Flanagan said five years after Bechler's death.

A year after his contract ran out as a team executive, Flanagan was hired in 2010 as a TV analyst for club-owned MASN. Tragically, while the Orioles were on the road August 24, 2011, Flanagan killed himself with a gunshot to the head outside of his home in Baltimore County. The 59-year-old reportedly had been dealing privately with depression for years. The incident sent shockwaves throughout the organization and sport. On the night of Flanagan's death, Hall of Fame pitcher Jim Palmer discussed his teammate and friend's legacy during an exceptionally moving MASN postgame show. "He was one of a kind," Palmer said, choking back tears. "I'm sorry for the people that knew him. This is part of being my age and having a chance to be with guys that were this special...It's devastating."

37 Ken Singleton

Ken Singleton and his Montreal Expos teammate Mike Torrez were hanging out together one evening in December 1974 when they began discussing a trade earlier that day, which had sent slugger Lee May from the Houston Astros to the Orioles. Singleton and Torrez talked about how the Orioles seemed to be reloading again; they needed a run-producing first baseman to replace Boog Powell, and Singleton felt they had landed one with May, the "Big Bopper."

The next morning, Singleton's phone rang at 6:00. It was Torrez, who said he had just been traded to the Orioles. "I said, 'Oh Mike, that's too bad, I'm going to miss you,'" Singleton remembered. "And he said, 'No, you don't understand. You're going with me to Baltimore.'"

Minutes later, Singleton's phone rang again. It was Expos general manager Jim Fanning, who confirmed that Singleton and Torrez had been dealt to the Orioles for rotation stalwart Dave McNally, promising outfielder Rich Coggins, and a minor leaguer.

Singleton vs. Baylor

In 1979 the American League MVP voting wasn't particularly close. California Angels outfielder/designated hitter Don Baylor basically ran away with the award, getting 20 of 28 first-place votes and compiling 347 points to 241 for Singleton.

Analyzed through today's statistical prism, though, you have to wonder if Singleton should have bested Baylor. They both played on clubs that won their division, but the Orioles were far superior. (They won 102 games and beat the Angels, who won 88 regular season games, in the ALCS.)

Baylor won all three Triple Crown categories against Singleton, besting him by one point in average, one homer, and 28 RBIs. He also stole 22 bases versus three for Singleton. But Singleton had a slightly higher slugging percentage and a much higher on-base percentage (34 points) while posting a 5.2 wins above replacement (WAR) compared to Baylor's 3.7. Plus, Singleton played 143 games in the outfield and just 16 at designated hitter compared to Baylor, who had 97 games in the outfield, 65 at DH, and one at first base.

One other note, if you lean heavily on the WAR statistic, then Singleton and Baylor both should have finished behind the Boston Red Sox's Fred Lynn (8.8 WAR, fourth-place MVP finish) and the Kansas City Royals' George Brett (8.6 WAR, third-place MVP finish).

Here's how Singleton and Baylor matched up in 1979:

Ken Singleton

Orioles (102–57 record)
159 games, 93 runs, 168 hits, 29 doubles, one triple, 35 homers, 111 RBIs, three stolen bases, 109 walks, 118 strikeouts
.295 (batting average)/.405 (on-base)/.533 (slugging)
.938 on-base plus slugging percentage (OPS), 5.2 WAR, .406 weighted on-base average (WOBA)
143 games outfield, 16 games at DH

Don Baylor

Angels (88–74 record)
162 games, 120 runs, 186 hits, 33 doubles, three triples, 36 homers, 139 RBIs, 22 stolen bases, 71 walks, 51 strikeouts
.296/.371/.530
.901 OPS, 3.7 WAR, .392 WOBA
97 games outfield, 65 at DH, one at first base

The 27-year-old Singleton had to feign his surprise—and suppress his enthusiasm. He was going from an organization that hadn't won in its first six years of existence to one that had one losing season in its last dozen. "I didn't want to sound too happy on the phone, but the Expos were more or less an expansion team in those days," Singleton said. "We had either players that were over the hill or players like myself that were still coming into their own. And to get traded to the Orioles, a very good team, I was really ecstatic."

Coggins played just 13 games for the Expos, and McNally pitched in just 12. Torrez ended up winning 20 games for the Orioles in 1975 before being included in the ill-fated Reggie Jackson deal in 1976. Singleton, however, became a fixture in right field and in the Orioles lineup for a decade. Although the June 1976 trade with the New York Yankees that yielded Rick Dempsey, Scott McGregor, and Tippy Martinez is considered to be the backbone of those great late 1970s and early 1980s teams, swiping Singleton from the Expos set the foundation. "We don't win without him," Dempsey said of Singleton. "He got more walks, had a much higher on-base percentage than anyone on our ballclub. He really was one of the great Orioles hitters of all time, and people forget how good this guy really was."

In 10 seasons with the Orioles, Singleton played in nearly 1,500 regular season games, compiling 1,455 hits, 182 home runs, and 766 RBIs—numbers that put him in the top seven in each category on the franchise's all-time lists. His .328 average in 1977 stood as the modern-day Orioles' best among qualifiers for 27 years until Melvin Mora batted .340 in 2004. Although he typically hit in the middle of the order, Singleton's batting eye was so good that manager Earl Weaver had him lead off 104 times in 1975 despite Singleton's lack of typical, top-of-the-order speed. Singleton responded with a .300 average and a .415 on-base percentage and won his first of three Most Valuable Oriole Awards.

In his Orioles career, Singleton walked 886 times and struck out 860 times—an anomaly for someone who consistently hit double-digit homers each season. Three times he batted .300 or better for the Orioles, four times he had an on-base percentage above .400, and in four consecutive seasons he hit 20 or more home runs. "This guy could take a walk, get a base hit, a home run, a double, whatever we needed. This guy was capable of anything," Dempsey said. "Everybody forgets about him, and he was the best hitter of them all."

Singleton made three All-Star Games and finished in the top 10 in the MVP voting four times, including once with the Expos. In 1977 he finished third in the AL MVP race and in 1979 he placed second, behind former teammate Don Baylor of the California Angels. In the current world of advanced statistics, Singleton may have finished ahead of Baylor; he had a better on-base percentage, higher slugging percentage, and his WAR (wins above replacement) outpaced Baylor's 5.2 to 3.7. (Boston's Fred Lynn, who finished fourth in the 1979 MVP race, had a 8.8 WAR.) But Baylor, who had one more homer and 28 more RBIs, received 20 of the 28 first-place votes and easily out-pointed Singleton 347 to 241. "A lot of people still, to this day, feel I should have won," said Singleton, who hit .295 with a .405 on-base percentage, .533 slugging percentage, 35 homers, and 111 RBIs for the American League champion Orioles in 1979. "They didn't really take in account on-base percentage in those days and the other numbers they do now like total OPS. I think, in this day and age, I would have had a better chance of winning than I did back in 1979."

Singleton received three first-place MVP votes that year, the same as his Orioles teammate, left-handed pitcher Mike Flanagan, who won the AL Cy Young Award. That was typical of Singleton's career. He was on so many good teams that his individual accomplishments often were overshadowed by other Orioles, such as Hall of Famers Eddie Murray and, eventually, Cal Ripken Jr. Never complaining about being underappreciated, Singleton just plugged along without much national fanfare.

Unlike good buddy Murray, Singleton never had any problems with the media. But he joked that he likely was viewed as boring by national reporters looking for a story. "Maybe it's because I didn't say all that much. I saved all my words for the broadcast booth," said Singleton, a native New Yorker and longtime color analyst for New York Yankees games. "Maybe I wasn't interesting. It's one of those things. And it's okay. I enjoyed every single minute of being a Baltimore Oriole because we won every year. We had a winning record every year and we were in the race every single season. And, as a player, that's all you can ask for."

38 The Jeffrey Maier-Aided Home Run

Tony Tarasco has a theory. He believes New York Yankees shortstop Derek Jeter was ticketed for greatness and the Orioles weren't able to stand in his way no matter what they did in 1996. Tarasco believes one unfortunate moment—which featured a flabbergasted Tarasco pointing skyward—paved the way for Jeter to become a champion as a rookie. "Sometimes there are other destinies meant to happen, and I think the destiny of Derek Jeter and the New York Yankees were meant to prevail," said Tarasco, an Orioles outfielder in 1996 and 1997. "That's the way I look at it. We were going against the universe. Things were in line for Derek. And his magnificent personality and his demeanor and his attitude day-in and day-out were meant to shine. And it had to start somewhere; 1996 was his rookie year, and that's when that happened."

Tarasco has one other personal take on Jeter's fly ball on October 9, 1996 that was redirected into a home run during the first game of the 1996 American League Championship Series, a chain of events that potentially altered the trajectory of two franchises. "I was robbed," Tarasco said.

The Orioles were leading 4–3 in the bottom of the eighth at old Yankee Stadium when Tarasco was sent in to play right field as a defensive replacement for Bobby Bonilla. With one out Jeter hit the first pitch from reliever Armando Benitez to deep right. Tarasco backed up to the wall and appeared to be camped under the ball when it didn't come down. Instead, 12-year-old Yankee fan Jeffrey Maier reached over the wall with his glove in an attempt to catch the fly, and knocked it into the bleachers. Tarasco looked stunned. Then he began pointing to the stands above. "The point thing was very after the fact. I didn't know who did it. I was completely thunderstruck by it because the ball was going into my glove," Tarasco said. "So at the last second it was like, *Wow, what happened?* But I immediately knew somebody had interfered with it.'"

TV replays showed clear interference by Maier, but umpire Richie Garcia missed it, and Jeter was awarded the homer. The game went into 11 innings before the Yankees prevailed on a walk-off home run by Bernie Williams against Randy Myers. The Orioles won the next game at Yankee Stadium but dropped all three at Camden Yards to lose the best-of-seven series in five. The Yankees beat the Atlanta Braves in a six-game World Series, capturing their first championship in 18 years. It was the beginning of a run in which the Yankees won four World Series in five years and appeared in seven October Classics in 14 seasons. The Orioles made it back to the ALCS in 1997 and then spiraled downward, failing to produce a winning record in their next 14 seasons. "You never know what could have happened. We won the next game, so coming back home with a 2–0 lead. I mean, they beat up on us pretty bad that series other than the second game," Tarasco said. "But you have to wonder if it had its effect."

Before the series began, Tarasco said the Orioles had complained about the fans in the right-field bleachers. Some had thrown objects at Bonilla, so Orioles manager Davey Johnson asked officials to keep a close eye on the group. The one fan who made the biggest difference, though, was a polite, round-faced pre-teen who became an instant celebrity in New York and an instant pariah in Baltimore. (Incidentally, Maier never caught that ball. It ricocheted off his glove and into the stands where another fan grabbed it.) After his initial media tour, Maier distanced himself from his moment of fame. But he continued to love baseball and played collegiately at Division III Wesleyan University in Connecticut before entering the business world. "When I was younger, it really did bring animosity out and, in some cases, a lot more hit-by-pitches in my games than I had previously," Maier told *The Baltimore Sun* in 2012. "I was more hesitant to embrace it. But as time has gone on…I think it helped me mature and hopefully grounded me and shaped me into the person I am today. It's a huge part of baseball history, either positive or negative depending on your allegiance. But it's part of history nonetheless. It's a fun story to recall when people are apt to hear about it. So I've come to embrace it—but not flaunt it."

It's a story that Orioles fans won't ever forget. Even those who weren't there at the time understand the significance of the Jeffrey Maier-aided homer. In the summer of 2014, Orioles manager Buck Showalter was asked to talk about the retiring Jeter. Showalter offered the usual platitudes but added this gem concerning the Yankees shortstop: "We were talking about what you give him as a gift. I would give him that big picture of the home run—well, it wasn't a home run; we know that. That's what I'd give him," Showalter said, "a big picture [of the Jeffrey Maier homer] and have the whole Baltimore Orioles team sign it. That's a good idea, and it's cheap too, right? Make it in bronze or something. Not that we remember that at all."

39 Harry Dalton

When Lee MacPhail quit in 1965 to become chief aide to baseball's commissioner, he left behind two parting gifts for Harry Dalton: his job as Orioles general manager and a close-to-fruition deal with the Cincinnati Reds that would bring former MVP Frank Robinson to Baltimore. Dalton, who was the Orioles' farm director under MacPhail and had been working in concert with him in trying to land Robinson, consummated the deal that December. It was Dalton's first major order of business and probably the most important. But Dalton orchestrated others that helped push the club to four World Series in his six seasons at the helm, including winning the organization's first world championship in 1966 in his initial year in charge of personnel.

Dalton was the one who promoted Earl Weaver from the minors to big league first-base coach and then inserted him as manager when Hank Bauer was fired in July 1968. Dalton also traded for Mike Cuellar and Pat Dobson, who became half of the famed quartet of 20-game winners in the 1971 rotation. The other two, Jim Palmer and Dave McNally, were products of Dalton's farm system—like most of the core for those title teams. "He was the farm director when I signed and he came to California to sign me out of high school. We were good friends through our whole relationship," said catcher Andy Etchebarren. "Harry had his guys, his scouts that he trusted around him, and they were all very good, friendly guys that cared about winning. Harry Dalton, I would think, was one of the successes in Baltimore."

Dalton grew up in Massachusetts, graduated from Amherst College, and earned a Bronze Star in the Korean War. He was briefly a sportswriter in Springfield, Massachusetts, before joining the Orioles in their inaugural 1954 season to be the assistant farm director for $45 a week. (He worked part time as a cabdriver for extra money.) His dedication and intelligence allowed him to ascend through the organization. "Everyone kind of knew that sooner or later Harry would be general manager," Hall of Famer Brooks Robinson told *The Baltimore Sun*. "He was just a little brighter than everyone else." He also had a knack for recognizing front office or field talent and assigning it to the right position. "Dalton was very sharp as far as people were concerned," said former Orioles player, minor league manager, and big league coach Billy Hunter. "Those of us that were hired and involved at that time considered ourselves part of 'The Dalton Gang.'"

The list of Dalton's protégés is impressive; he was the first to hire respected baseball executives such as former general managers Lou Gorman and Baltimore native John Schuerholz. After six seasons with the Orioles, Dalton left to try and turn around the California Angels. He was there for six years, never posting a winning record, before becoming the general manager of the Milwaukee Brewers. It was with Milwaukee that Dalton hired another kid out of Amherst College: Dan Duquette. "Harry gave me an opportunity with the Brewers, but he also gave me exposure to all his best baseball people and all the different facets of the team operations," said Duquette, who became the Orioles' executive vice president before the 2012 season. "So he really gave me a great opportunity and great training."

Dalton led the Brewers to their lone American League title in 1982. He retired in 1994 and received the Orioles' Herb Armstrong Award in 1997 for outstanding contributions to the franchise by non-uniform personnel. He was included in the Brewers' Walk of Fame at Miller Park in 2003. Dalton died in Arizona in 2005 at age 77 from Parkinson's disease. "Harry Dalton was a great listener, a really good listener," Duquette said. "He was generous with his time and he was also a real direct executive. You could tell where you stood with Harry pretty quickly."

40 Big Mac's Big Games

The first spring training bullpen session lefty Scott McGregor ever threw was at Fort Lauderdale Stadium in February of 1973, when he was just 19 and only months removed from being drafted in the first round by the New York Yankees. Known for his impeccable control as an amateur, McGregor couldn't buy a strike that day. Why? Well, he was throwing to Hall of Fame catcher Elston Howard. Yankees manager Ralph Houk was standing behind Howard. Everyone's boyhood hero, Mickey Mantle, was watching. So was Whitey Ford, one of the greatest pitchers of the 20th century. "I was going, 'Oh, my God.'" I had come out of high school and I had walked just one guy to every 100 guys I faced. And now I'm bouncing shit everywhere," McGregor remembered with a laugh. "Whitey said, 'Are you all right?' And I said 'No. You are standing here, and [Mantle] is leaning on the cage and I'm throwing to Elston Howard."

Ford assessed the situation and decided to give the nervous kid some advice. "Let me tell you something: three pitches or less [per batter], 12 pitches in an inning; 15 pitches are too many," Ford said to McGregor. "He said, 'Get them out fast.' And that just stuck in my brain for years." Certainly, McGregor was nervous again on a mound at some point; that happens when you spend 13 seasons in the majors. But armed with a definitive plan and a devastating change-up, McGregor pitched and won some of the most important games in Orioles history.

He got quick outs on huge stages. "I always thought he was our best, big-game pitcher," former Orioles outfielder Ken Singleton said. "In 1979, when we beat the Angels in the ALCS, we lost a tough one the night before. If we won that game, we are going to the World Series and we lost it. And before the reporters got into the clubhouse, Macky got up in front of everybody and said—loud enough so everybody could hear it—'I guarantee you we will win tomorrow.' He was pitching. And he went out there and shut them down the next day."

McGregor doesn't deny his "guarantee," but he remembers it slightly differently. In the bottom of the ninth inning of Game 3, sure-handed center fielder Al Bumbry dropped a fly ball that allowed the tying run to score. The next batter smacked a walk-off double, and the Orioles lost 4–3. As the team came off the field, Bumbry was distraught, and so McGregor, who was the scheduled starter for Game 4, decided to pick up his buddy. "'It's all right, Bee,'" McGregor said he told Bumbry. "'I guarantee we are going to win this tomorrow.' And Richie Dauer happened to hear it. And Richie just blared it to everyone: 'Mac guarantees we're winning tomorrow's game.'" At that point McGregor couldn't back down from his statement.

He also held a career trump card. A native Southern Californian who was a high school teammate of Hall of Famer George Brett at El Segundo High School, McGregor was always dominant against the Angels, going 20–7 with a 3.17 ERA and 11 complete games in 29 starts against the Angels. With a bunch of childhood and high school friends watching the next afternoon in Anaheim, McGregor extended his excellence there. He threw a complete-game shutout in which he allowed six hits, one walk, and struck out four as the

Orioles won 8–0 and returned to the World Series for the first time in eight years.

That may not even be considered his signature performance. Four years later McGregor took the mound in Philadelphia for Game 5 of the World Series with the Orioles leading three games to one. They were in a similar situation in 1979 and dropped three straight to lose the World Series to the Pittsburgh Pirates. McGregor threw well but was the losing pitcher in Game 7 of that 1979 World Series. He wasn't going to let history repeat itself in 1983. And he told his teammates that in another guarantee of sorts. "After he warmed up, he walked into the dugout in the old Vet in Philadelphia, looked up to us, and said, "Boys, the World Series is over,'" Singleton recalled. "And he went out there and threw another shutout."

McGregor pitched nine scoreless, allowing five hits and two walks while striking out six. When Cal Ripken Jr. squeezed Garry Maddox's liner for the final out, McGregor was mobbed by his teammates. It was the Orioles' first world championship in 13 years and last for more than two decades. "I was definitely at the top of my game in all those years. I wouldn't have been doing that in 1988, that's for sure. But I had everything going. I was very confident, arrogant, probably, in that way. But I knew I was good and I knew I could compete and win. And we had great teams," McGregor said. Years later McGregor was watching a ballgame on TV when a trivia question popped up: "Who is the only pitcher in baseball history to clinch two postseason series with complete-game shutouts?" McGregor said he was thinking about the answer when his name appeared on the screen. "I had no idea. I figured Whitey or someone else had done it."

McGregor couldn't overpower the opposition, so he focused on control, deception, changing speeds, and reading hitters' bats. His biggest weapon was a change-up he could throw at any time for a strike. "That pitch changed everything for me," he said. How effective was it? In the 1983 World Series clincher, he threw one curveball; all the rest were fastballs or change-ups. McGregor also experienced a breakthrough of sorts in 1977, when manager Earl Weaver told McGregor to practice on getting his curveball under 70 mph. McGregor slowed it down the best he could, and it was still at 75. "I'm like, *Holy crap, I've got to take 5 more miles off?*" So, in attempting to slow down his curve, he created a delivery with a slight pause while stretching his glove hand before he threw a pitch. "Having that hesitation and the glove sticking right at them and hiding the ball helped," he said. "I hid the ball well and I changed speeds, could throw curveballs in the 60s, fastballs in the mid to upper 80s, and the change-up in the 70s. I had a great arm speed, and that change-up/palmball was a swing and miss pitch. Guys couldn't figure it out."

Even his teammates couldn't. "You'd stand in the outfield, and every pitch looked the same," Singleton said. "You'd think, *How does he beat these people?*" The answer was simple. "A lot of guys were throwers," Bumbry said. "Scotty was a thinking man's pitcher."

In 13 seasons McGregor was 138–108 with a 3.99 ERA and remains sixth on the modern franchise's wins list. He was 3–3 with a tremendous 1.63 ERA in six postseason games and posted nine seasons with double-digit wins and six seasons with 200 or more innings pitched. In the Orioles' disastrous 1988 season, McGregor was released in May after making four starts and posting an 8.83 ERA. It was an emotional time in Baltimore. McGregor was such a huge part of the club's success for a decade.

General manager Roland Hemond broke down in tears when he gave McGregor the news. And McGregor, who was traded by the Yankees in 1976 but never pitched a big league game with anyone other than the Orioles, had the cry of his life later that afternoon. "I came back that day for a press conference and I was doing fine. I was holding it together before that pretty good," said McGregor, who has remained with the organization in various roles, including big league bullpen coach and minor league instructor. "Then I came into the clubhouse and I lost it. I started crying so bad. I went out and sat in the stands and cried so hard that for a week afterward my chest was just raw."

The Babe

Before he was the majors' home run king, before he was an American icon, before he inadvertently cursed the Boston Red Sox for 86 years, George Herman "Babe" Ruth Jr. was an Oriole. His first professional contract, signed in February 1914 at age 19, was with the International League Orioles, who were managed and run by Jack Dunn, a former major league utility man and pitcher who kept Baltimore baseball on the map for decades.

Dunn discovered Ruth, a Baltimore native, at St. Mary's Industrial School for Boys, a reform school the "incorrigible" Ruth had been attending since he was seven. The left-handed hitter and power pitcher was taught the game by the Xaverian Brothers, including the school's prefect of discipline, Brother Matthias. Dunn brought the 19-year-old kid with him to Fayetteville, North Carolina, in 1914 for the Orioles' spring training, and that's believed to be Ruth's first trip outside of Baltimore. At some point during that trip, Ruth was referred to as one of "Dunnie's babies" or "Dunn's Babe," and the nickname ultimately was shortened to Babe.

As an Oriole, Ruth hit his first professional home run in an intrasquad game at the Cape Fear Fairgrounds in Fayetteville on March 7, 1914. The blast to right field was estimated at 350 to 400-plus feet, depending on the report. There is a historical marker there to commemorate the feat. Ruth received attention almost immediately for his baseball prowess with the Orioles. He allowed 17 base runners in an exhibition against the defending world champion Philadelphia Athletics but still led the Orioles to a 6–2 victory.

According to *The Baltimore Sun,* Ruth made his official regular season debut for the Orioles on April 22 at Oriole Park on Greenmount Avenue and 29th Street. He shut out the Buffalo Bisons 6–0 while collecting two hits at the plate in front of about 200 spectators. At the time the city was smitten with the Baltimore Terrapins, a team in the new and short-lived Federal League. That league lasted just two years, but it hastened Ruth's departure from his hometown. The Terrapins attempted to sign Ruth, but due to his loyalty to Dunn, he stayed with the Orioles. Dunn's bills were piling up, however, and he couldn't compete attendance-wise with the Terrapins. So he had to start selling off players.

Several teams were interested in Ruth, but ultimately Dunn sold him and two others to the Boston Red Sox for a reported $16,000 in July of 1914. Ruth had won 14 of his 20 decisions on the mound for his hometown team but, according to *The Sun,* had hit just .205 (16-for-78) with no home runs. Dunn considered selling Ruth as the biggest regret of his career. Of course, it wasn't the most infamous sale of the Babe. That occurred in January of 1920, when Red Sox owner and Broadway theater producer Harry Frazee sold Ruth to the New York Yankees for $100,000 and an additional loan against the mortgage of Fenway Park. It changed the fates of two franchises—and the history of baseball. Led by Ruth, the Yankees became the sport's greatest team while the Red Sox went from 1918 until 2004 without winning a World Series. Before any of that happened, though, the Babe became the Babe as an Oriole.

42 Visit Babe Ruth Birthplace and Sports Legends Museums

There are plenty of worthy tourist attractions in downtown Baltimore, but if you are a sports fan and particularly a baseball fan, there are two spots about three blocks apart that you need to check out. And you can buy a combined ticket for both.

The first is the Babe Ruth Birthplace and Museum at 216 Emory Street, a restored, three-story row house, which was leased by Ruth's maternal grandfather. You can actually walk into the upstairs bedroom where baseball's most iconic player was born. The museum features memorabilia that chronicles Ruth's life from his days at the St. Mary's Industrial School for Boys all the way through his incomparable Hall of Fame career.

Ruth's first pro experience was with the International League Orioles in 1914. The museum has an extremely rare baseball card from Ruth's abbreviated season with those Orioles. In celebration of the 100th anniversary of Ruth's pro career, the museum has added artifacts, including his wedding certificate, the rosary he had at his side when he died in 1948, and a 1927 notched baseball bat—with the notches presumably Ruth's way of counting how many homers he hit with that particular stick. Despite playing in the major leagues for the Boston Red Sox, New York Yankees, and Boston Braves, Baltimore's favorite son will always have an undeniable connection with the Orioles and Camden Yards. One of the saloons run by Ruth's father was located on the site that is now shallow center field at Oriole Park at Camden Yards. And there is a statue outside the stadium—at Babe Ruth Plaza—that immortalizes his time with the International League Orioles.

Adjacent to Oriole Park is another must-visit site, Sports Legends Museum at Camden Yards. Located roughly three blocks from Ruth's birthplace, it's an easy walk. Sports Legends has plenty of baseball flavor with exhibits featuring the Orioles' Hall of Fame, as well as Baltimore's amateur, minor league, and Negro League histories. There's also a separate tribute to Ruth, the Maryland Athletic Hall of Fame, and displays dedicated to the pro football Ravens and Colts, and, specifically, Hall of Fame quarterback Johnny Unitas. The museum also has a kids activity zone, which includes a locker room where children can dress up in various uniforms.

Admission to the two museums can be purchased separately or together for a discounted price. (In 2014 admission for adults to Sports Legends was $8, to Ruth's birthplace was $6, and to both was $12.) Admission is discounted for children and seniors.

Brady Anderson

What has made Brady Anderson such an interesting subject to cover over the years is that he is not what he appears to be. The guy with the matinee idol looks, the sideburns, the sculpted body, and the California cool has dated actresses, models, a tennis star, and a rock singer. But there's also another side to Anderson. He's a tireless worker who continually seeks challenges. He's introspective and analytical, contemplating every question before answering it. He can be outgoing and quick-witted or quiet and aloof. He's part open book and part mystery. "I remember he pulled up in this primer-black Cadillac in the parking lot for a game," said former Orioles teammate Tony Tarasco about Anderson. "It was cold. And he got out and he had on black jeans, a black T-shirt with a long, black trench coat, the sideburns, black sunglasses on. I was like,

That is Batman. If that isn't Bruce Wayne right there, I don't know who is. So my image—to this day—of him is Batman. If anybody could play the role for the next Batman, Brady should definitely be auditioning for it."

Anderson arrived in Baltimore in July of 1988 along with pitcher Curt Schilling in a deal that sent right-hander Mike Boddicker to the Boston Red Sox. A 10th round draft pick in 1985 out of the University of California, Irvine, Anderson was an on-base machine in the minors, a five-tool talent that had just two months of big league playing time when he was traded. He wasn't an everyday player for the Orioles until his breakout 1992 season, when he became the club's exclusive leadoff hitter, smacked 21 homers, stole 53 bases, and made his first of three All-Star teams. When Anderson turned 28, the Orioles finally understood what they had. "I remember early in his career coaches trying to get him to hit the ball on the ground," said former Orioles pitcher Ben McDonald. "They screamed at him all the time: 'Hit ground balls; you can't hit fly balls.' And he ended up hitting 50 homers one year. That said a lot about him. He was very serious, worked out all the time."

Oh, the 50 home run season in 1996. It was the first time that hallowed mark was reached in franchise history. Frank Robinson never got there; Eddie Murray, Boog Powell, Rafael Palmeiro, and Jim Gentile didn't either. But Anderson, who had never homered more than 21 times in a season before that or 24 times in a season after that, hit 50 in one year. He had 20 by the end of May. "I had 30 home runs at the break, and only a few players in the history of the game had done that. But I wasn't thinking about it. I knew it was pretty good. I knew I was swinging the bat well, knew I was hot," said Anderson, who hit 12 homers that year to lead off a game. "I was aware of my numbers and everybody else's numbers in the league, but it seemed like that's what I was supposed to do."

Because his 50 home runs were anomalous for his career, because he was so muscular, and because it happened in the mid-1990s—the Steroid Era—there always will be whispers about how Anderson could have had such a lofty power surge in one season. Performance-enhancing drug testing didn't occur in Major League Baseball until

Outfielder Brady Anderson, whose Beverly Hills, 90210 *looks belied his gritty work ethic, poses in 1993.*

after he was out of the game, though he was tested in the minors in 2003. Anderson has always contended his 1996 season was the confluence of his talent, ability, and work ethic peaking together, noting that if his power surge had been chemically-based, wouldn't it have lasted longer, at least one more season along the way? "I would liken it to a lot of golfers out there who shoot 95 all the time and then, every now and then, they shoot an 80. Why? Why can they be so much better one day? If you make tiny little adjustments, if your swing is a little better, it maybe snowballs in a positive way," Anderson said. "Things can snowball negatively. You get on that spiral ever downward, I guess, when you are in a slump. When you are in a groove, things tend to work out in your favor, too. You are aware you are hitting the ball well. You are more conscious, and the pitchers are going to pitch you more carefully when you are more conscious. You can see the ball a little longer. You don't cheat 2–0 and you don't panic 0–2. I think it's a weird thing to say, but hormonally, it must do something to people in general to have a positive outcome in your life, day after day after day."

Anderson was known as a fitness freak in his playing days (and still is). He used the supplement creatine before it became popular and would bring his own blender into the clubhouse to make pregame or postgame protein concoctions. In 1996 he felt like he was in a tremendous groove most of the season; he said he'd wake up every morning excited to play that evening. Yet he's always pointed out that his 1996 power output was really just one more homer per week throughout that season. And it certainly didn't hurt his production that he had hitters like Roberto Alomar, Cal Ripken Jr., and Palmeiro batting behind him. (Seven Orioles had 22 or more homers that year.)

Perhaps the most impressive thing about Anderson's 1996 season is that he didn't die on the field. Yes, that's a bit dramatic, but on July 19 in Boston, Anderson felt tenderness in his lower abdomen. An ultrasound and MRI were taken, and he was diagnosed with appendicitis. He was told he needed to have his appendix removed as soon as possible. A respected surgeon at the University of Massachusetts suggested that if he didn't have an appendectomy and continued to play, Anderson could collapse and potentially die. But another doctor visited with Anderson and said the situation could heal in some cases without surgery. That's all Anderson needed to hear. He would have missed two weeks to a month or more if he had surgery. There were only 10 weeks remaining in the season. His team was in the expanded wild-card playoff hunt. He had 31 homers and was chasing franchise history. So he decided against surgery, missed four games, and incredibly played the rest of the year. He never did get the appendectomy, though the club had potential emergency landing spots mapped out for Anderson each time it flew at the end of 1996. "It sounds stupid now, but I really didn't care if I died on the field. I didn't care. I thought that when I got in the batter's box against Randy Johnson, too," Anderson said. "The first thing I thought of is: *I'd rather be carted off the field in a bag than be worried.* I wasn't married. I didn't have kids. My dad could get over it. I knew people would say something nice at my funeral."

But what about the teenaged girls with the shirtless Brady Anderson posters on their walls? The ones who oohed and aahed whenever the ballplayer with the *Beverly Hills, 90210* sideburns came near? Anderson said he never really contemplated the whole sex symbol thing as he concentrated on playing baseball. But he didn't run from it either. "I loved the fans. I was always flattered when anybody ever asked for an autograph," said Anderson, who in 2012 joined the Orioles front office as a special assistant and was named vice president of baseball operations in 2013. "Obviously, having female attention was right up my alley. That was fun. There was no doubt. I really did like my private life to remain private, but that certainly was terrific. What else can I really say about that?"

44 The Final Days of 1982

The 1982 season didn't start well, didn't have a catchy slogan, or an eventual championship. It is still one of the most memorable in club history for how it unfolded. In March it was announced that Earl Weaver, who had been the club's irascible and incomparable manager since midway through 1968, was retiring at the end of the season. The Orioles responded by going 6–12 in April, including a nine-game losing streak. By mid-August they were 61–57, seven-and-a-half games behind the American League East-leading Milwaukee Brewers. But Weaver's clubs always seemed to rally; the 1982 Orioles followed script, winning 33 of their final 44 for a frenetic pennant push that ended with four must-win games. "Looking back," said Cal Ripken Jr., a rookie shortstop on that team, "It might be the most exciting series that I've ever been a part of."

With 10 games left, the Orioles traveled to Milwaukee for three. They were blown out in the first, won the next two. The Sunday victory was highlighted by "the Throw" from 24-year-old center fielder John Shelby, a September call-up, in the bottom of the eighth. With the Orioles up 3–2, Shelby, who quietly had been dealing with bone spurs in an aching right elbow, caught a fly ball from Cecil Cooper and unleashed a perfect strike—while catapulting himself to the grass—to nab Bob Skube at the plate for a critical double play. The Orioles then dropped two of three in Detroit, setting up a scenario in which they were three games behind Milwaukee with four to play at Memorial Stadium to end the season. If the Orioles won all four, they'd capture the division; lose once and the pennant race was over. The Orioles swept a

Friday doubleheader 8–3 and 7–1 and hammered the Brewers the next day 11–3. "We beat them handily in the doubleheader and then we beat them handily the next game and all the momentum— if there is such a thing in baseball—was with us," Ripken said. "We were feeling pretty good." Before the winner-take-all Sunday afternoon contest, Weaver held a rare meeting in the clubhouse, telling the players to sit at their lockers and face the middle of the room. He wanted to applaud their effort. But second baseman Richie Dauer spoke before Weaver could: "Don't tell us you're not going to retire." Everyone laughed. "That kind of broke the ice," said pitcher Jim Palmer.

Palmer, the 36-year-old future Hall of Famer, had a bizarre season. He allowed four runs or more in each of his first four starts while dealing with neck stiffness and was pulled from the rotation. At the time Palmer said general manager Hank Peters announced he wouldn't start again. But as the club struggled, Weaver pushed for Palmer to return to the rotation. Palmer did at the end of May and at one point won 11 straight decisions. At 15–4 with an ERA just over 3.00, Palmer took the mound for the season finale with a chance to pitch his team into the playoffs and potentially win his fourth Cy Young Award. The Brewers countered with future Hall of Famer Don Sutton. More than 51,000 people rocked Memorial Stadium; many carried brooms in anticipation of an exhilarating sweep. It never materialized. A third future Hall of Famer, Milwaukee's Robin Yount, hit solo homers in the first and third against Palmer. In his other 73 career at-bats versus Palmer, Yount had just one home run. Cooper homered to lead off the sixth, and after a walk, Palmer was gone, having allowed four runs (three earned) in five-plus innings. "Everybody always said to me along the lines of, 'You were always able to win the big games.' Well, I couldn't win that one," Palmer said. "But you have to realize how good they were."

Sutton carried a 5–1 lead into the eighth when Terry Crowley delivered a two-out RBI single to draw the Orioles within three. With runners at the corners, pinch-hitter Joe Nolan, representing the tying run, sliced a ball down the left-field line that Ben Oglivie snagged with an outstanding sliding catch. Milwaukee scored five runs in the ninth and clinched the division. "We were still in the ballgame [until Oglivie's catch], and it could have changed the game at that moment," Ripken said. "To be a part of that and to experience that was out-of-this-world exciting. And it would have been really over the top if we could have come back and swept them."

When the game ended, the fans wouldn't go home. Weaver would later come out of retirement in 1985 and manage through 1986, but at the time, this was his official send-off. Tears streaming down his cheeks, the hardscrabble Weaver waved repeatedly to the crowd. The players—some of whom had to get dressed again—returned to the field to thank the fans. The next year the Orioles would win the World Series without Weaver. Ripken said that 1983 team was particularly focused because they understood what one extra win during the course of a season could mean. But on October 3, 1982, all the fans knew was that the great Weaver was retiring and that they had just witnessed a tremendous run—even if it had ended with a loss. And the team and the crowd had to soak it in together. "You are bearing witness to one of the most remarkable scenes maybe that you'll ever see in sport," ABC broadcaster Howard Cosell said that day. "The fans have stayed. They have stayed to cheer and to honor the retiring manager of the Birds of Baltimore, a man who in 15 years has become an absolute legend."

2012: BUCKle Up

Center fielder Adam Jones left Baltimore at the end of a dreadful, 93-loss season in 2008, his first with the Orioles, and wondered what had just happened. "I was like, 'Wow. What is going on? What is the mind-set of this team?'" The next year they dropped 98, the year after that 96. During that 2010 season, though, Jones said something changed. It was both obvious and subtle. In July the Orioles hired a new manager: Buck Showalter, a proven winner with a reputation as a demanding perfectionist. The Orioles lost 93 games again in 2011, Showalter's first full season with the Orioles. But this time Jones went home thinking his club had turned the corner. "You can't give all the credit to Buck, but a lot of it does start with him because he made the whole organization feel accountable for everything that they do," Jones said. "Every person and facet that has to do with the Orioles is sharper because of the demands from Showalter."

The Orioles closed 2011 by beating the Boston Red Sox in two of their final three games, ending Boston's playoff chances. In the season finale, the Orioles rallied for a walk-off win with two runs in the ninth inning. Infielder Robert Andino hit a two-out sinking liner to left to score Nolan Reimold and seal the victory. The Orioles celebrated as if they had just made the playoffs —and not kicked the Red Sox out. Afterward, Andino fired this shot: "Make Boston go home sad, crying—I'll take it all day." Unofficially, the Orioles' return to respectability the next season began with that game—forever known in Baltimore as "The Curse of the Andino."

The Orioles started off 2012 playing well, winning 18 of their first 27, good enough for first place in the American League East on May 6 as they tried for a sweep at Fenway Park. They hadn't swept a three-game series in Boston in 18 years. It was on that Sunday afternoon when the 2012 season officially turned surreal, when long-suffering Orioles fans who had endured 14 consecutive losing campaigns began thinking that maybe this one would be a little different. That's what happens when your club beats a division rival on the road in a 17-inning, six-hour-and-seven-minute saga in which the winning pitcher is the designated hitter who had gone 0-for-8 with five strikeouts. "People have asked me about how cool was it to run out there to the mound at Fenway, and at the time, I wasn't thinking about it that way," slugger-turned-temporary hurler Chris Davis said. "Really, I was pissed off because I had had such a horrible day at the plate and I was really out to seek revenge."

The Orioles and Red Sox were tied through 15, and Showalter had used all seven available relievers. He asked Davis, who hadn't pitched since junior college roughly six years before, if he wanted to take the mound. "I'm like, 'Sweet,'" Davis said after that game. "I get to try something different today because hitting ain't working." Davis retired the first two batters in the 16th—including striking out Jarrod Saltalamacchia on an 83-mph change-up—and the third out came when a relay throw from Jones to shortstop J.J. Hardy to catcher Matt Wieters nailed Marlon Byrd trying to score from first on a double. Jones then hit a three-run homer in the top of the 17th against Boston's designated hitter Darnell McDonald. Davis allowed a single and a walk in the bottom of the 17th but struck out Adrian Gonzalez and induced McDonald into a game-ending double play to become the first AL position player to record a win in 44 years. "It's something I'll never forget. I've always said it was something I'd never want to do again," said Davis, whose fastball hit 92 on the stadium radar gun. "But now I kind of would like to go back out there and maybe throw a few sliders this time."

It was one of 18 extra-inning contests the Orioles played in 2012. They won 16 straight after losing their initial two in the season's first week. The Boston marathon wasn't even their longest game of the year innings-wise; the Orioles won in 18 in Seattle in September. Seven times the club was victorious in its last at-bat with the most dramatic example occurring July 14 on national TV. Reserve catcher Taylor Teagarden, who had been out all season with a back injury, hit a two-run, walk-off homer in the 13th inning against the Detroit Tigers; it was his second at-bat of the year.

Those unexpected comebacks, combined with Showalter telling a story during a daily press briefing about being on a roller coaster, led to the 2012 season's slogan: BUCKle Up. "You'd have an 18-inning game, a 17-inning game, and it was like, 'All right, what are we doing here?' And then there'd be another one that was 15 innings," Wieters said. "It was like a fighter that's out on his feet, but he just keeps fighting. That's what it felt like. Those were some of the most rewarding games, where you feel like you had nothing left to give and yet you are still up fighting. I think that's what that season was more about for me than anything else."

The Orioles were supposed to be overmatched; their roster seemed inadequate compared with other contenders. But Dan Duquette, in his first year as club executive vice president after roughly a decade away from the majors, kept finding players to fill holes. He signed starter Miguel Gonzalez as a minor league free agent, grabbed outfielder Nate McLouth after he had been cut loose by the Pittsburgh Pirates, and made under-the-radar trades for pitcher Joe Saunders and designated hitter Jim Thome. When the Orioles needed defensive help at third base, the club promoted 20-year-old shortstop prospect Manny Machado, changed his position, and made him a starter on a playoff squad.

The Orioles officially learned they had made the playoffs while sitting on a tarmac in Jacksonville, Florida, after a minor malfunction forced their charter plane to make an emergency landing on their way to Tampa Bay for the final series of the year. BUCKle Up *indeed*. Things didn't get simpler when the postseason began.

The Orioles played in the AL's first one-game wild-card playoff. They had to go to Texas to face the Rangers, the two-time defending American League champs. Saunders, a Virginia native acquired in a late August deal with the Arizona Diamondbacks, was handed the Orioles' first postseason start in 15 years. It was in Rangers Ballpark, where the veteran lefty was 0–6 with a 9.38 career ERA in six games. So, naturally, Saunders allowed just one run in five and two-third innings to lead the Orioles to a 5–1 victory. "It was just one of those things that was meant to be. I was meant to pitch that game," Saunders said. "I always considered myself a guy that likes the ball in a big moment in a big situation and I tried to take advantage of it."

The good fortune expired in a five-game loss to the New York Yankees in the American League Division Series. They matched up well, but Yankees ace CC Sabathia shut them down twice and they lost the other one in extra innings, the first time they had done that since April. The end result, though, didn't dampen what the season meant to the franchise and to Baltimore. "That was a terrific year because the team went from 69–93 to 93–69. And that just doesn't happen all that often," Duquette said. "When things get turned around that quickly, it's like magic."

46 Diamond Jim's Great Season

The season that Orioles first baseman Jim Gentile put together in 1961 still stands as one of the greatest offensive performances in modern franchise history. In 148 games, Gentile blasted 46 homers and drove in 141 runs—both club records at the time—while batting .302 with a .423 on-base percentage and a .646 slugging percentage. The argument can be made that in 60 years of Orioles baseball what Gentile did in 1961 may have been surpassed only by Frank Robinson's Triple Crown year in 1966, Chris Davis' record-setting campaign in 2013, and maybe Brady Anderson's 50-homer season in 1996.

Yet Gentile finished a distant third in the 1961 American League MVP vote because the top two guys just happened to be competing for a spot in baseball history. Diamond Jim's season for the ages happened the same year that New York Yankees sluggers Roger Maris and Mickey Mantle battled to break Babe Ruth's longstanding record of 60 home runs. Maris ultimately hit 61; Mantle hit 54. That allowed Maris (seven of 20 first place votes) to best Mantle (six first place votes) 202 to 198 in the MVP race. Gentile received five first-place votes, 157 total points, and became a footnote to baseball immortality. "I always said a player has a career year some time. That happened to be mine," Gentile said of 1961. "If I would have done that the year after, it would have been wonderful. There would have been more prestige for the Orioles, would have been more prestige for me. But I'm fine with it. I had my career year. It helped me, it helped the Orioles, and we kept going for a couple more years."

In 1962 Gentile had a solid campaign, hitting 33 homers, driving in 87 runs, and batting .251 while making his third consecutive All-Star team. After a similar season in 1963, Gentile was dealt to the Kansas City Athletics for first baseman Norm Siebern partially because future Orioles first baseman Boog Powell was biding his time in left field. In four years with the Orioles, Gentile batted .272 with 124 homers and 398 RBIs—not bad for a guy who had spent eight seasons in the minors and previously had just 36 at-bats in three seasons with the Brooklyn/Los Angeles Dodgers.

The Orioles initially bought him from the Dodgers, but Gentile assumed he wasn't going to stay after a rough spring training in 1960. Orioles manager Paul Richards met with the left-handed Gentile toward the end of that camp and told him that no player could be as bad as he looked. So he was going to keep him on a trial basis and give him 120 or so at-bats in the first month of the season to prove himself in a platoon with right-handed hitting Walt Dropo. And if Gentile didn't hit, he'd be going back to the Dodgers. Gentile seized the opportunity, batting .290 in April, .339 in May, and then slugging eight homers in June.

By 1961 he was the Orioles' starting first baseman on his way to an historic season. He hit five grand slams that year, which still stands as an Orioles record. On May 9 he hit a grand slam in the first inning and another in the second inning off two different Minnesota Twins pitchers. He was the first player in big league history to hit grand slams in consecutive at-bats in a game. He added a sacrifice fly in the eighth inning for a nine-RBI game—matched only one time since (Eddie Murray in 1985). Gentile eventually tied for the 1961 RBI crown, though it took 49 years. In 2010 baseball researchers took an RBI away from Maris' total because they discovered a run actually had scored on an error on July 5, 1961. So Maris' RBIs dropped to 141, and he fell into a first-place tie with Gentile all those years later. Maris actually took the lead—or what was thought to be the lead—in the final game of the 1961 season when he homered for the record-breaking 61st time. Gentile had three plate appearances in his final game that year, walking once and striking out twice, including one time with runners on second and third. He came out of the game early since it was the end of the season; he said he really wasn't thinking about winning the RBI title.

Frankly, as great as his 1961 season was, Gentile said he didn't really enjoy it. Having been up and down with the Dodgers, Gentile never felt like he could ever allow himself to be comfortable in the majors. "I was always waiting for the left shoe to drop," he said. "That was me. I was always worrying about not doing it and not helping my team and not helping myself and the next thing I know they would say, 'We're going to send you to Rochester.'"

Some teammates accused Gentile of brooding. Others, like his good buddy Gus Triandos, would tell him to stop "pissing and moaning." Pitcher Milt Pappas said Gentile was a good guy, a good teammate, and a tremendous ballplayer, but he was "his own worst enemy." "Every time he was going good, he'd walk in and he'd say, 'Oh man, I'm going to go into a slump,'" Pappas said. "I'd look at him and say, 'What are you talking about? Will you just shut the hell up and go play? You are talking yourself into a slump.' And, of course, he'd go into a slump. It just irritated the living hell out of me."

Gentile laughs now at those memories. He said as time went on, he learned to enjoy life—and his tremendous accomplishments. "I got better after I got out of the uniform," Gentile jokes. "I was a real nice guy if I had a suit on."

47 Tito's Great Blast

It's arguably the greatest home run hit in Orioles history. And it was delivered by a guy who had gone deep just once as an Oriole. His next at-bat for the club didn't come for another five years— partially because he was part of one of baseball's more bizarre trades. And that's a story worth mentioning, too. But, more critical in the world of Orioles baseball, Tito Landrum forever will be known for one swing—a solo home run in the 10th inning of the fourth game of the 1983 American League Championship Series to break a scoreless tie and propel the Orioles to a 3–0 victory and into the World Series. "I don't know if it was the most important, but it was probably the most unexpected home run for an Oriole," said Landrum, who was generously listed at 5'11" and 175 pounds and hit just 13 regular season homers in parts of nine big league seasons. "I know we kidded about my size at that time. I looked like the bat boy compared to the guys nowadays."

Landrum, a fourth outfielder whom the Orioles had acquired on August 31, 1983, had been 0-for-7 in the ALCS before singling to lead off the sixth against Chicago White Sox lefty Britt Burns. Playing in a typically brutal wind at Chicago's old Comiskey Park, Landrum struck out against Burns in the eighth and then, with one out in the top of the 10th, he faced Burns again for his fifth at-bat of the game.

He remembers talking to hitting coach Ralph Rowe during that series about what he might be doing wrong, and Rowe told him to stop trying to pull everything to left and just concentrate on squaring balls up the middle for line drives. Landrum, after all, had homered just three times in 230 previous big league games and had just one home run in 1983. So Landrum said that was his plan in the 10th. "I was just trying to get on base, just set the table, and have someone drive me in," he said.

Burns was approaching 150 pitches, and the sense was that Landrum, who was hitting second, might be his final batter with future Hall of Famers Cal Ripken Jr. and Eddie Murray due up next. The national broadcast team said as much, adding the caveat that Landrum wasn't the kind of player who could do damage with one swing.

White Sox manager Tony La Russa decided to keep riding Burns, who had a solid, eight-season career but never again pitched in the postseason. Burns retired John Shelby to start the 10th, and Landrum took the first pitch for a ball. He then waited on the second offering and whacked it toward the left-field bleachers. There had been a few clouts earlier in the game that were blown back into play and caught. So Landrum didn't take anything for granted—even though his blast ultimately hit the upper deck before falling to the bleachers below. "I was watching the video a while ago and I don't think I touched the ground," Landrum said, laughing. "I was racing around those bases. I think if they put a clock on me you would have thought I was trying to break a speed record."

As the ball flew in the air, Landrum inadvertently nearly injured one of his teammates. "The wind was blowing in really hard that day. It was a typical, cold Chicago early fall day. And when he hit it, and I saw it hit the seats, I jumped up and I almost knocked myself out," said Orioles outfielder Ken Singleton. "I hit my head on the ceiling of the dugout. I was stunned for a moment there. I saw stars while I was jumping up and down."

Landrum didn't get to the dugout unscathed either. "When I got to home, Eddie Murray gave me such a hard high five," Landrum said. "I got a bone bruise on my hand."

Burns was pulled after what ultimately would be the greatest start of his career; he lasted nine and one-third innings and allowed just one run on six hits and five walks while recording eight strike-outs. Right-hander Salome Barojas entered and allowed consecutive singles to Ripken and Murray and a RBI base hit to Gary Roenicke. A sacrifice fly by Benny Ayala gave the Orioles a 3–0 lead in the 10th, and Tippy Martinez, pitching in his fourth inning of relief in the game, finished it off. The Orioles went on to win the World Series against the Philadelphia Phillies in five games.

Landrum's homer cleared the path for the Orioles' championship run and it also guaranteed that the club wouldn't have to face White Sox ace LaMarr Hoyt in a deciding Game 5 on the road. Hoyt won 24 games in 1983 on his way to the American League Cy Young Award. In the first game of the ALCS, the White Sox won 2–1 at Memorial Stadium on the strength of a complete-game, five-hitter by Hoyt. "We had talked about that in the dugout," Landrum recalled. "We said, 'We need to win today. We know we can beat LaMarr, but it is going to be a tough challenge. Let's go and finish it off tonight and not have to worry about LaMarr tomorrow.'"

Landrum would never hit another home run for the Orioles. He wouldn't get an at-bat in the 1983 World Series, entering three games as a pinch-runner/defensive replacement and picking up a stolen base in Game 2. He then was traded back to the St. Louis Cardinals in one of the ultimate wink-and-nod moves in franchise history.

In the summer of 1983, the Cardinals needed a third baseman, and the Orioles were looking for a reserve who could play each outfield position well. So the Cardinals traded a player to be named later for Orioles catcher/third baseman Floyd Rayford. They completed that deal in August, when Landrum was sent to the Orioles as the player to be named. What wasn't said at the time was that both sides wanted their original player back—and that apparently was agreed to at the time of the first deal.

During spring training in 1984, the Orioles played the Cardinals and, after the game, Landrum approached a friend of his who coached for St. Louis and wished him luck in the upcoming season and said, "I'll see you later." The coach responded by saying, "You never know, T."

The meaning of that was a mystery for Landrum until he was traded back to the Cardinals a few days later for a minor league pitcher named Jose Brito. It seemed a bit strange that the Orioles would deal away a postseason hero for a pedestrian minor leaguer who never made it to the big leagues. Five days after that trade, the Orioles purchased Rayford's contract from the Cardinals. In essence, the duo was swapped for itself. "It wasn't until 1993, when they had the All-Star Game in Baltimore, that former manager [Joe] Altobelli came up to me and said, 'Did you know you were the player to be named later in your own trade?'" Landrum said. "'I said, Get out of here.' And he said, 'No, we had arranged all of that.'"

Landrum went on to be a playoff hero for the Cardinals in 1985, hitting .385 in 12 postseason games. In 1988, as his career came to a close, Landrum returned to the Orioles and had three hits in 24 at-bats before being released. He never played in the majors again. Landrum finished his nine-season career with just 82 plate appearances for the Orioles. But with one swing, he should never have to buy a beer in Baltimore again. "If you really look at it, you have to consider me a Cardinal," Landrum said. "But I was really fortunate to come be an Oriole for a short stay. Birds of a feather flock together, I guess."

48 Davis Crushes the Home Run Record

In one sense it shouldn't have been a huge surprise. Chris Davis hit 33 home runs in 515 at-bats in 2012, his first full season as an Oriole. While with the Texas Rangers organization in 2008, he smacked 40 homers between the minors and the majors. So it wasn't as if the prodigious power came out of nowhere. But, still, did anyone expect the then-27-year-old first baseman to break out in 2013 with the greatest home run display in the 60-season history of the Orioles?

Frankly, Davis didn't. "I thought 2008, as far as my career was concerned, was the best year I'd ever have," Davis said. "I hit over .300 at three different levels. I had 40 home runs, drove in over 130 runs, got called up to the big leagues, and thought then, *This was it. This is the best it is ever going to be, statistically speaking.* I was like, 'I don't ever know if I will be this locked in again.'"

All that changed in 2013, when Chris Davis officially became alter ego Crush Davis—a twist on Kevin Costner's character Crash

Davis from the baseball movie *Bull Durham*. Crush Davis homered in the Orioles' first four games in 2013, picking up 16 RBIs in that span. A hot streak, for sure, but four games don't make a season. He then hit two more homers in the next week and three more before April ended. He was named American League Player of the Month for April with nine homers, 28 RBIs, a .348 average, and a 1.171 on-base plus slugging percentage (OPS). He was just a tad better in May with a 1.210 OPS and 10 homers. June was actually his best power month with 12 homers and 30 RBIs. By the All-Star Break, Davis was hitting .315 with 37 homers and 93 RBIs—tremendous numbers for a full season, let alone 95 games.

A guy who just two years earlier was traded by the Rangers as part of a package deal for reliever Koji Uehara was rewarded by the fans with a starting spot in the All-Star Game and more total votes—8.2 million—than any other player in the majors. "That was crazy. That didn't really sink in until they presented the award at the All-Star Game," Davis said. "I just remember sitting there thinking, '*Holy cow, dude. I have been sent down numerous times to the point where I thought about giving up baseball, got traded over to Baltimore, was just trying to establish myself as an everyday player, finally got the opportunity to play every day, and now I am accepting the award for most votes of any player at the All-Star Game.* I'm just like, 'I think this is good enough right now.'"

Next up was chasing history, both nationally and locally: the all-time home run record of 73 set by the San Francisco Giants' Barry Bonds in 2001, the American League mark of 61 set by the New York Yankees' Roger Maris in 1961, and Orioles vice president Brady Anderson's franchise record of 50 in 1996. Davis actually caused a mini-controversy that July when he said he considered Maris' home run record to be the lasting target, dismissing the marks set by Bonds, Mark McGwire, and Sammy Sosa due to the performance-enhancing drug scandal. "When McGwire and Sosa did what they did in 1998, it was awesome to watch. And then when all the stuff came out with the PEDs and all of that, it was really disheartening," said Davis, who has denied ever using performance-enhancing drugs. "And if there are people that want to get upset with me saying that 61 is still, in my opinion, the single-season record, I'm entitled to my own opinions and own beliefs. I was a fan before I played this game at the big league level and I think what Roger Maris did is still considered by a lot of people to be the legitimate home run record."

In an ironic twist, Davis was suspended 25 games in September 2014 after testing positive for amphetamines. He said he took the prescription drug Adderall, knowing he didn't have a therapeutic use exemption for it. Davis has been diagnosed with ADD in the past and at one point had an Adderall exemption. But he didn't have one in 2014, a season in which he hit just .196 with 26 homers in 127 games. His decision to take the medication cost him a chance to play in the playoffs and disappointed teammates, fans, and the organization.

In 2013, though, he could do no wrong. And, for a while, Davis used Maris as his benchmark. But as the second half progressed, it became obvious that goal was out of reach. Teams started pitching Davis differently—if they pitched to him at all. He was getting fewer and fewer mistakes to hit and, in his frustration, when the mistakes were made, he wasn't hitting them out of the park. He homered just seven times while batting .211 in July. He rebounded in August with nine homers and he began picking off the top single-season home run leaders in franchise history one-by-one.

On August 28 he homered against Boston's John Lackey for his 47th of the season, passing another slugging first baseman, Jim Gentile (1961) for third most on the O's list. Gentile sent an email of congratulations to Davis and told him to keep going until he put a first baseman at the top again. With a blast against New York's Ivan Nova on September 10, Davis tied Hall of Famer Frank Robinson at 49. Three days later Davis homered in the Rogers

Centre against Toronto reliever Steve Delabar to tie Anderson and become the second Oriole to ever hit 50 homers. In the sixth inning on September 17 at Fenway Park, Davis hit his historic homer against Ryan Dempster. He had knocked off three of the more prolific sluggers in club history in the span of three weeks. "That was the coolest part about it. I had met Frank before. I ended up meeting Jim about a week after I passed him. Obviously, Brady and I are pretty close, having known each other for years now and spending quite a bit of time together," Davis said. "It was cool, but it was kind of humbling to look at the company I was in and really put into perspective what I had done over the course of a season."

He finished third in the American League MVP voting behind Miguel Cabrera of the Detroit Tigers and Mike Trout of the Los Angeles Angels after adding two more home runs for good measure, including his final one at Camden Yards on the Friday before the season he ended. When the dust settled, Davis had hit a major league best 53 homers, driven in 138 runs—most in the majors in 2013 and the fourth highest total in franchise history. "I had never thought about hitting 50 home runs. I didn't know if it was in reach. The most I had hit was 40," Davis said. "It wasn't a goal that I had, and even as I got close, I was thinking, *You know, this has been a great year regardless if I hit 50 or more home runs.* But then once I hit 50, I wanted to hit 51. It was kind of crazy the way my perspective changed throughout the year."

Dempsey's Rain Delay Theater

No matter how long he played the game or the accolades he achieved, former Orioles catcher and 1983 World Series MVP

Rick Dempsey is best known as the guy who clowned around on drenched tarps during rain delays.

Dempsey played in 1,766 games in a 24-year big league career and he performed his "Rain Delay Theater" just a handful of times. No matter. He'll always be the goofy guy dressed as Babe Ruth or Robin Yount slipping and sliding to the joy of soggy patrons. He's fine with that. Orioles fans, though, may not be fine with this: Dempsey's unforgettable antics were inspired by (gulp) a New York Yankee.

When Dempsey was with the Yankees, his teammate, reliever Sparky Lyle, would throw baseballs into the crowd at the end of a season. Major League Baseball frowned on the practice, but Lyle loved how the fans would go crazy as he pitted one section of the stadium against another, riling each up until throwing a ball into the loudest part. Lyle would tell Dempsey that one day he wanted to throw baseballs into the crowd during a rain delay and then pantomime Babe Ruth calling his home-run shot and slide around the tarp. "He never did it," Dempsey said. "But I kept thinking, *Boy, that would be cool.*"

In the final game of the 1977 season at Fenway Park in Boston, Dempsey got his chance. The Yankees had eliminated the Red Sox and Orioles, who were tied for second, from playoff contention. It was raining that afternoon in Boston and it was unclear whether the game would be played. Toward the end of batting practice, Dempsey was throwing some balls into the loudest section of the stands, Sparky-style, when the rain began pouring. The players headed to the dugouts, and Dempsey noticed one more ball sitting on the tarp.

"I said to myself, 'I'm going to get that ball out there, throw it to the people in the grandstand because it doesn't look like we are going to play this game,'" he said. "And then the organist started playing 'Raindrops are Falling on My Head' while I was out there. So I started to lead the people singing and, at the same time, I was starting to slide around the tarp. Then I threw the ball and left."

After Dempsey went back into the clubhouse, the rain subsided some, and the bored, wet crowd wanted more Dempsey. "They started beating on the stadium. And if you are underneath Fenway in the locker room and people start beating and stomping in that stadium, it is almost deafening," he said. "So Richie Dauer came in and said, 'They want you to come back out. What can you do?' And I remembered what Sparky Lyle said."

So Dempsey put pillows inside his uniform jersey for Ruthian girth, went out onto the tarp, stood at the plate, pointed to the outfield fence, and corkscrewed a pantomime homer. He then jogged up the first-base line, gyrating for the imaginary ball to stay fair, the way Boston's Carlton Fisk did in the 1975 World Series. Dempsey splished and splashed around the diamond and then sprinted down the third-base line, sliding headfirst into home plate, causing a mini-geyser on the tarp. "I went out there and did that, and obviously everybody liked it, and that was the beginning of it," Dempsey said.

He did it again at Fenway and also Milwaukee's County Stadium and at Baltimore's Memorial Stadium. In Milwaukee in 1983, he borrowed a Robin Yount No. 19 jersey and pantomimed Yount's two-homer day in October 1982 against Orioles' right-hander Jim Palmer. Orioles reliever Sammy Stewart re-created the part of Palmer, wearing a No. 22 Orioles jersey and a pair of under-wear—Palmer was a Jockey spokesman—over his uniform pants. In Baltimore Dempsey again mimicked Ruth, a Baltimore native, calling a home-run shot. He said he felt he owed it to Orioles fans to perform his rain delay antics at his home park.

They went crazy, too, while the fun-loving Dempsey had a blast. "I couldn't sit around and do nothing. I didn't mind being that guy. I think every team kind of needs one," Dempsey said. "We were winning a lot so we were afforded that opportunity to have more fun than a lot of teams."

Rex Barney

Oftentimes when someone with strong ties to Baltimore sports passes away, the Orioles hold a moment of silence at Camden Yards. On August 12, 1997, the Orioles held a game of silence. There were no between-inning announcements, no player introductions, and no pitching change information. It was the ultimate tribute to the man whose voice was Memorial Stadium and Camden Yards: public address announcer Rex Barney.

When Barney, who had battled myriad ailments in the latter stages of his life, was found dead at age 72 at his home that morning, the Orioles decided they wouldn't replace his voice that night. So after a pregame message to the fans from his close friend, Orioles Hall of Fame radio and TV announcer Chuck Thompson, the in-stadium microphone sat silent, and Barney's chair in the first row of the Camden Yards press box remained empty. "I thought the way they handled it was great. I think that was as nice of a tribute as you could do. Just leave it silent," said Jim Henneman, a longtime Baltimore sportswriter and friend of Barney's. "People knew why. The ballplayers knew, the visiting ballplayers knew. They understood because he really was kind of a tradition here."

Barney never played for the Orioles; his six-season career was spent exclusively with the Brooklyn Dodgers. Armed with one of the best fastballs in baseball history, the 6'3" right-hander from Omaha, Nebraska, could be overpowering. On September 9, 1948, Barney threw a no-hitter against the New York Giants at the Polo Grounds despite having to wait out a rain delay of about an hour before pitching. He made the majors at age 18 and he started Game 5 of the World Series against the Yankees at 22, striking out Joe DiMaggio with the bases loaded and no outs in the first inning. He allowed just two runs in four and two-third innings in that game, but he walked nine—typical of a career in which he struggled with his command. By age 25 Barney's major league career was over. He finished with a 35–31 record and a 4.31 career ERA while walking 410 and striking out 336 in nearly 600 big league innings. He ended up in broadcasting, doing some radio play-by-play and filling in as PA announcer at Memorial Stadium before getting the full-time gig in 1974. He stayed in that job until his death. "His voice was almost like a security blanket," the late Orioles pitcher Mike Flanagan told *The Baltimore Sun* in 1997. "Being announced by Rex always gave me a quiet confidence, almost like the voice of a baseball god. He made you feel like everything would be all right."

Also a sports radio talk show host known for his politeness and patience with callers, including children who would phone in to talk baseball, Barney had two special catchphrases: "THANK Youuuu" and "Give That Fan a Contract." Both have seemingly endured after his death, at least in the memories of Orioles fans. "THANK Youuuu" started simply enough. According to Barney's 1993 autobiography, appropriately titled *THANK Youuuu*, at the end of a promotional spot in the late 1970s, he decided to emphasize the first word of that phrase and stretch out the second for no apparent reason. Some friends who heard it that day told Barney that they liked it. So he mixed it in more often, and the response grew to the point that strangers would come up to him and say, "THANK Youuuu" or ask him to say it. And it stuck.

Barney's other catchphrase was less spontaneous. In the 1970s Orioles executive Jack Dunn III held a meeting with employees, asking for suggestions to get the fans at Memorial Stadium more involved. When it was his turn, according to his autobiography, he told Dunn that when he was playing in the minor leagues there was an announcer in Raleigh who would say, "Give that fan a contract," whenever a fan caught a foul ball. And then the fan would be presented with a token contract. Barney wrote that the other employees thought it was corny, but Dunn liked it and decided to try it. Initially, the statement was gender specific—give that man, lady, boy, or girl—a contract. That changed when a ball was caught in front of the press box by what Barney thought was a long-haired woman. So he said, "Give that lady a contract." Later, he wrote: "The ugliest, toughest-looking guy I have ever seen, long hair down his back and a long straggly beard, turned around and showed me the ball and gave me the dirtiest look…From then on, it was: 'Give that fan a contract.'"

The next year at the spring meeting, the Orioles decided to scrap the idea. But Barney began receiving calls and letters wondering what happened to it. So the club re-instituted the program, and it remained until Barney's death. If a catch was made beyond Barney's view, an usher would signal to him to let him know what had happened. Once a "qualifying" catch was made, the stadium ushers would get the name and address of the fan, and the organization would send them a mock contract signed by Barney and the general manager at the time. The only time a fan wasn't awarded a contract was if they caught a home run ball. Barney didn't think it was appropriate to celebrate a fan's catch after the opposition homered. He wanted the focus to stay on the players at that time. Barney had fun with the concept, though, even giving the occasional fan an error if they dropped an easy foul ball. In turn, everyone seemingly loved Barney, and when he unexpectedly passed away, it was a tough blow for the Orioles community.

The club didn't name a permanent replacement until the next year. And a plaque bearing his name and the words, "Thank Youuuu," remains behind the PA announcer's seat at Camden Yards. "He had a great connection with the fans," Henneman said. "He was everybody's friend it seemed like."

51 The Managers: The Good, the Bad, and the Ugly

The Orioles have had a fairly strange managerial history. Earl Weaver lasted parts of 17 seasons, won one World Series, and was inducted into baseball's Hall of Fame. Hank Bauer and Joe Altobelli each won a World Series with the Orioles and were fired within two full seasons of their championships. Both were replaced by Weaver.

Cal Ripken Sr. managed both of his sons in the majors in 1987 but was canned six games into the next season. Dave Trembley had his interim tag removed in August 2007 only to have his team lose 30–3 later that afternoon. Then there was Davey Johnson, who won the 1997 American League Manager of the Year Award and resigned the same day in a dispute with club managing partner Peter Angelos, who has employed 10 managers in the two-plus decades he has owned the club.

Weaver's tenure is by far the longest of the modern franchise's 17 skippers (plus two interim managers). Weaver managed 2,541 regular season games. The next closest is Paul Richards, who managed six full seasons and part of a seventh for a total of 1,063 games. Richards had the unusual distinction of being field manager and general manager simultaneously for four seasons.

Only two men besides Weaver and Richards have managed more than four seasons for the Orioles: Bauer and current skipper Buck Showalter, who hadn't previously lasted beyond four seasons in any of his three previous gigs. Luman Harris, who stepped in for Richards at the end of 1961 and went 17–10 in his brief stint, has the shortest tenure of any as O's manager and the best winning percentage (.630). Weaver is second at an incredible .583 clip in 17 seasons.

Richards and Weaver have their own chapters in this book. So do Frank Robinson and Johnson, who were key Orioles players, and Ripken Sr., who was considered the backbone of the organization. Here's a brief look at the other full-time managers in club history:

Hank Bauer
1964–68
A World War II veteran, Bauer had a tough exterior, but his young players viewed him as a father figure. He expected personal accountability and, otherwise, let a talented team play. In 1966 he became the first Orioles manager to win a World Series but was fired in 1968. Bauer clashed with GM Harry Dalton, who wanted to give Weaver a chance.

Joe Altobelli
1983–85
He skippered the Orioles in between stints by Weaver. That included the 1983 World Series team. Weaver basically told Altobelli not to screw things up in 1983. And he didn't. Altobelli was fairly hands-off, but he did push the right buttons with his pinch-hitters.

Buck Showalter
2010–present
He once described his managerial career as similar to raising a daughter and then watching someone else walk her down the aisle. In his three previous jobs, the man who replaced him ended up in the World Series, and two of them won titles. Showalter was brought in to take a talented but undisciplined club to the next step. In his second full season, the Orioles made the playoffs for the first time in 15 years.

Mike Hargrove
2000–03

This was a high-profile hire; Hargrove had just been fired by the Cleveland Indians after leading them to five straight postseasons and two World Series. But Hargrove didn't have the same talent in Baltimore, especially after Albert Belle was forced to retire due to a hip condition.

Johnny Oates
1991–94

A seasoned baseball man who had the Orioles playing at a .563 level before the strike hit in 1994, Oates didn't make it through the work stoppage. He was fired by Angelos, who was openly critical of Oates' managerial decisions.

Dave Trembley
2007–10

The ultimate good guy and baseball lifer who spent two decades in the minors before finally getting his big break, Trembley went through growing pains with a rebuilding team and was canned by Andy MacPhail as the club continued to struggle.

Billy Hitchcock
1962–63

Like Trembley, Hitchcock was considered a good man, but his Orioles teams went backward, and Lee MacPhail wanted a stronger presence, hiring Bauer.

Ray Miller
1998–99

One of the greatest pitching coaches in baseball history, he was elevated to manager by Angelos after Johnson resigned. He wasn't supported by general manager Pat Gillick or by a veteran club-house, and his teams underachieved greatly.

Sam Perlozzo
2005–07

He was the players' choice the previous two times the job came open and he finally got it in 2005. But the transition from teacher and confidant to boss and disciplinarian was a rocky one, especially with an inferior cast.

Lee Mazzilli
2004–05

This was a strange fit from the beginning. A New Yorker with no big league managerial experience, Mazzilli nailed the job interview, but he never seemed to warm to the position and became a casualty of the great implosion of 2005.

Phil Regan
1995

Also a strange fit, Regan, known for his intellect and scouting sense, was not the high-profile manager that Angelos desired. The club was interviewing candidates even before he was fired.

Jimmy Dykes
1954

A former All-Star infielder who managed six different big league teams, Dykes was hired for the transition to Baltimore. He lost 100 games in his lone season.

52 The Ripken Family

Both brothers remember the quote. They weren't surprised by what their father said publicly. He was, by all accounts, an exceptionally fair man and wouldn't give the impression he had favorites. So in July 1987, when second baseman Bill Ripken received the major league call from the Orioles to play next to his big brother, shortstop Cal Jr., their father, Orioles manager Cal Ripken Sr. downplayed the historic combination. "We just happen to be in the same business at the same place. Maybe years from now, I'll smile about all this," the skipper said. "But for now they're just a second baseman and a shortstop on this ballclub."

His boys understood the sentiment; they didn't buy it. "I know a little better than that," Bill Ripken said. "If you ask Cal, he knew a little better than that." In fact, if you ask Cal, the Hall of Famer will tell you he'd get a little ticked when he heard one particular line from his dad. "One quote for me that was personal was he would say, 'I look at all the guys as my kids.' And I'm thinking, 'Noooo, we're your kids,'" Ripken Jr. said, laughing.

Only seven times in history has a man managed his son in the big leagues; Ripken Sr. is the only one to have managed two simultaneously. On June 13, 1985, he became the third big league skipper to manage one son—joining Connie Mack and Yogi Berra—while holding the interim tag for one game, which occurred between Joe Altobelli's firing and the re-hiring of Earl Weaver. The Orioles won that one 8–3, and Ripken Jr. had two doubles to help his father pick up his first big league managerial win. When Weaver retired for good after the 1986 season, Ripken Sr. took over the club's reins after more than a decade as an Orioles coach and even more years managing and playing in the franchise's minor league system.

From left to right, Billy Ripken, Cal Ripken Sr., and Cal Ripken Jr. were part of the 1987 Orioles. (AP Images)

Even before the elder Ripken managed the Orioles, he and his namesake shared several lasting moments on the field. They were together for Ripken Jr.'s debut on August 10, 1981. When the son hit his first Orioles home run in his first at-bat on Opening Day of 1982, it was his father in the third-base coach's box who had the pleasure of first congratulating him. "You hit the ball and you ran until it was out of the ballpark, and then the first person's hand you shook was the third-base coach's hand," Ripken Jr. said. "I could tell by the gleam in his eye and the happiness that came over him—it was different." The father hadn't been able to watch his son succeed on the diamond much before that. "I think he saw parts of two of my games from ages of eight to 18," Ripken Jr. said. "He didn't see me play because his baseball schedule didn't allow for that."

On July 11, 1987, Ripken's youngest son, 22-year-old Billy, made his debut, starting next to his big brother. Four years apart, they had never played organized ball together except for maybe a few innings in a spring training game. "You get to be called up to the big leagues, and your name is written in the lineup by your father. And, oh by the way, when you go out there and stand for the national anthem of your first game ever, you are standing with your big brother. That's pretty cool," Bill Ripken said. "There are a lot of people that get to the big leagues and there has only been one—or I guess three—that you could say have done what we've done so far in the history of Major League Baseball."

It did create an interesting situation. What do two big league ballplayers call their dad when he is their manager? The answer: any accepted baseball moniker—but nothing fatherly. Bill Ripken said he called his father "Bub" because that was his dad's nickname for most people, or "Senior." "I never called him 'Dad' on the baseball field. I don't think that would have gone over too well," Bill Ripken said. "That probably would have opened the door for me to get ragged a little bit more than I wanted."

The Ripkens' unique experience didn't last very long. The trio spent three months of the regular season together in 1987 and then the first week of 1988 before Ripken Sr. was unjustly fired after six losses to begin that year. (The Orioles lost 15 more consecutively after the managerial change.) Senior returned to the organization to do some scouting that summer and in 1989 he was back coaching third base, partially to work with his sons again. After the 1992 season, Ripken Sr.'s contract was not renewed; Bill Ripken was released that December. He came back to join his brother for one more season in 1996. Cal Ripken Jr. retired in 2001 as one of the

The F--- Face Bat

Bill Ripken swears it was a combination of convenience, locker room humor, and bad timing that led to one of the most controversial baseball cards of all time. It wasn't a prank and it wasn't purposeful. His infamous 1989 Fleer baseball card is a posed shot with Ripken in uniform, half-smiling and holding a bat. But neatly printed on the knob of the bat are two words: the last is Face. The first is a common, four-letter profanity that begins with F. Alliteration was being represented that day. For years it was believed that someone set up Ripken, a notorious jokester himself. Or maybe he was messing around. Neither, Ripken said 25 years later. Here's his "F--- Face" explanation.

In 1988 Ripken received a shipment of bats that he liked, but the grain patterns made them too heavy. He decided to keep one for batting practice and began using it routinely. Since the bats were often thrown together in a grocery cart, he thought it would be smart to write something on the knob so he could quickly identify it. Why he picked the particular phrase he used, he's not sure. He thought it was funny; he was 23. So that's how "F--- Face The Bat" was created.

As for the photo, he was at Fenway Park and had just finished a round of batting practice and a run around the bases when a photographer representing Fleer tapped him on the shoulder and asked him if he could take his baseball card shot. Ripken obliged, grabbed his bat, and the photo was snapped.

He said he didn't think anything about that picture until an Orioles public relations representative called him in January with news about his baseball card. "It was my bat, my writing, only meant for clubhouse humor, only meant because I wanted to know where my bat was for batting practice. It never was intended to be on a picture," Ripken said. "And I still say to this day that Fleer, when they took the picture and they proofed it and saw it, they probably twisted it and turned it right and probably enhanced it because I don't write that good."

More than 25 years later, he's still asked about it. He said it's neither funny nor annoying to him. It's just over. "I find nothing in it now, anymore," Ripken said. "Twenty-five years, we should let it go. Time to move on."

greatest Orioles ever—and the only one who had two members of his immediate family with him in uniform for part of the ride. "You realize the value of having a trusted family member in the form of a dad, where you could go to him for advice and direction and those sorts of things when you didn't know what to do. The same is true when you have a brother there," Ripken Jr. said. "But you don't realize it as you are going through it. You take it for granted. And when it's not there anymore, it's a big hole that you miss."

53 Sing "Thank God I'm a Country Boy"

The vast majority of Orioles fans don't know how to whittle. They can't play a tune on the fiddle. They may have never had cakes on the griddle. And, in this hectic, modern world, they probably don't view life as a funny, funny riddle. It doesn't matter, though, at least not for a half an inning 81 times in the spring, summer, and fall in Charm City. After the Orioles retire the side in the top of the seventh at Camden Yards, everyone lauds a higher power that he or she is a country boy.

There's no really good explanation as to why late country music star John Denver's mid-1970s hit, "Thank God I'm a Country Boy" has resonated so much and for so long in Baltimore, a decidedly un-country town. (Remember, this is a city that was abuzz for days in June 2014 when a 750-pound steer escaped a slaughterhouse and galloped about two miles in and around downtown before police shot and killed the animal. It was like a four-legged Elvis sighting.) So, yes, it's fairly bizarre for so many city dwellers and suburban types to proclaim their country boyness on a nightly basis during the seventh-inning stretch. But so it goes with tradition.

Denver's live version of "Country Boy" hit the top of Billboard's country and pop charts in late spring of 1975. It was about that time Orioles executive Frank Cashen was getting tired of organ music being played at games and wanted to infuse more current tunes to interest the younger set at Memorial Stadium, according to a story in *The Baltimore Sun*. The stadium experimented with several different seventh-inning stretch songs. Orioles shortstop Mark Belanger and his wife, Dee, were fans of Denver and pushed for "Country Boy" as an option, according to the website of John Sommers, who wrote the song and played fiddle and guitar in Denver's band. The song received the best response that season. Then, in 1976, it took on a new life.

Three Orioles, Doug DeCinces, Tim Nordbrook, and Tony Muser, started to have a little fun with the song when they were stuck on the bench during games. They'd grab bats and towels; turn them into guitars, fiddles, and microphones; and form a pantomime country band. Muser played his bat upright, used the towel as a bow, and strummed an imaginary bass. It was just a silly thing to do to pass the time, DeCinces said. One day in 1976, however, the Orioles were losing a one-run game, and the trio decided not to mess around in the dugout. Suddenly, Hall of Fame manager Earl Weaver was standing before them. "Weaver said, 'What the hell are you guys doing? Get your shit ready.' That's exactly what he said," DeCinces said, laughing. "Weaver was so superstitious. And we had been doing that for a while, so all of the sudden Earl wanted it. I mean, we thought, *Well, we shouldn't be doing this today because he was mad about a lot of stuff…*From that point on, we just did it the rest of that year."

No one messed with the Weaver mojo. The song became a staple at Memorial Stadium, and pretty much every time the Orioles tried something new, it was rebuffed by fans. In 1980 "Orioles Magic," a catchy and campy tribute to the 1979 Orioles, was played during the seventh inning stretch and was booed. It's happened several times. In the second half of the 1986 season, the Orioles used catcher Rick Dempsey's cover of "Old Time Rock and Roll," and early in 1987, several songs were tested during the seventh inning. Fans kept clamoring for "Country Boy," and they got their wish until 1988, when owner Eli Jacobs ordered that the Andrews Sisters version of "Take Me Out to the Ballgame" be played in the middle of the seventh inning. Despite negative fan reaction, it stayed that way until local attorney Peter G. Angelos bought the team in 1993. "Country Boy" returned and has stayed since. Nowadays, "Take Me Out to the Ballgame" starts the seventh-inning stretch followed immediately by Denver's crooning and the foot stomping of the Camden Yards crowd.

Denver was born in New Mexico, lived all over the country, and is known for his love of Colorado. But he embraced his connection to the Orioles. He attended the first game of the 1983 World Series and received a huge ovation when he was introduced to sing the national anthem. Then, during the seventh-inning stretch that night, Denver belted out the song from the top of the Orioles dugout to the delight of the fans—something ABC sportscaster Howard Cosell called "a lovely scene."

In September of 1997, Denver was performing at a benefit concert in Baltimore and paid a surprise visit to Camden Yards, dancing on top of the dugout with the Oriole Bird. The fans again loved it. Roughly three weeks later, on October 12, 1997, Denver was killed when the plane he was piloting crashed into the Pacific Ocean. The Orioles won Game 5 of the American League Championship Series the next night, and then, in a weird twist of fate, the franchise didn't win another playoff game for 15 years. The Curse of the Country Boy ended on October 5, 2012 with the Orioles' 5–1 win against the Texas Rangers in the first AL wild-card play-in. The game was in Arlington, Texas, not far from where Denver went to high school in Fort Worth.

54 Gus Tremendous

Brooks Robinson was the first face of the Orioles franchise, but the first real star of the club was a plodding, hulking catcher with a hangdog mug and the strange sense that he couldn't fully satisfy his fan base despite its obvious adulation. Gus Triandos was originally signed by the New York Yankees as an amateur free agent in 1948 and made it to the big leagues four days after his 23rd birthday. He played just 20 games with the Bronx Bombers in 1953–54 before he was involved in the landmark 17-player trade between the Yankees and Orioles in the winter of 1954. Although the deal ultimately favored the Yankees—they landed Bob Turley and Don Larsen—it was a blessing for Triandos, who was blocked in New York at catcher by Yogi Berra.

In Baltimore, Triandos—who was known as Gus Tremendous or Big Gus—started as a first baseman, but by 1957 he was catching exclusively. And his powerful arm and explosive bat quickly made him one of the best all-around backstops in baseball. He made the American League All-Star team in three consecutive years from 1957 to 1959. In 1958 he hit a career-best 30 homers, at the time tying Berra's American League record for home runs by a catcher while setting the Orioles franchise mark for any position player. Hitting 30—which stood as the Orioles' record until Jim Gentile shattered it with 46 in 1961—was particularly impressive given how cavernous Memorial Stadium was. Each of his first five seasons with the Orioles, Triandos led the team in homers.

He was so popular that a Gus Triandos Fan Club was created in Baltimore. In 1962, when he moved his family into a new development in Timonium, Baltimore County, a street was named after him—Triandos Drive. Yet Triandos never felt truly appreciated in

Charm City. Whether it was his size—he was 6'3" and heavier than his listed 215 pounds—or his comical lack of speed, he just felt like fans were disappointed in him, which mystified his teammates. "He was the star," Gentile said. "But he always said the fans didn't like him there. I'd say, 'They love you in Baltimore.' And he'd always say, 'No, they don't like me.' He just had this feeling that the fans didn't care for him, and I don't know why. The times I was there they always clapped for him. But he always had that in the back of his mind that he wasn't liked."

He also, at times, felt like he had the worst job ever: the unenviable task of trying to catch Hoyt Wilhelm's jolting, dancing, dipping knuckleball. Triandos would say later that pitch almost ruined his career. Manager Paul Richards eventually devised an oversized catcher's mitt, flat and round like a pizza pan, to assist Triandos. Wilhelm's famous pitch also factored into one of Triandos' career highlights. On September 20, 1958, Wilhelm pitched and Triandos caught the Orioles' first no-hitter, and it was against the mighty Yankees, the club that had traded away Triandos. Making the situation even sweeter, the Orioles won 1–0 on Triandos' 425-foot homer in the seventh inning at Memorial Stadium. Years later, he joked about that day to *The Baltimore Sun*, "Catching Hoyt was such a miserable experience [that] I just wanted to end the game."

"Gus was funny, quiet, and slow, oh boy, was he slow," said former teammate Joe Durham. "But he was a good guy to have around." Triandos played in more than 1,200 games in a 13-season career and he had just one stolen base on one attempt. It came on the final day of the 1958 season when the Yankees were resting their regulars. Triandos made it to second standing up. He also was considered one of the tougher players in the game. He was constantly covered with bruises from getting hit with foul tips or Wilhelm's knuckler. "I don't think one foul ball ever missed him," Gentile said. "He was bruised on his arms and his shoulders, everywhere. He was just so big back there the ball would always hit him."

Triandos got revenge by smacking the ball with a ferocity and a repetition the Orioles hadn't seen before, making him a fan favorite—whether he knew it or not. He was inducted into the club's Hall of Fame in 1981 and died from congestive heart failure in March 2013 at age 82.

"Gus and I were dear friends. We used to have a lot of fun," Gentile said. "He went his own way and didn't bother anybody. He never talked bad about anybody."

Hall of Famers

In their modern-day history—from 1954 until the present—six men have gone into the National Baseball Hall of Fame as Orioles. They are the all-time greats, the ones with their uniform numbers retired and statues at Camden Yards: Earl Weaver, Jim Palmer, Eddie Murray, Cal Ripken Jr., Brooks Robinson, and Frank Robinson. But the modern Orioles franchise also had eight more of its players make it to the Hall of Fame with other logos on their caps: Roberto Alomar, Luis Aparicio, Whitey Herzog, Reggie Jackson, George Kell, Robin Roberts, Dick Williams, and Hoyt Wilhelm.

Williams, an infielder/outfielder who had three stints with the Orioles (1956–57, 1958, 1961–62), and Herzog, an Orioles outfielder in 1961–62, both made it into the Hall as managers. Neither, however, managed the Orioles. Hall of Fame outfielder Larry Doby technically counts as an Oriole, but he never played a regular season game with the club. The Orioles received him in a deal with the Chicago White Sox in December 1957 and then flipped him to the Cleveland Indians on April 1, 1958, two weeks before the season started.

Here's a look at the six who played for the modern-day Orioles and were inducted into the Hall—as players—while representing other clubs:

Roberto Alomar

He played three seasons with the Orioles (1996–98), was the starting second baseman on the mid-90s playoff teams, and hit a combined .312 in his tenure, the highest of any Oriole with at least 1,200 at-bats. His time in Baltimore was tainted by his suspension for spitting on an umpire in 1996.

Year of induction: *2011*
Cap on plaque: *Toronto Blue Jays*

Luis Aparicio

He played five seasons with the Orioles (1963–67). The speedy, slick fielding shortstop was the first Oriole to have a plate appearance in a World Series, leading off Game 1 of the 1966 World Series against the Los Angeles Dodgers with a fly out against Don Drysdale. His 166 stolen bases are tied for fifth on the Orioles' all-time list with Mark Belanger, the man who replaced Aparicio as the club's starting shortstop.

Year of induction: *1984*
Cap on plaque: *Chicago White Sox*

Reggie Jackson

He played one season with the Orioles (1976). In an eight-season span from 1971 to 1978, Mr. October only missed the postseason once—his lone year with the Orioles. Jackson was acquired April 2,

1976 as part of Oakland's fire sale and initially held out for more money from the Orioles. After a late and then dreadfully slow start, he eventually put up numbers in the second half. He hit 27 homers and stole a career-best 28 bases for the Orioles.
Year of induction: *1993*
Cap on plaque: *New York Yankees*

George Kell
He played two seasons with the Orioles (1956–57). Kell ended his career with the Orioles, batting .278 in 201 games and making the All-Star team both seasons. But his most important contribution was tutoring another young third baseman from Arkansas: future Hall of Famer Brooks Robinson. Kell was one of Robinson's heroes growing up, and Robinson said he learned how to be a big leaguer from Kell.
Year of induction: *1983*
Cap on plaque: *Detroit Tigers*

Robin Roberts
He played four seasons with the Orioles (1962–65). Roberts picked up 42 of his 286 career victories with the Orioles, posting a 3.09 ERA in 113 games. He also played a crucial mentoring role. He was future Hall of Famer Jim Palmer's first road roommate in the majors in 1965, when Palmer was just 19 and Roberts was 38.
Year of induction: *1976*
Cap on plaque: *Philadelphia Phillies*

Hoyt Wilhelm
He played five seasons with the Orioles (1958–62). The seemingly ageless knuckleballer pitched until he was 49, so the Orioles basically got him in his prime—from age 36 to 40. He won more games with the Orioles (43 of 143 wins) than with any of his other

eight teams. He only started 52 of the 1,070 games he pitched in his career, but 43 of those starts were with the Orioles. He pitched the club's first no-hitter on September 20, 1958 against the New York Yankees at Memorial Stadium.

Year of induction: *1985*

Cap on plaque: *New York Giants*

56 Magnificent Moose

When the Orioles signed veteran Rick Sutcliffe to anchor the 1992 rotation, they had only two returning pitchers with at least 20 starts: Bob Milacki and Ben McDonald. The *Baltimore Sun* speculated that the rotation's fourth spot would go to the team's top pick from 1990: a slender, good-looking right-hander out of Stanford named Mike Mussina. One brief look and Sutcliffe quickly concurred. "There was an article saying Mussina was penciled into the rotation," Sutcliffe said. "And I said, 'You can do that with a Sharpie.'"

Known for his quiet confidence, expressionless mound demeanor, and pinpoint command, Mussina excelled from the beginning. He rolled through the minors with a 2.43 ERA in 28 starts and was in the majors 14 months after he was drafted. In 12 games with the Orioles in 1991, he posted a 2.87 ERA. By the time Sutcliffe met Mussina, the sense was the kid had the goods to stay in the big leagues. Mussina was hopeful but not convinced. "I knew I could pitch a little bit, but I still had a whole lot to learn. Being on a team with a veteran pitcher like Rick really helped because I didn't know what I was doing," Mussina said. "I didn't know how to play a six-month season. I didn't know how to make adjustments from one team to the next or one at-bat to the next. There was no way I felt like I was ready. I just felt lucky to have the chance."

That season, at age 23, Mussina emerged as one of the American League's best pitches, going 18–5 with a 2.54 ERA and making the first of five All-Star teams. He finished fourth in the AL Cy Young voting and would place in the top six eight other times, though he'd never win the award. Instead he won games—270 in an 18-season career, including 147 with the Orioles. "Moose was in that rare category that you feel comfortable whenever he took the mound," said shortstop Mike Bordick. "It was like 'Okay, we've got a chance today and a really good chance.'" Mussina thrived by precisely locating his low-90s fastball and befuddling batters with a wide array of offerings, including a knuckle curve, which Chris Hoiles said was one of the two most unhittable pitches he ever caught—along with Gregg Olson's curveball. Hoiles remembers one start when Mussina decided to throw a conventional knuckleball. "I already use all five fingers on my right hand to call your pitches," Hoiles told Mussina. "How do you want me to call a knuckleball?'"

With an economics degree from Stanford and a penchant for completing crossword puzzles in the clubhouse, Mussina was one of the most erudite Orioles. His quiet, no-nonsense style was interpreted by some as standoffish. But his teammates considered him trustworthy and genuine. "People get a misread on Mike if you don't know him," said reliever Alan Mills. "He is not going to have much to say unless he knows or trusts you. But I played with him for a while, and he's a really good person. There's nothing fake in him."

Mussina's public image changed dramatically in the 2000 offseason when he signed a six-year, $88.5 million deal with the New York Yankees. The Orioles, who were in full rebuilding mode, reportedly fell $10 million short in their final counter. Since Mussina wanted to remain in the AL and close to his hometown of

Montoursville, Pennsylvania, the Yankees were the obvious choice. "It was hard to make that change. Human beings by nature don't like to change a lot if they can help it," Mussina said. "I loved playing in Baltimore. It was a great experience, a great time, and, at the time, all I knew. I probably wanted to stay, but a change was probably the best thing."

Orioles fans understood Mussina's yearning to win but felt betrayed when he chose the Yankees. They let him hear it, turning the "Mooose" cheers into boos when he visited in pinstripes. "I

Mussina vs. Palmer

The argument is moot. Mike Mussina left the Orioles after 10 years, and the rest of his 18-season career was spent with the New York Yankees. But had he stayed and put up the same numbers—pure conjecture since the Orioles were awful after his departure in 2000, and the Yankees were tremendous—would he have surpassed Jim Palmer as the greatest pitcher in franchise history?

The career numbers sure are close. In 537 regular season games, Mussina was 270–153 with a 3.68 ERA, walking 785 and striking out 2,813 in 3,562⅔ innings. In 558 games through parts of 19 seasons, all with the Orioles, Palmer was 268–152 with a 2.86 ERA, walking 1,311 and striking out 2,212 in 3,948 innings. Palmer was better in the postseason, but both pitched well. Palmer was 8–3 with a 2.61 in 17 playoff games; Mussina was 7–8 with a 3.42 ERA in 23 playoff games.

Both were outstanding defenders. Mussina won seven Gold Gloves; Palmer won four. Palmer, however, won three Cy Young Awards and was in the top five in voting eight times; Mussina won none, but was in the top five in voting six times (and placed sixth on three other occasions). Palmer won 20 or more games eight times and had 211 complete games; Mussina won 20 games once (18 or more six times) and completed 57 games. Palmer was on three championship clubs and played in six World Series; Mussina never won a title but was in the World Series twice with the Yankees. Palmer was inducted into the Hall of Fame on his first ballot in 1990; Mussina has the numbers to get there at some point.

knew people were not going to like it. I know how fans are," he said. "Ultimately, though, I had to make the best decision for myself." He spent eight years with the Yankees and played in seven postseasons and two October Classics. "Good things happened in both places," he said. "I can't sit here and say I favor one over the other."

In 2012 the Orioles inducted Mussina into their Hall of Fame; he was cheered during an on-field ceremony. Mussina played a role in many of the most memorable moments at Camden Yards. He started the night Cal Ripken Jr. broke the consecutive-games played streak. He nearly threw the first perfect game in club history in May 1997, falling two outs shy on a single by Sandy Alomar Jr. The Cleveland Indians catcher also participated in another unforgettable—and frightening—incident involving Mussina roughly a year later. Alomar hit a liner that struck Mussina in the face, fractured his nose, and left a gash above his right eye. Mussina missed roughly three weeks but returned in June. "It was hard to go back out there," he said. "Every time somebody swung, I thought it was coming right at me."

Perhaps the most lasting image of Mussina in an Orioles uniform is the least significant in terms of his career: throwing in the bullpen in the ninth inning of the 1993 All-Star Game. It was the second All-Star Game ever held in Baltimore, and fans were psyched to see their 24-year-old homegrown ace on the big stage. Ripken was the only other Oriole on the roster. Meanwhile, the defending champion Toronto Blue Jays had seven All-Stars and manager Cito Gaston. With the AL winning 9–3 in the ninth, Gaston chose his closer, Duane Ward, to pitch, turning the crowd's chants from "We Want Mike" to "Cito Sucks." Gaston, who thereafter was treated harshly in Baltimore for the slight, said he believed Mussina got up on his own and that he wouldn't have pitched unless the blowout had gone into extra innings. Mussina maintains he was told by the Orioles coaching staff at the park to use the ninth as an in-between-starts session. "I was a kid and I didn't really realize what was going to happen. So it didn't turn out too good," he said. "It's a shame it happened that way, but I can't go back and change it." One good thing came from it, Mussina said. Players from host cities always seem to appear in the games now.

Tippy's Pickoffs

Pretty much wherever he goes, Tippy Martinez is asked about August 24, 1983 and one of the strangest innings a pitcher has ever encountered. If he only could have a dollar for each time it is brought up. "Residual income, I'd like to have it. But you don't get anything anymore other than a pat on the back and more reminiscing," Martinez said with a big grin. "But it is a lot of fun to be remembered."

Felix Anthony "Tippy" Martinez came to the Orioles in 1976 as part of the blockbuster trade with the New York Yankees that also yielded pitcher Scott McGregor and catcher Rick Dempsey, strengthening the foundation for those great Orioles clubs of the late 1970s/early 1980s. Martinez pitched 14 seasons in the majors, including 11 in Baltimore. His 499 appearances are second most in club history—behind only Jim Palmer—and the most for a reliever. Listed at 5'10" and 180 pounds and armed with a knee-buckling curve, Martinez saved 105 games with the Orioles. He posted his best season in 1983, when he went 9–3 with a 2.35 ERA, saved a career-best 21 games, and threw a career-high 103⅓ innings. And yet when Orioles fans think about Martinez, one crazy 10th inning in the heat of summer comes to mind: the time Martinez picked off three Toronto Blue Jays in one inning.

A little background is needed. The Orioles entered that night in a dogfight in the American League East. With a loss the previous evening to the Blue Jays, the Orioles had fallen out of first place and were a half-game behind the Milwaukee Brewers, who had edged the Orioles out of the division crown the previous year. The Blue Jays and Detroit Tigers were tied for third, just one game behind the Orioles, and the always dangerous New York Yankees were in fifth, three-and-a-half games out of first. So with just a quarter of the season remaining, every game was crucial. And Orioles manager Joe Altobelli was managing that way. Trailing 2–1 in the bottom of the seventh, the Orioles loaded the bases with one out, and Altobelli brought in reserve catcher Joe Nolan to pinch hit for starter Rick Dempsey. It didn't work; Nolan popped out. The Jays escaped that inning without allowing a run and then scored another in the top of the eighth to make it 3–1.

In the bottom of the ninth, the Orioles rallied, and Altobelli used all of his tricks. With one out and a runner on first, outfielder Gary Roenicke entered to pinch hit for Rich Dauer, who had been moved from second base to third in the previous inning. Roenicke struck out. Then Lenn Sakata, who had entered in the eighth to play second base, walked. With two on and two outs, Altobelli went for it. He pinch hit for Nolan with outfielder Benny Ayala, who singled home a run. Al Bumbry followed with a single to score Sakata and tie the game at 3. But when Dan Ford struck out to end the frame, the Orioles were stuck. They entered extra innings with no catcher and five outfielders. So Sakata, a light-hitting middle infielder who had never caught in a real game as a professional, was sent behind the plate. Roenicke, who had never played third base, went to the hot corner, and John Lowenstein, whose infield days seemed behind him, moved from left field to second base. Reliever Tim Stoddard entered for the Orioles and immediately surrendered a home run to Cliff Johnson to make it 4–3 Blue Jays. After Stoddard allowed a single to Barry Bonnell, Martinez was summoned to pitch. That's when the fun really began. "When I came in the game, there was a guy on first base already," Martinez said. "We had a catcher who had never caught before in his entire life, which was Sakata. We had Roenicke playing third base, [and] we probably had to show him where third base was at. And we had John Lowenstein, who had the range of a dime, playing second."

Truth be told, Martinez was part of this perfect storm for potential base runners, too. For a lefty Martinez did not have a particularly good pickoff move. And with his looping curve, runners would challenge him. Eager to get a good jump on Martinez and steal on Sakata, Bonnell broke to second prematurely and halted. Martinez threw to first baseman Eddie Murray, who chased down Bonnell and tagged him for the first out. The next batter, pinch-hitter Dave Collins, walked.

Collins got to first and Blue Jays first base coach John Sullivan gave the runner simple instructions: don't get picked off. But Collins took about a four-step lead, and Martinez fired to Murray, who tagged a stunned Collins standing up. *Out No. 2.* The announced crowd of 25,882 was going crazy, Blue Jays manager Bobby Cox was seething, and the Orioles bench was stunned. "I couldn't believe they were that stupid," Dempsey said of Toronto's base runners. "It wasn't a great move. It wasn't one of the most effective moves. I think they were just trying to get such a good jump off Sakata that they took a little more liberty than they should have."

The next batter was slugger Willie Upshaw. Martinez was afraid to throw curveballs because he wasn't convinced Sakata could catch them. Sakata admitted later he had trouble seeing out of his mask. Upshaw singled on a ball that Martinez believes a regular second baseman like Dauer would have reached. "The ball was hit to Lowenstein, and I figured the play was going to be made because that's what we are built on, pitching and defense," Martinez said. "But I had Lowenstein playing second, and it was an infield hit."

Upshaw took a minimal lead at first. Legend has it that Sullivan told Upshaw, "whatever you do…" But before Sullivan could utter, "don't get picked off," Martinez threw to Murray, who put the tag on Upshaw's hand for the third out. The quick-witted Lowenstein later said: "The reason Tippy kept throwing to first base was because Eddie was the only guy he recognized."

"I would have to say that was probably one of my better moves that I have ever had in my entire life. Put it that way," Martinez said. "I'm really not known for picking people off. But, anyway, things kind of came together. You might call it more of a balk move, but it really wasn't a balk."

To finish the Hollywood script, the Orioles came to bat in the bottom of the 10th, and Cal Ripken Jr. led off with a homer to tie the game at 4. Then, with two on and two outs, Sakata, of all people, hit a three-run, walk-off homer. It was just his second homer of the season, it was one of only two walk-offs in his career, and it came in the only inning in his 11-season big league career that he played catcher. "Everybody just sat there in disbelief. How did we just do that?" Dempsey said. "It just happened. No one could explain it."

The next game Martinez allowed a solo home run to Bonnell in the 10th inning to break a scoreless tie, but the Orioles delivered another walk-off on Ford's two-run double. Those two dramatic victories ignited an eight-game winning streak, which catapulted the Orioles into first place. They never fell off the top perch again and ultimately won the World Series. It was almost as if they were destined to win it all after the improbable heroics from Sakata and Martinez.

58 Roenicke and Lowenstein

It's difficult to mention one former Orioles outfielder without the other; they seemingly were intertwined. Gary Roenicke and John Lowenstein. John Lowenstein and Gary Roenicke.

It's the most famous platoon in club history and it was supposedly one of the things that made Hall of Famer Earl Weaver a genius. The common belief is that the great Weaver realized the importance of lefty-righty splits and that he turned Lowenstein and Roenicke into a two-headed monster—maybe even a three-headed monster with Benny Ayala tossed in there on occasion.

There's some truth to that theory and some hindsight embellishment. Weaver was a master of juggling his lineup—perhaps the best of all time. In 1979 Weaver used 140 different lineups—never utilizing the same order more than three times—and the Orioles won 102 regular season games. He was always looking for match-ups, flipping through his index cards with hitter-versus-pitcher statistics to create the best lineup and optimum pinch-hitting situations. But that doesn't mean he used a straight platoon with the right-handed hitting Roenicke and the left-handed hitting Lowenstein. In fact, at a reunion banquet years after they played, Roenicke was introduced as half of Weaver's tremendous left-field platoon. As soon as the dinner was over, the always excitable Weaver made a beeline to Roenicke. "Earl comes up to me afterward and says, 'I didn't platoon you. What is all that about?'" Roenicke said. "I said, 'I know. But that's how I'm labeled.' Earl didn't play me against the real tough right-handers like Nolan Ryan. But with most of the other right-handers, he did play me."

In 1979 Roenicke played in 133 games and started 109 while Lowenstein played in 97 games and started 48—not numbers of a typical platoon. Their traditional platoon didn't really occur until 1983 when Joe Altobelli took over the managerial reins from the retired Weaver. In 1982, which was Roenicke's and Lowenstein's best combined season, the duo started together 39 times under Weaver, just about a quarter of the season. From August 1 until the end of the year, they were in the starting lineup together 18 times. Under Altobelli in 1983, they started just seven times together all season. Out of 162 games that year, either Roenicke or Lowenstein started in left 136 times. The two ended up with the exact same number of plate appearances in 1983: 366 each. And what an effective combination it was. Together they hit .270 with 34 homers, 124 RBIs, and 97 runs scored. They actually experienced a dip in production from 1982, when they played together much more often. That year the two combined for 861 plate appearances, 45 homers, 140 RBIs, 127 runs scored, a .292 average, and 124 walks.

"They were fantastic. They were something that one guy would pick up where the other guy left off," former Orioles outfielder Ken Singleton said. "They didn't play together in games a lot, but when they did, they just continued to push. John was a great fastball hitter, one of best I've ever seen. He really could turn on anybody's fastball. And Roenicke, you talk about an underrated player. Tremendous fielder, he could play center field as well as left field, very good arm, good on the bases. And he had a stroke that was perfect for Memorial Stadium. He could pull all of his home runs down the line in left field. We used to joke that if one person had a season ticket for that seat he was going to get 25 home run balls a year from Roenicke."

"Rhino" and "Brother Low," as they were known, got along well but were different in many ways. Roenicke, a former first-round pick of the Montreal Expos, seemingly was built to play baseball. At 6'3", 205 pounds, he had speed, power, and a rocket throwing arm. And he was tough. He took a fastball to the upper lip in 1979 and only missed six games. Although unfailingly polite to fans, he had a competitive streak and a keen knowledge of the game. It came as no surprise that he spent years as a scout after his playing days.

Lowenstein was a 6'0", 175-pounder who was taken in the 18th round of the amateur draft by the Cleveland Indians. He didn't have prodigious power, but he did hit 24 homers in 1982. He wasn't a burner, but he stole 36 bases for the Indians in 1974. He could be quiet and introspective, but he possessed a tremendous wit and had a unique perspective on practically everything. It was no surprise he became an Orioles TV analyst before eventually moving full time to Las Vegas and distancing himself from his previous baseball life. Perhaps Lowenstein's biggest strengths were his versatility—he played every big league position except pitcher and catcher—and his desire to win.

Singleton remembers one game in which the Orioles offense was being shut down by the Oakland A's, when Lowenstein told Singleton he was going to make something happen in his next at-bat. Lowenstein walked to lead off the inning, stole second on the next pitch, and stole third base right after that. "I'm on the bench thinking he is not going to do it. And sure enough, John tries to steal home on the next pitch and he gets thrown out by an eyelash. He almost made it," Singleton said. "He comes back down, sits next to me, and says, 'I told you I was going to make something happen.' 'Yeah you did,' I said, 'but here he comes. Here comes Earl.' And Weaver walks down, looks at John and says, 'I hope you got that out of your F'ing system.' And then Weaver turned around and walked away."

Singleton often sat across from Lowenstein on the club's charter flights and was always entertained by his off-the-wall teammate's theories—like the one about commercial airlines. Lowenstein rationalized that places no one wanted to go to like Cleveland and Detroit took an hour or so to fly to, but a flight to a popular destination such as Hawaii lasted hours upon hours. "He said, 'Well, I bet you Hawaii's not that much farther away than Cleveland or Detroit. The airlines just get you up in the air, fly you around longer, and then charge you more money,'" Singleton recalled Lowenstein saying. "And I said, 'Well, John, I've never thought of it that way.' That was John."

Lowenstein was much more comfortable being a role player, while Roenicke admits he never fully embraced the label. Yet the two—so different but with one common goal in mind—will forever be mentioned in the same breath. And that's fine with Roenicke. "Absolutely," Roenicke said. "John was a character. We were entirely different people. I don't think I ever saw him take a bad swing. I was at times hot and cold; it seemed like he was a little bit steadier than I was. He was a great guy to have on this team. He kept people loose and he could hit."

59 Brother Low Rises to the Occasion

John Lowenstein played parts of seven seasons with the Orioles and batted .274 with a .365 on-base percentage during that time. He had some huge clutch hits in those days, prompting signs throughout Memorial Stadium that read, "Tonight, Let It Be Lowenstein," a word play on the popular beer slogan, "Tonight, Let It Be Lowenbrau."

Lowenstein was as popular for his goofy personality as he was his baseball talent. And though Orioles fans won't forget his 10th inning, three-run homer in Game 1 of the 1979 American League Championship Series that helped propel the club into the World Series, it wasn't the snapshot moment of Lowenstein in an Orioles uniform. That came in the bottom of the seventh on June 19, 1980, against the Oakland A's at Memorial Stadium.

Trailing 3–2 with runners on first and second and one out, Lowenstein pinch hit for Lenn Sakata and drove a Rick Langford pitch into right field to score Mark Corey to tie the game. Lowenstein, who was hobbled by an Achilles' tendon injury, tried to turn the hit into a double, but Oakland first baseman Jeff Newman caught the relay and threw to second. Lowenstein would have been out, but Newman's throw struck Lowenstein in the back of the neck. The ball caromed into the outfield, allowing Al Bumbry to score the eventual winning run. Lowenstein was safe at second, but he was also out—as in knocked out. He reportedly lost consciousness for about 20 seconds. Medical personnel rushed to his aid and moved his motionless body to a stretcher as a pall drew across the announced crowd of 15,491. The Orioles players were a bit confused. "We were all thinking, *How could he get hurt on that play?* That was the first thing I thought," said fellow outfielder Gary Roenicke. "Then I'm like, 'Now they are going to bring a stretcher out?'"

What the fans and players didn't realize was that Lowenstein was no longer unconscious, but was being told to remain still by the staff working on him. He adhered to that advice for a little while, but always with a flair for the dramatic, Lowenstein had another plan. As the stretcher approached the home dugout, Lowenstein shot upright, thrusting his arms and fists upward. It took a moment to realize what had happened, and then the crowd roared its approval. "As we got to dugout, I suddenly raised up with my fists and yelled, 'Awwwwright,'" Lowenstein told John Eisenberg in *From 33rd Street to Camden Yards*. "And the doctor who was carrying the stretcher reared back like I was some wild mountain lion."

Lowenstein said he had witnessed former Detroit Tiger Norm Cash pull the stunt years earlier and Lowenstein vowed he'd do the same if ever put in that position. What resulted was probably the loudest ovation in Orioles history for a player removed from a game due to injury. "The place just totally went crazy. You could hear a pin drop until I reared up, and the fans went nuts," he said. "God, it was worth every second of all the planning and all the years it took for me to do that."

The Orioles' dugout was in shock—and then stitches. "The whole stadium went silent. I thought maybe he got killed," said Orioles outfielder Ken Singleton. "He was a piece of work. It was typical John."

"It was hilarious," Roenicke said. "When I saw him yelling, I'm like, 'Oh my gosh. That's John.'"

60 Grab a Sandwich at Boog's

A few times each season a reader will ask where he or she should eat at Camden Yards before a game. There's never a hesitation in my response. If it's your first time visiting Camden Yards—or your 50th—you have to stop by Boog's Barbecue on Eutaw Street.

You can get an overstuffed pit beef, turkey, or pork loin sandwich for $10—$15 if you go crazy and order double meat. Pit beef in itself is a Baltimore tradition, just a notch below crabs, oysters, and corn for things you have to eat in a Maryland summer. Crab feasts and bull and oyster roast celebrations dot the Baltimore landscape all year. But there's another reason a stop at the Yards isn't complete without Boog's Barbecue.

John Wesley "Boog" Powell played for the Orioles from 1961 to 1974. A four-time All-Star, he played first base in four World Series with the Orioles, won the 1970 American League MVP, and finished in the top three of voting two other times. His 303 home runs are third most in Orioles history, and his 1,063 RBIs are fourth all-time. Before almost every Orioles home game these days, Powell hangs out at his barbecue stand as Camden Yards' unofficial greeter. "I try to go out there every game, signing autographs and being an ambassador for the Orioles and for pit beef and getting an opportunity to talk baseball," said Powell, now in his 70s.

Even if Powell weren't one of the greatest ballplayers in club history, the stand would probably still be a local institution. It opened when Camden Yards did in 1992. It initially was located behind the bullpens beyond left field, but Powell didn't like the spot. He felt there weren't enough people passing through, and so it was moved that first season to just beyond the right-field flag court on the pedestrian walkway that divides the park from the B&O Warehouse. It's fair to say there's enough foot traffic now. "Our biggest problem has been our lines are so long, people were waiting too long, and we couldn't figure out a way to get people through the line faster," he said. "So we added a couple more cashiers. And the next thing we know, we have six full-time cashiers working and we still had a line. But that's about as good as we can do."

While you wait, there's plenty of reading material. The stand is located next to the Orioles Hall of Fame display with plaques for every player, field staffer, and front office member elected to the franchise's Hall. And as you get closer to the stand, the real payoff is meeting Powell, a big man with a hearty laugh and a massive handshake. "I sign everything. I sign shirts, bats. The only thing I won't sign is skin. But I will sign shirts or tickets or whatever anybody's got. And if someone wants to bring a book out (his *Baltimore Baseball & Barbecue with Boog Powell: Stories from the Orioles' Smokey Slugger* came out in 2014), I'll sign it, too."

Powell's been grilling ever since he can remember. When he was a pre-teen living in Florida, he and his brother would go camping, dig a hole, burn wood in the hole, then place a refrigerator grate over the opening and cook out. Years after he retired, Powell was

Though younger Orioles fans may only know Boog Powell for his barbecue stand at the stadium, the slugger was a four-time All-Star while playing for Baltimore from 1961 to 1974.

living in Florida, running a boat and marina business and wanted a change. He often had kicked around the idea of opening a barbecue joint. After having some drinks following a charity golf tournament in Baltimore one evening, a buddy of his who had handled concessions at Memorial Stadium said he would set up a meeting to see if he could make Powell's vision a reality. The idea was a hit.

With the help from a chef during the 1991–92 offseason, Powell picked the menu, developed the rubs, and devised the baked bean and cole slaw recipes. Early on, he was involved in most aspects of the business. Now he's more about quality control: making sure the food meets his standards, that his workers are smiling, and that his customers keep coming back. The stand has become so popular that there's a second one on Camden Yards' club level. And he has opened up a Boog's on the Ocean City, Maryland, boardwalk that is run by his son.

Boog Powell's main responsibility these days is just being Boog Powell, the former All-Star and legendary sandwich guy. "I get a lot of kids that come out there now that don't even know I played baseball. It's, 'Hey Daddy, let's go see the barbecue man,'" Powell said. "And the dads will tell their kids, 'You know, he played baseball, too.' And the kids will say, 'Okay, but let's go get a sandwich.'"

61 Elrod

He hit .220 in parts of 12 years—almost all with the Orioles—in the big leagues. He never had more than 365 plate appearances or 12 home runs in a season. Yet when former Orioles catcher and coach Elrod Hendricks died unexpectedly of a heart attack a day before his 65th birthday in 2005, Brooks Robinson, arguably the greatest Orioles player ever, said this: "We lost the most beloved Oriole of all time. He has touched more lives in this town than anyone else."

It's not an overstatement. No one worked more tirelessly to embrace fans than Hendricks, who spent a record 37 years, the final 28 as bullpen coach, in the franchise's uniform. No one cared more about being an Oriole. And no one—absolutely no one—signed more autographs. He was everywhere: playing Santa Claus at the team Christmas party for underprivileged youth, shaking hands at offseason banquets, and holding pregame court at "Ellie's Place," the spot behind the Orioles on-deck circle where he would chat with fans. "He was the best ambassador for baseball that the Orioles ever had," said former Orioles outfielder Ken Singleton. "Elrod was very personable, outgoing, always talking to fans, always signing autographs. Even in those years that the Orioles weren't playing well, he'd be the only one on the field, talking to fans. That's just the way he was. Most players aren't like that. But I always felt that if Elrod was a politician, he'd definitely win his elections."

A native of the Virgin Islands, Hendricks joined the Orioles before the 1968 season as a 27-year-old rookie who had been languishing in the minors. His winter league manager in Puerto Rico was new Orioles first-base coach Earl Weaver, who convinced the club to give Hendricks a shot. It wasn't easy early on; Hendricks was viewed as a "Weaver guy," while manager Hank Bauer was still in charge. Known as an excellent handler of pitchers who threw out 38 percent of would-be base stealers in his career, Hendricks made the 1968 team as the third catcher, the last player on the 25-man roster. His playing time increased dramatically once Weaver replaced Bauer at midseason. Hendricks cut into the starts of incumbent starting catcher Andy Etchebarren and by 1969 he was playing a little more than Etchebarren. There was no conflict. "Elrod and I got along great," Etchebarren said. "That was fine with me what Earl did as long as we were winning."

Hendricks' reputation as a team player was cemented June 26, 1978 in Toronto when the player/coach answered the bullpen phone and was asked how long it would take to get ready to pitch. "You're speaking to Elrod," Hendricks replied. A half-bemused Weaver knew, but his team was losing 24–6 in the fifth inning, and outfielder Larry Harlow was on the mound getting shelled. Hendricks agreed to pitch. He had a plan: throw as slow as you can to mess up their timing, throw inside, hope they pull the ball, and get out of the way if it is hit up the middle. Throwing in the 45-mph range, the 37-year-old survived, allowing one hit and one walk in two and one-third innings. When Weaver took him out after the seventh, the crusty old manager thanked Hendricks. "I'm thinking, *Yeah, but don't think about it again*," Hendricks told *The Baltimore Sun* years later. "I'd like to say it was fun, but it really wasn't."

Hendricks is best remembered nationally for his role in the sixth inning of Game 1 of the 1970 World Series, when he accidentally became tangled with home-plate umpire Ken Burkhart after fielding a chopper in front of the plate. Hendricks lunged at Cincinnati Reds runner Bernie Carbo, who was sliding home, and tagged Carbo with his glove, but the ball was in his hand. A tumbling Burkhart missed it and called out Carbo, who never touched home plate anyway. An inning earlier Hendricks had hit his lone World Series home run in an eventual Orioles win. Swinging a ridiculously heavy 38-ounce bat, Hendricks had some pop, homering a dozen times each in 1969 and 1970.

His most lasting contributions, though, were with his mind and mouth. Singleton called Hendricks "the old sage of the team," and Palmer said, "Ellie was like truth serum. You'd come out of the bullpen and you'd go, 'Okay, what do I have?' And if you didn't have anything, he'd tell you." Hendricks was just as frank with fans. If an over-eager one screamed for a souvenir ball, he'd flash his 1,000-watt, disarming smile and tell the fan to "calm the hell down." Eventually, he'd give away the ball—but on his terms. He could get away with saying things no one else could because he was Elrod, the bow-legged, shin-guard-wearing Orioles institution.

Months after he had suffered a mild stroke, his coaching tenure ended following the 2005 season. The Orioles decided to reassign him in October, but they never gave him a clear idea of his future role, something his family said was crushing. Hendricks died several weeks later after having a heart attack in a parking lot of a hotel/restaurant. His legacy of giving back, however, continues. The organization's annual community service award for minor leaguers is named after Hendricks. "He was a huge figure in the city of Baltimore and beyond," former Orioles catcher Chris Hoiles said. "He was just loved."

Cy Stone

If you have a friend who is a know-it-all baseball fan, here's a question than could stump him or her and maybe win you a beer or two. Ask which Orioles pitcher holds the franchise record for most wins in a season. Give a hint and say the guy became a broadcaster after his playing days. Add in that he won a Cy Young Award. Jim Palmer is the obvious answer. Or Mike Flanagan. Mike Cuellar? Maybe Rick Sutcliffe? Fine guesses, but all wrong.

The answer is right-hander Steve Stone, who had a solid big league career and one tremendously special season in 1980, when he went 25–7 with a 3.23 ERA and won the American League Cy Young Award with the Orioles. "If you would sit down at the beginning of any baseball season and write down everything you would want to have happen, the best way it possibly could happen, that's exactly what 1980 was like," Stone said. "It seemed like the ballclub would never let me lose, certainly not too often."

The Orioles signed Stone as a 31-year-old free agent before the 1979 season, and he came as advertised. He was 11–7 with a 3.77 ERA in 32 starts that year, pushing his career record to 78–79 over nine seasons. He had won 10 or more games four times in his career but never more than 15 in one season. He began 1980 in unspectacular fashion; after a loss to the Minnesota Twins on May 5, Stone was 2–3 with a 4.74 ERA in five starts. Then everything changed. The Orioles' offense, which had tallied two runs or fewer in each of Stone's three losses, scored four or more runs in 22 of his next 23 starts. Eight times in that span the Orioles scored eight runs or more.

Stone did his part, too, allowing four earned runs or more in just five of those 23 outings. And the wins piled up. He went 19–1 in that 23-game stretch, winning 14 straight decisions, losing one, and then winning five more. His 20th win occurred on August 19, the earliest mark for a 20-game winner in modern franchise history. The Orioles won 100 games in 1980, missing the playoffs because the New York Yankees won 103. Stone and lefty Scott McGregor (20 wins) were credited with 45 percent of the Orioles' victories in 1980. Only one other time since then has an Oriole pitcher won 20 games: Mike Boddicker in 1984.

"Everything just went perfectly that year. In fact, it was so good that my relievers only blew one save for me, and it was the last game of the season," Stone said, "That shows you what a remarkable year it really was because those kinds of things just don't happen. And they did."

With Earl Weaver managing the American League All-Star team, Stone got the call to start the 1980 Midsummer's Classic. In the lone All-Star Game appearance of his career, he faced nine batters in three innings and retired all of them. He struck out sluggers Dave Parker and Dave Kingman and pitcher Bob Welch, who, incidentally, is the only hurler in the two-plus decades since Stone to win at least 25 games in a season; Welch won 27 in 1990. "Not Randy Johnson, not Roger Clemens, not Greg Maddux or Tom Glavine. Not any of the great pitchers hit [25 wins]," Stone said. "So it tells you how rare it really is."

Former Orioles catcher Rick Dempsey said what he remembers most about Stone in 1980 is how he threw all of his pitches for strikes, especially his knee-buckling curve. "He had such great control of that curveball and he had fantastic control of the fastball, the change-up. He could move them in, he could move them out," Dempsey said. "He just went for it all in one year. And if he had to throw five curveballs all in a row, he did."

Stone said once in 1980 he threw 73 curveballs in one game and 75 in the next—just a mind-boggling number these days. The next year, Stone started on Opening Day and beat the Kansas City Royals, but his arm didn't feel right. He had chronic tendinitis inside his right elbow and he couldn't overcome it. Stone ended up 4–7 with a 4.60 ERA in just 15 games (12 starts) in 1981. "After that 1980 season was over, he threw his last curveball, and that was really it, career basically over," Dempsey said. "He was pretty much done. But he went on a run that he knew he was never, ever going to be able to duplicate again for the rest of his life."

Stone didn't emerge from the disabled list in 1982 and retired. "It was my 14th year of professional baseball. I had accomplished everything I had wanted to accomplish. I knew I wasn't a great pitcher, but I did borrow greatness for a short period of time. I wouldn't have had it any other way. I wouldn't have traded that year for another five or seven years of winning 12 games and being just one of the guys. It was nice to be *the* guy for just one year."

Big Ben

Ben McDonald knows that whenever his name is brought up in baseball circles it often includes a cautionary tale about how overuse—or really abuse—on the amateur level can negatively affect even the most talented pitchers. McDonald, the only No. 1 overall pick in Orioles history, shrugs off the criticism surrounding his surgically repaired right shoulder. "Abused isn't the right word. I think I was a product of my times," said McDonald, who pitched parts of nine seasons in the majors, including seven with the Orioles. "We didn't know then what we know now."

As a 16-year-old high school junior growing up in small-town Denham Springs, Louisiana, McDonald threw 221 pitches in a game once. When he was 17, he pitched all 14 innings of a state playoff. The heavy workload continued in college. From his sophomore to junior year at Louisiana State University, including the summer in between in which he starred for the 1988 U.S. Olympic gold medal-winning squad, McDonald estimates he threw 352 innings. "You look back on it. Yeah, it was probably too much," McDonald said. "And it probably led to an early breakdown. A lot of doctors said I was probably fortunate to pitch as long as I did before something finally did happen."

But he said he never turned down an opportunity to pitch. And, really, he doesn't regret that. "Five times I threw nine innings at LSU and then closed the next day," McDonald said. "Did it feel good? No, it hurt at times. But I was such a competitor that I wanted to do that. If the coach said, 'Can you do that?' I'd always say, 'I can,' and I'd go do it. I don't know if I would change that. I really don't."

McDonald was arguably the best college pitcher ever. He won the 1989 Golden Spikes Award for baseball's top amateur, was inducted into the College Baseball Hall of Fame in 2008, and the Louisiana State Hall of Fame in 2010. The 6'7" McDonald also played two years of basketball at LSU before switching full time to baseball for his junior year, a season in which he struck out 202 batters in 152⅓ innings, both SEC records. He also set a conference record with a streak of 44⅔ scoreless innings. It set him up to be the super-hyped No. 1 overall pick in the 1989 draft.

It seemed like tremendous good fortune for the Orioles, who otherwise have never selected first overall since the draft was instituted in 1965. But the club's historically dreadful 107-loss season put them first overall. Things didn't start well. The Orioles and McDonald's agent, Scott Boras, locked horns on what ultimately resulted in the first multi-year major league deal for a recently drafted amateur. It took until August for a contract to be signed, and after two minor league appearances, McDonald was promoted to the majors. He was the sixth—and last—No. 1 overall pick to play in the big leagues in the same season he was selected. He is the only one to ever do it in the middle of a pennant race. "Because everybody already had their roles, the rotation was set, and the bullpen roles were set too. So I only got six outings in September, and they were all in relief and I think it was more to get my feet wet than anything," McDonald said. "So I just kind of sat back and enjoyed it. And I didn't appreciate it at the time that that would be the closest I would get in my career to the playoffs."

The Orioles were eliminated by the Blue Jays on the second-to-last day of the season. The next game, in the year's finale, McDonald threw one scoreless inning in relief and picked up his first major league win. It was supposed to be one of hundreds for the can't-miss, flame-throwing right-hander. In truth, it was the first of 78 in his career—just 58 with the Orioles. It's unfair to call McDonald a draft bust. Three times in his Orioles career, he won

13 or more games in a season and twice he pitched more than 220 innings. He also had a rebound season with the Milwaukee Brewers in which he won 12 games and threw more than 220 innings. For his career he was 78–70 with a 3.91 ERA in 211 big league games,

McDonald's Rapid Ascent

Since Major League Baseball began its first-year player draft in 1965, only six players made the majors the same season in which they were selected as the No. 1 overall pick. Only one, right-hander Ben McDonald out of Louisiana State University, made his debut the year he was drafted in the middle of a pennant race.

To earn the right of selecting first overall, a club has to be the worst in the majors the previous year, and the Orioles were the embodiment of terrible in 1988, losing 21 straight to begin the season on their way to a club-record 107 losses.

Usually clubs that pick first stay awful for a while, but the Orioles turned around their fortunes in the incredible "Why Not?" year in 1989 when they won 87 games and finished two behind the Toronto Blue Jays for the American League East crown.

McDonald wasn't a force that year. He pitched in only six games, posted an 8.59 ERA in seven and one-third innings, and his only decision was a one-inning victory in the season finale after the Orioles had been eliminated from the pennant race.

Still, just a couple months removed from college, McDonald was in a playoff chase in the majors. No other top pick can boast that. The other five played for cellar dwellers during their respective debuts. Since McDonald debuted in 1989, no top overall pick has played for the big league team that selected him in that same calendar year.

Here are the six overall No. 1 picks who made it to the majors the year they were selected.

INF **Dave Roberts**, San Diego Padres, 1972
LHP **David Clyde**, Texas Rangers, 1973
INF **Bill Almon**, San Diego Padres, 1974
DH **Danny Goodwin**, California Angels, 1975
INF **Bob Horner**, Atlanta Braves, 1978
RHP **Ben McDonald**, Baltimore Orioles, 1989

a solid showing for mere mortals. But not what was mapped out for Big Ben. "There were a lot of expectations obviously, and I think if I could have stayed healthy I could have achieved a lot of those expectations," McDonald said. "It was tough."

Recurring shoulder problems ended his career at age 29 after three surgeries. Toward the end of his run, his frayed right rotator cuff was completely torn. "That's the sad thing about it. I was just 29 years old. I was just starting to really figure it out. That's when pitchers start to really figure it out. And that's when I was out of the game," McDonald said. "But I tell people all the time: don't feel sorry for me. I lived the dream. I did what I wanted to do and I did it for nine years and accomplished some really cool things."

Among his teammates McDonald was known as a hard-working and fun-loving country boy who never really left the Bayou. On two different occasions, McDonald caught alligators and brought them indoors to freak out fellow ballplayers. Once, during instructional league in Sarasota, Florida, he put an alligator in the bathtub, taped its mouth shut, and waited for unsuspecting teammates to take a shower. "I heard an awful, horrendous scream as you can imagine," McDonald said, chuckling. "They had no idea what an alligator was, so they were very scared of it. They ended up half naked in the parking lot."

He caught a three-foot alligator during one spring training and sneaked it into the Orioles' clubhouse in a duffel bag. "I kind of put the bag down by my side and unzipped the bag. It crawled out and started going through the clubhouse," McDonald said. "And I mean guys were on top of lockers, screaming and hollering. I got into a little trouble about that. I was warned by the animal rights people to not do that anymore."

64 Four Men and One No-Hitter

Bob Milacki still remembers the feeling in his right hand during the sixth inning on July 13, 1991. His four fingers were swelling up, the result of a Willie Wilson comebacker that struck Milacki's pitching hand and deflected off his leg before the ball rolled innocently to Randy Milligan at first for an out. No one came out to check on Milacki's health. The belief was that the ball just glanced off his leg—no big deal. But as he continued to pitch, he said the baseball felt like "a softball in my hand. I just didn't have a good control of the ball." With two outs in the inning, Milacki walked Dave Henderson on five pitches and then struck out the dangerous Jose Canseco on a 2–2 count.

As Milacki entered the visiting dugout at Oakland Coliseum, he knew he had to say something about his swollen hand. He was removed from the game. That would normally be an obvious decision—except Milacki hadn't yet allowed a hit in six innings. "It's not like I had impeccable command that day anyway. I think I was effectively wild," said Milacki, who had issued three walks. "I knew what was going on, but the no-hitter doesn't really come into play until you start getting into the eighth and ninth innings. I'm just trying to compete and win the game at that point." Milacki retreated to the athletic trainers' room to ice his hand and watch the remainder of the game on TV with the Orioles clinging to a 2–0 lead against the Oakland A's. "Then something magical happened over the next three innings," Milacki said.

What happened was something that had occurred just one other time in baseball history and only three times since: a combined no-hitter thrown by four or more pitchers. Veteran left-hander Mike Flanagan was the first reliever to come in. He issued a two-out walk but otherwise threw a scoreless seventh. Set-up man Mark Williamson followed, getting a foul pop and two ground-outs to complete the eighth. Then it was up to Gregg Olson, the Orioles closer, to preserve history. "That was the most nervous I had ever been in my life," said Olson, the 1989 American League Rookie of the Year and all-time Orioles saves leader.

Olson had pitched in big games previously, but he never had to close out a no-hitter. At that point only two other pitchers in baseball history had ever recorded no-hitter saves. Olson had been watching the scoreboard from about the seventh inning. By the ninth inning, he knew he'd be facing three of the more feared hitters in the AL: Henderson, Canseco, and Harold Baines. "It was kind of bizarre, but with the first hitter Henderson, I kind of had this out-of-body experience," Olson said. "I was going through it, but I wasn't fully involved. I wasn't making great pitches. And then Henderson hit a ground ball to Ripken's backhand, and Cal threw him out. And I stood on the mound as the ball was being thrown around the infield and I'm going, *You are two outs away from a no-hitter. Will you please wake the hell up?* After that, everything kicked in, and the pitches after that were as about as nasty as I could throw to Canseco and then Baines. It was as ugly as I could get."

He struck out Canseco and, with the no-hitter on the line, faced Baines, a pure hitter whom Olson fanned just once in their careers. It came at the perfect time. "I wasn't thinking about striking him out or doing anything ultra-special. It was just, *How do I get Harold Baines out?* It was one of the rare times in my life where I don't remember the sequence. I just remember the last pitch, a really good curveball at his back foot that I got a check swing with for strike three."

That's when things got really bizarre. Orioles catcher Chris Hoiles squeezed Olson's last pitch, the only no-hitter he would ever catch. Hoiles jumped out of his crouch, jogged to the mound, handed Olson the ball, and shook his hand. That was it. Everyone

Other O's No-Hitters
The Orioles have had five no-hitters in their first 60 years and have
been no-hit for at least nine innings six times. They've never been
involved in a perfect game, and only one no-hitter has been thrown
at Camden Yards: Hideo Nomo of the Boston Red Sox on April
4, 2001. Each of the Orioles' five no-hitters has held significance
beyond the obvious. Two were by future Hall of Famers, one was
by a local product, one was in a losing effort, and one was by the
aforementioned quartet.

September 20, 1958 versus the New York Yankees at Memorial Stadium
Knuckleballer Hoyt Wilhelm pitched the Orioles' first one against
a Yankees lineup that included Mickey Mantle and Elston Howard.
Wilhelm, who was 36 and wasn't a starting pitcher until that season,
walked two and struck out eight. His final out was a pop-up by
Yankees leadoff hitter Hank Bauer, who later managed the Orioles.
Baltimore won the game 1–0 on a seventh-inning homer by catcher
Gus Triandos, who joked that he just didn't want to prolong catching
Wilhelm's impossible knuckler that day.

April 30, 1967 versus the Detroit Tigers at Memorial Stadium
This was the second ever and first American League no-hitter to end
in a loss. Orioles left-hander Steve Barber didn't allow a hit, but he
walked 10 batters and hit two more in eight and two-third innings. He
took a 1–0 lead into the ninth but allowed three walks and permitted
the tying run to score on a wild pitch. Stu Miller entered and induced
a potential inning-ending force out, but Mark Belanger dropped the
feed and a run scored. Miller picked up the final out to preserve the
no-hitter, but they lost 2–1.

April 27, 1968 versus the Boston Red Sox at Memorial Stadium
Local boy Tom Phoebus energized the home crowd on a rainy
afternoon against Hall of Famer Carl Yastrzemski and the Red Sox.
The Baltimore native and Mount St. Joseph's alum had turned 26
earlier in the month. He was superb on the day, allowing three walks
and striking out nine. He had a scare in the eighth, but third baseman

Brooks Robinson dove and caught a sinking liner to keep the no-hitter intact. Robinson also had three RBIs in the 6–0 win.

August 13, 1969 versus the Oakland Athletics at Memorial Stadium
This was the only no-hitter for Jim Palmer, the greatest pitcher in franchise history. It wasn't his smoothest game; he struck out eight but walked six batters, including A's slugger Reggie Jackson three times. Palmer walked Jackson to start the ninth, then got two quick outs, including one that initially appeared to be a double-play ball. He walked two more to load the bases before former teammate Larry Haney grounded into a force to end the game. It was Palmer's second outing after missing nearly six weeks due to injury. Brooks Robinson homered, and the Orioles won 8–0.

else shook hands as if it were just a normal Saturday victory on the road and not the fifth no-hitter ever thrown by an Oriole (or Orioles). The club hasn't had a no-hitter in the 23 years following that strange gem. "Nobody knew what to do. It was a no-hitter, but it wasn't my no-hitter. It wasn't Milacki's no-hitter. It was kind of a team no-hitter," Olson said. "So Hoiles came out, and I don't know if mine and his reactions tempered everyone else's. It was like, *Hey, that's cool.* I'm sure it was a lot funnier to watch, but I can't explain it."

There was no fanfare around Milacki in the locker room either. There was one thing, however, that made the day a little more special. Oakland's clubhouse manager presented each of the four pitchers and Hoiles with a bottle of champagne. They all signed the bottles. "Being able to have all five guys, including myself, sign the bottle and have it as a memento of what we did, that was pretty cool," Hoiles said. "I still have that in my office to this day." Olson still has the game ball. He said he offered it to Milacki, but Milacki told him to keep it. Milacki's champagne bottle is in his trophy case at his home. "It's the main object in there," Milacki said. "It's the centerpiece."

Who knows what would have happened if Milacki hadn't been forced to leave the game after the sixth? It's possible he could have had the glory to himself and been at the bottom of a dog pile on the mound. Instead he was the starter in one of baseball's 11 combined no-hitters. And he's perfectly fine with that. "The way I look at it is that it doesn't happen very often in the major leagues, so it turned out to be an even better thing for me," Milacki said. "Essentially your name is in the Orioles' record book. So that's kind of special. It is always neat to show the kids. *Look, your dad is here. No, he wasn't one of the super, superstars, but his name is here.* But I also showed them all the little plaques on [Eutaw] Street behind right field where I gave up home runs. So I guess it all equals out."

65: 2014: We Won't Stop

Baseball teams don't usually mesh in February. Players are just getting to know each other, and managers are figuring out what they have. After two consecutive winning seasons, the 2014 Orioles expected to be good heading into spring training. Those prospects improved in late February when the club added outfielder Nelson Cruz to a one-year, $8 million deal. Cruz had compiled five straight seasons of 22 or more homers but had enough baggage to make a multi-year contract unattainable. He had turned down a qualifying offer from the Texas Rangers, meaning the Orioles relinquished a draft pick to sign Cruz. Also he had been suspended 50 games in 2013 for his involvement in the Biogenesis performance-enhancing drug scandal. When the club announced the signing, eight Orioles attended Cruz's news conference to show support, including outfielder Nick Markakis and first baseman Chris Davis,

The 2014 American League Manager of the Year, Buck Showalter, guides his team during Game 2 of the ALDS. Under Showalter's watch the Orioles reached the ALCS.

who previously had been critical of PED users. "That means they care about their teammates," Cruz said of the turnout. "I know the closer you are to your teammates, the better you're going to perform on the field. We are now a family and we're going to stick together the whole time."

That moment set the tone for the Orioles, who posted their best season in 17 years despite continual adversity. They won 96 games, ran away with the American League East title, and swept the

Detroit Tigers in the American League Division Series. For the first time since 1997, the Orioles hosted league championship games at a frenzied, ear-splitting, orange-towel-waving Camden Yards. The Orioles' "We Won't Stop" season stopped abruptly, however, in the American League Championship Series with a four-game sweep by the Kansas City Royals. It was a jolting and disappointing finish to a year of remarkable resiliency.

In May they lost All-Star catcher Matt Wieters to an elbow injury that eventually required surgery. Budding star Manny Machado didn't make his season debut until May 1 after recovering from left knee surgery and was shut down August 11 with a right knee injury. In between, the young third baseman was suspended five games in June for intentionally tossing his bat onto the field in a game against the Oakland A's. Right-hander Ubaldo Jimenez, who signed a four-year, $50 million deal in February, was yanked from the rotation in August. Reliever Tommy Hunter started the season as closer but lost the role in May. In September, Davis, who was hitting a paltry .196, was suspended for 25 games for testing positive for amphetamines. He later said in a statement that he took the ADD drug Adderall without an exemption. It was an ironic twist given his outspokenness about PEDs (though amphetamines are not considered performance-enhancers). In response to Davis' suspension, Cruz was particularly supportive. "We have his back with whatever has gone on," Cruz said.

On the field Cruz shouldered the Orioles at times. He hit a career-best and major-league-leading 40 home runs and was named Most Valuable Oriole. Others exceeded expectations, too. Rookie catcher Caleb Joseph and veteran Nick Hundley, who was acquired in a May trade, handled catching duties. Steve Pearce, whom the Orioles released in April and re-signed days later, took over the first-base job from Davis and smacked a career-best 21 home runs. Zach Britton, a starter most of his career, became the closer in May and excelled. Lefty reliever Andrew Miller was outstanding after coming over in a July 31 deal from the Boston Red Sox. And journeyman Delmon Young batted .302 in 83 games, was 10-for-20 in the regular season as a pinch-hitter, and delivered the highlight of the year in Game 2 of the ALDS. His bases-loaded, pinch-hit double in the eighth inning against the Tigers gave the Orioles a 7–6 victory "Every player on this team has been through some shit at some point this season," Hunter said. "To come together like all these guys have, everybody has stepped up when they needed to step up, guys coming over via trades, guys coming up from the minor leagues, everybody contributed throughout the year."

Manager Buck Showalter, whose steady guidance and deft use of his bullpen produced consistent results, was recognized with his third Baseball Writers' Association of America (BBWAA) Manager of the Year Award, becoming the sixth to win it at least three times and the second to win it for three different franchises. He also won it with the 1994 New York Yankees and the 2004 Texas Rangers. Executive vice president Dan Duquette, who made a bevy of under-the-radar moves that paid dividends, was named *The Sporting News* Executive of the Year. It was the second time he has won the award, receiving it in 1992 with the Montreal Expos. The Orioles also won three Gold Gloves in 2014, the third consecutive season they had done that. "It's been an unbelievable year," center fielder Adam Jones said after the ALCS loss. "To get this far with this group of men has been an honor. Everyone in here has meant the world to myself and to each other and to each other's families."

66 The 10 Most Notable Trades

With the exception of the successful teams in the mid-1990s that featured an infusion of key free-agent signings, the Orioles' blueprint for success over the years has been building from within and supplementing that core with trades.

For the most part, the Orioles have been fairly strong at recognizing when to deal a player at a high value and when to swoop in for an undervalued asset. Arguably the greatest swindle in baseball history—or certainly one of them—occurred in December 1965 when the Orioles dealt pitcher Milt Pappas and two others to the Cincinnati Reds for Frank Robinson, who helped lead the Orioles to four World Series in the following six seasons.

That franchise-changing move was mentioned by Annie Savoy as she explained her "tutoring" of minor leaguers during her "Church of Baseball" soliloquy in the movie, *Bull Durham*. "Sometimes it seems like a bad trade, but bad trades are part of baseball. Now who can forget Frank Robinson for Milt Pappas, for God's sake?" Susan Sarandon's character stated. "It's a long season, and you gotta trust it."

Here's my take on the 10 most notable deals (good and bad) in Orioles history:

1. Frank Robinson from the Cincinnati Reds for pitchers Milt Pappas and Jack Baldschun and outfielder Dick Simpson
December 9, 1965
The Reds needed a top-of-the-rotation starter, and Pappas had won 110 games by age 26. Robinson, a former National League Rookie of the Year and MVP, was perceived by Reds president Bill

DeWitt Sr. as "not a young 30." Well, Robinson won the American League MVP with a Triple Crown season in 1966 on his way to finishing off a Hall of Fame career. Pappas was solid with the Reds, 30–29 with a 4.04 ERA, before being dealt to the Atlanta Braves in 1968. The other two each played parts of two pedestrian seasons for Cincinnati.

2. Glenn Davis from the Houston Astros for outfielder Steve Finley and pitchers Curt Schilling and Pete Harnisch
January 10, 1991

The perception was that the missing ingredient for the Orioles after their "Why Not?" season in 1989 and their sub-.500 campaign in 1990 was a legitimate power hitter. Davis, 29, had hit 20 or more homers in his past six seasons despite playing his home games in the roomy Astrodome. Orioles executive Roland Hemond knew he was giving up a lot, but he thought it'd be worth it. Injuries, bad luck, and extensive slumps limited Davis to just 24 homers and 185 games in three seasons, drawing the ire of booing Orioles fans. Making matters worse, the trio the Orioles dealt away became All-Stars. Finley won five Gold Gloves, and Schilling emerged as a potential Hall of Famer.

3. Catcher Rick Dempsey and pitchers Scott McGregor, Tippy Martinez, Rudy May, and Dave Pagan from the New York Yankees for pitchers Doyle Alexander, Ken Holtzman, Grant Jackson, and Jimmy Freeman and catcher Elrod Hendricks
June 15, 1976

If the Robinson trade is credited for taking the franchise to the top, this one needs to be recognized for putting it back there. Dempsey won the 1983 World Series MVP Award, McGregor clinched the deciding Game 5, and Martinez was the bullpen glue for years. There's been a longstanding rumor that the trade could have been better, but the Orioles chose Pagan over eventual Cy Young Award winner Ron Guidry because they already had three lefties in the deal. Former executive Hank Peters said it was never that simple. Guidry's name was discussed in trade talks, but it wasn't an either/or situation with Pagan, according to Peters.

4. Pitcher Mike Cuellar from the Astros for outfielder Curt Blefary and shortstop Enzo Hernandez
December 4, 1968

In retrospect, this one may have been the most significant in terms of unexpected lopsidedness. Blefary was Rookie of the Year in 1965 and was whom the Reds most coveted when they were discussing the Robinson deal. The Orioles held onto the outfielder in 1965 and then dealt him to the Astros for a 31-year-old journeyman who became one of the best starters in Orioles history. Cuellar won a share of the 1969 Cy Young Award and compiled six straight seasons with 18 or more victories and an ERA 3.50 or lower. Blefary played one year for the Astros before being traded to the Yankees, never recapturing his old form.

5. Outfielder Adam Jones and pitchers Chris Tillman, George Sherrill, Kam Mickolio, and Tony Butler from the Seattle Mariners for pitcher Erik Bedard
February 8, 2008

Former president of baseball operations Andy MacPhail was known as a patient man and he just waited this one out until he got what he wanted. That included Jones, who became the cornerstone of the Orioles teams in the 2010s, and Tillman, who eventually emerged as the staff's best pitcher. Sherrill was an All-Star closer for the Orioles before he was dealt away. The oft-injured Bedard was 28–16 in 61 starts for the Orioles in 2006–07; he was 15–14 in 46 starts from 2008–11 for the Mariners.

6. Outfielder Reggie Jackson and pitchers Ken Holtzman and Bill VanBommell from the Oakland A's for outfielder Don Baylor and pitchers Mike Torrez and Paul Mitchell

April 2, 1976

The Orioles made this deal knowing Jackson was a pending free agent and the homegrown Baylor was a potential future MVP. But

Pappas' Side of the Trade

The December 1965 trade with the Cincinnati Reds that brought Frank Robinson to the Orioles for Milt Pappas, Jack Baldschun, and Dick Simpson will go down as the most important move the Orioles have ever made, lifting the club from very good to a champion. And it re-energized Robinson's career, thrusting him toward Cooperstown. Orioles fans know the Frank Robinson end of it. But what about the trade from Pappas' side?

A former bonus baby out of a Detroit high school, Pappas was 26 at the time of the trade. The right-hander was 110–74 with a 3.24 ERA in nine seasons. He made two All-Star teams, including 1965, when he was 13–9 with a 2.60 ERA. Pappas knew the Orioles had some good young pitchers coming and he thought they might trade a starter. But he didn't think it would be him.

Pappas said that on the trip home from Cleveland to end the 1965 season, lefty Steve Barber loudly demanded a trade to manager Hank Bauer and anyone else who would listen. "The thought of me getting traded never entered my mind after that blowup by Steve Barber," Pappas said.

In December, Pappas was in Florida as part of the player representative meetings when his wife called him. She said there was a story in the newspaper that he may get traded to San Francisco. He said he was worried, but later that day, he saw an Orioles contingent, including Bauer, coming into the hotel. He stopped them and asked if he was going to be traded. He was told, "You are our No. 1 pitcher. You are not going anywhere." Pappas was relieved. The relief didn't last long: "Two days later, I got traded." When he talks about the deal years later, he jokes about the present he gave Robinson: "That was nice of me to give him a World Series, huh?"

they thought they had a chance to sign Jackson to a long-term deal. They didn't. (He ended up going to the Yankees and cementing his reputation as Mr. October.) Jackson held out for more money after the trade to Baltimore, missing the club's first 16 games. (The Orioles went 6–10.) He didn't heat up until the second half. The case can be made that he cost them the pennant, but his overall numbers were good: 27 doubles, 27 homers, 28 steals, and a .853 on-base plus slugging percentage (OPS). Baylor won the AL MVP in 1979 with the California Angels. Torrez won 16 or more games in four different seasons after the deal.

7. Outfielder Ken Singleton and pitcher Mike Torrez from the Montreal Expos for pitcher Dave McNally and outfielder Rich Coggins
December 4, 1974

McNally was a stalwart in the O's rotation for years, but his career was ending when this deal was made. Singleton, however, was entering his prime and became a steady force in the middle of the Orioles lineup for a decade. Torrez won 20 games for the Orioles in 1975 but was dealt away in the ill-fated Jackson trade with Oakland. The Expos were deliberating between Coggins, who stopped playing after 1976, and Al Bumbry, who became a quality center fielder and leadoff hitter. So the Orioles won this trade on several levels.

8. First baseman Chris Davis and pitcher Tommy Hunter from the Texas Rangers for pitcher Koji Uehara
July 30, 2011

When we were first tipped this trade was going down, I asked my source to make sure he had it right. Hunter *and* Davis for Koji? Uehara was a quality reliever and helped the Boston Red Sox to the 2013 World Series. But he seemed like a bad fit in the Texas heat, and both Davis and Hunter had major upside. Hunter became a solid reliever for the Orioles, but Davis was the one who exploded, setting a franchise record for homers with 53 in 2013.

9. Catchers Gus Triandos and Hal Smith; infielders Willy Miranda, Kal Segrist, and Don Leppert; outfielder Gene Woodling; and pitchers Jim McDonald, Harry Byrd, and Bill Miller from the Yankees for pitchers Bob Turley, Don Larsen, Mike Blyzka; infielders Billy Hunter and Dick Kryhoski; catcher Darrell Johnson; and outfielders Jim Fridley and Ted Del Guerico

November 17–December 1, 1954

This one is noteworthy for its sheer volume: the 17-player deal is still the largest in major league history. It was so big it happened in waves. The Orioles got Triandos out of the deal, and he became the club's first star, making three All-Star Games. But the Yankees made out better on this one; Turley won the 1958 Cy Young Award, and Larsen pitched the only perfect game in World Series history in 1956.

10. Shortstop J.J. Hardy and infielder Brendan Harris from the Minnesota Twins for pitchers Jim Hoey and Brett Jacobson

December 9, 2010

There are other trades I considered for this spot—giving up Davey Johnson and Pat Dobson, among others, to the Braves for catcher Earl Williams in November 1972 didn't pan out—but getting Hardy for two minor league pitchers who weren't in the Orioles' plans and then signing him to an extension was one of MacPhail's best moves. Hardy won a Gold Glove and a Silver Slugger in 2013, an impressive combination. Hoey pitched in 11 games in relief for the Twins, and Jacobson never made the majors.

67 The End of the Streak

It's probably the greatest three-word quote in Orioles history. Certainly, given the context, it's the most humorous. Depending on whom you ask, it was uttered by a rookie with a "deer-in-the-headlights" look. Or it was said in jest, an attempt to make light of an intimidating situation. Regardless, on the night of September 20, 1998, minutes before the Orioles were to play the New York Yankees in the home finale of the season, Orioles manager Ray Miller grabbed promising infielder Ryan Minor in the Camden Yards hallway and told the rookie that he'd be starting at third base that night.

In other words, Minor, who had made his major league debut a week earlier, would be replacing Cal Ripken Jr., who wouldn't be starting an Orioles game for the first time in more than 16 years. Minor asked one three-word question to Miller about Ripken sitting: "Does he know?"

Ripken, of course, knew, and Minor said later he was joking, just trying to ease an awkward moment.

When the official lineup card was presented to the umpires and Yankees manager Joe Torre, it had a large black smudge at the sixth spot between designated hitter Calvin Pickering and left fielder B.J. Surhoff. Initially, it read Ripken, but that was redacted, and Minor's name was written to the right of the smudge. Ripken had been considering ending the streak on the final day of the 1998 season in Boston's Fenway Park. He wanted to do it on his own terms when he was still healthy enough to play every day and figured he wouldn't have to go through another offseason hearing about the merits of keeping the streak alive. But then he and his wife, Kelly, decided that they wanted the streak to finish in Baltimore, where it began 16 years prior. "If this is gonna end, let it end in front of the best fans in baseball," Ripken said at his postgame news conference. "This isn't a sad thing. I wanted it to be a festive, happy thing."

Once the opposing Yankees realized Ripken was sitting on purpose, the visitors in pinstripes stepped onto the top dugout step and began to applaud in the first inning. Ripken's teammates also began clapping, and the announced crowd of 48,013 figured it out, too, and rose, cheering. After Chuck Knoblauch made the first out, Ripken exited the home dugout, tipped his cap several times, and returned to the bench. The fans continued to cheer, and he came out again, took a bow, and then motioned to Orioles starter Doug Johns to pitch. There would be no 22-minute delay this time.

Minor, who was once the organization's top prospect and an All-American basketball player at the University of Oklahoma, played in just 142 major league games (87 for the Orioles) over parts of four seasons in his big league career. But he'll always be remembered in Orioles history for one moment and one game. "I actually kind of felt like I was on a pedestal with Cal that night. It was kind of fun being in the press conference with him," Minor told *The Baltimore Sun*. "That was kind of neat. I will always remember that."

After his playing career, Minor became a minor league manager in the Orioles organization. He's not the only future skipper to replace Ripken and end an impressive streak. Ripken also holds the longest consecutive innings played streak—or is at least believed to since it wasn't a record officially kept years ago—of 8,243 from June 4, 1982 until the eighth inning of an 18–3 loss to the Toronto Blue Jays at Exhibition Stadium on September 14, 1987. That streak spanned 903 games. (The Society for American Baseball Research has calculated Ripken's innings streak at slightly higher, 8,264, which it states eclipsed George Pinkney, who played 5,152 straight innings in 1885 to 1890 for the Brooklyn

Ripken's Unintended Foul Shot

Like many stadiums Oriole Park at Camden Yards offers pregame tours. They always stop in the press box, and while the fans snap pictures, the guides spin yarns. They discuss late public address announcer Rex Barney and point out where the official scorer sits. They'll often tell a story about Ken Rosenthal, a former sports columnist for *The Baltimore Sun* and longtime baseball insider for Fox Sports and MLB Network. The way the story is spun, Rosenthal was writing a column or had just written a column that Cal Ripken Jr. needed to end his consecutive games streak because it was hurting the team. Then Ripken hit a foul ball into the press box and destroyed Rosenthal's laptop. Depending on the creativity of the tour guide, the tale may include details like it happened on the day Ripken broke the streak or that Ripken looked back and smiled or pointed—sort of a called shot in reverse.

It's become legend. And, frankly, it's only partially true. "I want to set the record straight," Rosenthal mock screamed when asked about what happened. Here's the real story: on June 17, 1998, *The Sun* printed a column by Rosenthal with the headline, "Ripken-less game is calling, but O's can't bear to listen." Ripken, 37, had broken Lou Gehrig's consecutive games streak nearly three seasons earlier. He was in a 10-for-54 slump. He had walked twice in the month of June. Rosenthal never said Ripken must sit but suggested it should be considered. He referred to "the Streak" as "a runaway train."

Fast forward nearly a month and two homestands later to July 13, 1998. Rosenthal was writing about how the Orioles' recent hot streak in a woeful season shouldn't make them think they were buyers at the trade deadline. In the sixth inning with Toronto's Juan Guzman pitching, Ripken fouled a missile straight back into the press box. It hit Rosenthal's computer, sending the laptop flying to the wall behind his seat. It was destroyed; his column was lost. As good as Ripken was, he couldn't aim a foul ball behind him. No one can. The Iron Man also didn't look back. He was all business at the plate like usual. Afterward, Ripken was informed of the incident and apparently smiled and said, "Nice." So, yes, Ripken killed Rosenthal's computer. No, it wasn't out of spite. It was purely coincidental and a hazard of the job.

> Rosenthal, meanwhile, borrowed a laptop from *Sun* colleague Roch Kubatko, who had already filed his story. And Rosenthal re-wrote his column on the Orioles' trade-deadline path. The most important detail, Rosenthal says, is that he still made his deadline. He also had a little fun with the misadventure, amending his column to add these lines: "The Orioles are so hot, Cal Ripken hit a foul ball last night that disabled his favorite columnist's computer permanently. We had just typed 'sit' and were about to add 'down' when Ripken's heat-seeking missile headed straight into the press box, causing yours truly to dive for cover."

Grays and Brooklyn Bridegrooms of the American Association and National League.)

Ripken batted in the top half of the eighth in the 1987 blowout versus Toronto, but then his father and manager, Cal Ripken Sr., decided to end that streak so his son wouldn't have to answer the consecutive innings questions anymore. Plus, the Orioles were down 14 runs at the time, and as Ripken Sr. put it, he wasn't expecting his son to hit a "20-run homer." So Ripken came out and infielder Ron Washington, who later led the Texas Rangers to two World Series as a manager, replaced Ripken.

On several occasions Ripken's consecutive games streak was threatened by potential injuries, whether it was a sprained ankle in 1985, back spasms in 1997, a broken nose during an All-Star photo shoot in 1996, or the closest call of all.

On June 6, 1993, Seattle Mariners catcher Bill Haselman charged Orioles pitcher Mike Mussina in the seventh inning of a 5–2 Orioles win. The benches cleared, and Ripken, running toward the pile of players, slipped and twisted his right knee. He woke up the next morning with a knee so sore and stiff that he talked with his wife about ending the streak at 1,790 games, which would have left him 340 games behind Gehrig. Instead, Ripken went to the ballpark, tested it in batting practice, and then had a single and two walks in four plate appearances. The rest, of course, ended up as history.

But Ripken still maintains that if the streak had ended in 1993 because of the brawl, he would have accepted it. "I know people don't believe me, but I never thought of it in the terms of how to end the streak or if the streak would have ended. If it would have ended for whatever reason, that's the way it is supposed to be. You don't stop playing. You don't stop living. You don't stop running up the Metrodome steps. You just do what you do. You don't play easy. You just play," Ripken said. "When the brawl came on, my only feeling was I couldn't let the Seattle Mariners' bench jump on Mussina. And I thought for a minute that I could stop them."

Davey Johnson

Orioles left-hander Dave McNally was having trouble spotting his pitches in a game when second baseman Davey Johnson tried to help. Johnson approached McNally and asked if he had ever heard of the unfavorable chance deviation theory. A perplexed McNally said no, and Johnson explained that McNally was trying to throw his pitches on the outside corner, and they were running farther outside or over the middle of the plate, causing the unfavorable chance. "So what you need to do is when you are in that kind of situation, aim for the middle of the plate, and it will go outside," Johnson told McNally, the perennial 20-game winner. "And then once you get into a favorable chance situation, then you can start throwing outside again." Orioles Hall of Famer Jim Palmer remembers what happened when that conversation occurred. "McNally said to Davey, 'Go back and play second base,'" Palmer recalled. "When Mac came in [to the dugout], I said, 'What was Dumb-Dumb saying?'" When McNally responded with the theory Johnson espoused, Palmer retorted: "Oh, I know he's gonna manage someday."

Palmer was right. Johnson, who certainly belied his Dumb-Dumb nickname, managed 17 seasons in the majors following a 13-season, big league playing career in which he won three Gold Gloves and made four All-Star teams. Johnson played eight seasons for the Orioles from 1965 to 1972, finishing third in the American League Rookie of the Year voting as a 23-year-old in 1966. He had his best offensive season with the Orioles in 1971, when he batted .282 with 18 home runs. He also developed into a premier defender thanks to two Hall of Famers. He watched third baseman Brooks Robinson take 100 ground balls every day and he threw 15 minutes a day with shortstop Luis Aparicio to build arm strength. "You learn from the veterans. You learn how to play," Johnson said. "I won three Gold Gloves because of Brooks and Aparacio."

Since manager Earl Weaver coveted catcher Earl Williams, and infielder Bobby Grich was ready to start, Johnson was traded after the 1972 season to the Atlanta Braves. After dealing with a shoulder injury for more than a year, Johnson said he was healthy again in 1973, hitting a career-best 43 homers. He eventually played two seasons in Japan, finished up with the Chicago Cubs in 1978, and began managing the next year in the minors.

In 1984, at age 41, Johnson landed his first big league managerial job with the New York Mets, a club he led to 108 regular-season wins and a World Series title in 1986. As a manager Johnson won 1,372 cumulative games for five organizations, compiled an impressive .562 winning percentage, garnered Manager of the Year awards in both leagues and finished second in the voting four times. At age 70 Johnson ended his managerial career in 2013, retiring from the Washington Nationals. Not a bad resume for a guy called "Dumb-Dumb." "I used to always say the reason they call me 'Dumb-Dumb' is because I hesitate to articulate for fear that I might deviate from the true course of rectitude. In short, I don't know," Johnson said, using an old vaudeville line. "Back then, any time anybody had a brain in their head, they were called 'Dumb-Dumb.' That's just the way we treated each other."

Johnson definitely had a brain in his head—and a different way of looking at baseball. He initially went to college at Texas A&M but left to sign with the Orioles, his absolute first choice. Although he initially wanted to be an oceanographer or veterinarian, Johnson completed his bachelor's degree in mathematics from Trinity University in San Antonio while playing pro ball. While in Baltimore he discovered the book *Percentage Baseball* by Earnshaw Cook, a Johns Hopkins mechanical engineering professor. It was the first nationally recognized study of baseball statistics, and Johnson loved it. He and Cook had a two-hour lunch, and Johnson began formulating his own theories that he'd eventually use as a manager, such as the importance of on-base percentage. Johnson took a computer course at Johns Hopkins and created a program that would simulate 100 games in a few seconds, allowing him to determine the Orioles' optimal lineup. It had him batting second to take advantage of his on-base capabilities. Johnson presented the printout to Weaver. "He looked at it and he threw it in the garbage can," Johnson said, laughing.

Roughly three decades later, Johnson had his chance to manage the Orioles. In 1996 he led them to a wild-card berth and their first playoff appearance in 13 years. The next year they were in first place the entire season, won 98 games, and made it to the American League Championship Series before losing to the Cleveland Indians. Johnson won his first Manager of the Year Award, but there was no celebration. He submitted his resignation that same November day due to a dispute with team owner Peter Angelos.

Part of the tension between the two was a July incident in which Johnson directed second baseman Roberto Alomar to pay a $10,500 fine to a charity for which Johnson's wife, Susan, raised funds. Alomar submitted the money to another charity, and Angelos backed the player, believing Johnson had created a conflict of interest. Johnson felt he and his wife's integrity were attacked. Angelos has always contended that Johnson attempted to leverage his manager's award into an extension, overplaying his hand. "I didn't push for an extension. I just didn't like him berating my wife," Johnson said. "It got to the point where I guess he didn't respect me and I didn't respect him. That's the bottom line." Regardless of the reasons, the working relationship between two proud men was severed, Johnson walked away from a $750,000 salary for 1998, and the Orioles began a spiral of 14 losing seasons. In Johnson's two years managing the Orioles, he posted a .574 winning percentage, the second highest in franchise history—behind only Weaver—for anyone who managed at least one full season.

69 "Wild Bill" Hagy and the Roar from Section 34

William "Wild Bill" Hagy would stand in the upper deck, far above shallow right field at Memorial Stadium, waving his cowboy hat with the Orioles logo until the fans in section 34—his people—were frenzied. Then the bearded cabdriver from Dundalk, Maryland, with the tank top stretched over his beer belly and tucked into a pair of cutoff jeans would begin contorting his body into letters: O-R-I-O-L-E-S. Eventually, he progressed to doing his spelling on the top of the Orioles' dugout. By the end of 1979, he had become a nationally recognizable figure embodying the Everyfan. "He was the perfect peer-group leader. He's the kind of guy you wanted to hang out with," said Marty Bass, a longtime Baltimore TV personality who spent many nights with Hagy in Section 34. "You know in college there's always a guy in the dorm that everybody kind of rallied around? That was Bill. It was just a different dorm."

Hagy loved the Orioles so much that he once refused to take a fare because the college students who entered his cab were wearing New York Yankees hats. When they wouldn't take off their Yankees caps, he made the kids get out. He was a die-hard fan who hoped to energize the stadium in the same way that Leonard "Big Wheel" Burrier did at Baltimore Colts games. Hagy asked Burrier if it would be okay to replicate his body-spelling cheer for the Orioles, and Big Wheel gave his blessing. By mid-1978 the movement was gaining steam. Hagy selected an area of the upper deck for two practical reasons. The seats were among the cheapest in the park, and just down the ramp was the men's restroom, an imperative for nine innings of beer guzzling.

By the 1979 Oriole Magic season, Hagy had become an adjunct of the team. The Orioles invited him to go to the American League Championship Series in California and to Pittsburgh for the World Series. His profile increased. One night, Hagy was standing near the stadium's Hit and Run Club restaurant signing autographs when a player shuffled up in stocking feet. "'Wild Bill,' can we talk?" the guy said. Hagy looked up and responded, "Take a hike, Reggie." And future Hall of Famer Reggie Jackson walked away. The mercurial right fielder played with the Orioles in 1976 but left as a free agent the next season for the Yankees. When he would return to Baltimore, he'd be verbally harassed by Hagy's rowdies. So Jackson likely wanted to make a plea that night to temper the "Roar from 34." Hagy wasn't interested. "Reggie went scurrying away," said Wayne Kaiser, a Section 34 regular who eventually roomed with Hagy for a decade. "I couldn't believe it."

It wasn't the only example of a superstar player seeking out Hagy. Bass had set up an on-field interview with his buddy before

"Wild Bill" Hagy spells out the "O" in Orioles to energize the Memorial Stadium crowd during Game 2 of the 1979 World Series. (AP Images)

a 1979 World Series game. Pittsburgh Pirates legend Willie Stargell ran out to them before the segment started and offered Hagy a "Stargell Star," one of the now famous embroidered yellow stars that the team captain handed out to his teammates when they did something well. Bass said Hagy was confused, saying he thought it was a Pirates-only thing. "Stargell explained it was about baseball—nothing more and nothing less," Bass said. "Stargell said, 'You deserve that as much as anybody. It's a pleasure to meet you' and Stargell shook his hand and ran back to the dugout." Hagy put the Stargell Star on his cowboy hat.

The emergence of "Wild Bill" and Section 34 seemed serendipitous. The Orioles were an up-and-coming team in the late 1970s, a few years removed from the dynasty led by Brooks and Frank Robinson. In 1979 a hip rock-and-roll station, WFBR, secured the Orioles radio rights away from buttoned-down WBAL. With morning show personality Johnny Walker, a shock jock pioneer, leading the way, the Orioles became cool again. Section 34, with its beer drinking, friendly carousing, and rhyming chants—"Hey Dauer, Show Us Your Power," "Come on Ken, Hit it in the Pen"—emerged as the cool place to be. "It became more about the camaraderie, the fun of going to the game and not just sitting there watching every pitch and falling asleep after about five innings because baseball is a slow game," Bass said. "What made it work was the camaraderie and fun, which became as much a part of the event as the game."

All good things eventually end. Hagy grew weary of the constant interruption during games to greet the stream of people coming up to Section 34. Then, in 1985 the Orioles banned fans from bringing their own beer into the stadium. The night before the new rules took effect, Hagy decided to have a little public protest. After the game ended and the crowd was leaving, he threw his five-gallon cooler onto the field, was arrested, and fined. Urban legend is that he swore off baseball and didn't return for a decade. Kaiser said that's not true.

Hagy still went to games but not as frequently and not as a public cheerleader. He emerged every now and then over the years, including September 6, 1995 at Camden Yards, the night Cal Ripken Jr. broke baseball's consecutive games streak. Hagy performed his "O-R-I-O-L-E-S" cheer to the delight of the sold-out crowd. The last time he did the cheer was July 29, 2007 in Cooperstown, New York, when Ripken was inducted into the Hall of Fame. Three weeks later Hagy died at his Arbutus home at age 68. The Orioles have kept his memory alive. An annual fan award is named after Hagy, there was a "Hagy 34" T-shirt giveaway in

2008, and Hagy cowboy hats were handed out at a game in 2014 that drew over 40,000 fans. "The Orioles meant everything to him," Kaiser said. "That's not an overstatement."

70 Road Trip to Cooperstown

This isn't just a "To Do" directive for Orioles fans. Really, if you love the sport and haven't been to the National Baseball Hall of Fame and Museum in Cooperstown, New York, you have to fix that. And fix it soon. It's a fairly easy and picturesque drive from Baltimore to the baseball-centric village along the Susquehanna River in upstate New York; it takes roughly five hours. I've been three times. The first was in 1992, when I wasn't yet a sportswriter and my then-girlfriend took me for a weekend getaway, thinking that it would be a destination that would earn her some brownie points. In case you were wondering, yes, I absolutely married that amazing and perceptive woman.

The other two times I went to the Hall were to cover the induction ceremonies of Eddie Murray (2003) and Cal Ripken Jr. (2007). I'd go every year if it were possible. Attending an induction ceremony in Cooperstown should be at the top of every baseball fan's bucket list. But just strolling through the museum at any time of year is a thrill. Orioles fans should be particularly enthralled since their club is so exceptionally well represented.

Where else can you see baseball equipment that was worn by Orioles greats such as Brooks Robinson, Cal Ripken Jr., and Felix Pie? Yes, Pie's in the Hall of Fame—or at least his shoes are. The cleats that Pie wore on August 14, 2009 are among the items in the "Today's Game, Baltimore Orioles' Locker" display. Pie, the talented but tremendously inconsistent outfielder, became the fourth player in modern Orioles history to hit for the cycle in 2009, joining Robinson (1960), Ripken (1984), and Aubrey Huff (2007) in picking up a single, double, triple, and homer in one game. Pie's cycle, which came against the Los Angeles Angels at Camden Yards, was the seventh of eight hit that season in the majors, the most big league cycles in one year since 1933. There are cool things like that throughout Cooperstown. And plenty have an Orioles bent. There's the 1999 jersey that 42-year-old lefty reliever Jesse Orosco wore when he set the career appearances record. There's the cap that first baseman Chris Davis wore when he pitched two innings—and got the win in the 17th—at Fenway Park on May 6, 2012. There's even a celebratory handkerchief from the 1894 National League-pennant winning Orioles.

The museum continually updates its exhibits to keep things fresh and relevant. Plus, it features temporary displays and loaner pieces, so it's difficult to offer a complete list of Orioles items at the Hall at any given time. But you're sure to see artifacts from some of the most important moments in franchise history. Brooks Robinson's glove from the 1970 World Series is there. So is the bat that Dave McNally used to become the only pitcher in World Series history to hit a grand slam. One of the baseballs that Jim Palmer used in his 1969 no-hitter is on display, as is Murray's bat from his two-homer performance in Game 5 of the 1983 World Series. There's the official scoresheet from September 20, 1998, with Cal Ripken Jr.'s name scratched out, marking the end of his consecutive games streak. There are some cool but obscure items, too. There's a baseball from when the Orioles played in Cuba in 1999, a jar of infield dirt from Memorial Stadium, and, in the women in baseball exhibit, a hard hat worn by Janet Marie Smith, one of the primary visionaries behind Camden Yards' retro look and feel. There's also a section dedicated to Baltimore native Babe Ruth, the game's most recognizable character.

For me, though, the best part of the Hall of Fame is the legendary plaque room, where you can check out information on the six men who went into the Hall as Orioles: Brooks Robinson, Frank Robinson, Palmer, Murray, Ripken, and manager Earl Weaver. You can spend hours in that room, losing yourself in baseball history. And you never know who you may run into. In 2003, during the weekend of Murray's induction, I was reading the plaque of Cincinnati Reds great Tony Perez when I was tapped on the shoulder. It was Perez, who playfully asked me if he thought the artist did a good job with his plaque. The artist did. And I left with a cool story from an incredible place.

71 Bruising a Strawberry

When former Orioles reliever Alan Mills was in college in the 1980s, he had a poster of Darryl Strawberry on his dorm room wall. He loved the way the outfielder played the game. That, of course, didn't come into play on May 19, 1998 at Yankee Stadium, when Mills and Strawberry were forever linked in one of the ugliest brawls in baseball history. "I admired Strawberry as a player coming up when I was an amateur, so it was a little more for me than the typical brawl," Mills said. "I had admired what he had done on the field."

Mills wasn't a fan of what Strawberry did that evening: sucker punching Orioles reliever Armando Benitez, who had been ejected for plunking Tino Martinez with a fastball, one pitch after serving

More Melees

The Orioles-Yankees melee in 1998 is probably the most famous basebrawl in club history, but it certainly isn't the only one. Every few years, the club mixes it up with another team, and it usually doesn't amount to much more than dugouts emptying and some pushing and shoving. Here are three, though, that stand out:

June 6, 1993 versus the Seattle Mariners at Camden Yards

In the seventh inning of a 5–2 Orioles win, Mariners catcher Bill Haselman charged the mound after he was hit in the shoulder by a fastball from Mike Mussina. Haselman had homered in his previous at-bat, and Mariners starter Chris Bosio had thrown pitches behind Mark McLemore and Harold Reynolds to lead off the fifth and sixth innings. Haselman tackled Mussina, and Orioles catcher Jeff Tackett jumped on Haselman, igniting the main event of a brawl that caused a 20-minute delay. When play resumed the umpiring crew had ejected seven players and Seattle manager Lou Piniella, who was ticked that Mussina wasn't thrown out.

Among the players who were involved in the series of mini-fights were Orioles reliever Alan Mills and the Mariners' Tino Martinez, Jeff Nelson, and Norm Charlton—all of whom played roles in the infamous Orioles-New York Yankees brawl five years later. The most significant part of the Mariners' dustup didn't come to light until later that week when it was revealed that Orioles shortstop Cal Ripken Jr. ran onto the field during the altercation, tried to change direction, and twisted his right knee. The next morning his knee was so stiff that he told his wife he might have to miss that evening's game—which would have halted his consecutive games streak 340 shy of Lou Gehrig's record. "I was still unsure when I got to the ballpark, but I took some batting practice and fielded some balls, and it felt all right," Ripken later said. He played that night and ultimately shattered Gehrig's record. That was the closest he came to sitting during the streak.

May 31, 1971 versus the Chicago White Sox at White Sox Park

In the second game of a doubleheader in which the Orioles won 11–3, leadoff hitter Don Buford was hit by a pitch in his first at-bat and homered in his second and third. He then was plunked again in his fourth at-bat in the sixth inning. Buford started toward Chicago reliever Bart Johnson while dragging his bat. The sides converged, order was restored, and no one was ejected. Buford later apologized for not dropping his bat, and the umpire stated he never thought Buford intended to use the bat if he had reached Johnson. When Buford returned to left field for the next two innings, he told reporters that fans were throwing things at him, including pieces of wood that they had ripped off their seats. In the top of the ninth, Buford was on deck when, according to an Associated Press report, kids in the stands threw apple cores and paper cups at him. He approached the group to warn it to stop, and one fan grabbed him from behind. His teammates quickly came to his rescue, and the accosting fan was taken by police to the first aid room with a bloodied nose and mouth. According to the AP report at the time, the fan took off from the room before he could be identified.

July 8, 2011 versus the Boston Red Sox at Fenway Park
As far as brawls go, it was tame. What made it significant were the combatants: two very big and very proud men. With the Orioles trailing 10–3 in the bottom of the eighth, Orioles 6'6", 250-pound closer Kevin Gregg threw three consecutive inside pitches to Boston designated hitter David Ortiz, who is 6'4" and weighed 275 pounds in 2011. Ortiz really took exception to the third pitch, pointing at Gregg and walking toward him with his bat in his hand. Gregg took several steps toward the plate, the benches emptied, and the sides were warned. On the next pitch, Ortiz hit a lazy fly to center and jogged out of the batter's box, prompting Gregg to scream at him to run. The behemoths made contact for a moment, but neither landed a punch before they were separated. Screaming and jawing continued, and there were four ejections, but it didn't escalate. Gregg, in his first year as closer, was often a target of boos at Camden Yards, but he gained some fans that night while picking up further respect from his teammates, who felt like the Red Sox were trying to bully them.

up a game-changing, three-run homer to Bernie Williams. In a flash the Orioles had gone from up 5–4 to down 7–5, thanks to Williams' titanic blast to the upper deck in right. Benitez took out his frustration by hitting Martinez between the 2 and the 4 on his back. The decision wasn't appreciated by Martinez, who was hit by Benitez three years earlier on a pitch directly after Benitez served up a grand slam.

Martinez walked toward the mound, and the dugouts emptied. Benitez was clearly at fault at that point. "The emotions he wore on his sleeve got the best of him," said Orioles catcher Chris Hoiles. "Back then, it was a little bit different game. I think that was the way [some] guys were brought up and taught. You give up a home run, and the next guy is going down. But to me, you also have to look at the quality of pitch he made. And he did not make a very quality pitch [to Williams]. So to me that doesn't warrant the next guy getting a baseball right between the numbers...I did call for a fastball, but it definitely wasn't for the middle of the back. It was an unfortunate situation for everybody."

Hoiles rushed to get between the Yankees and Benitez, who dropped his glove and put his arms out to each side, as if to say, "Who, me?" One of the first Yankees to reach the mound was Strawberry, a 36-year-old reserve, who in his career had been suspended for cocaine use and arrested for failure to pay child support. All he did was jaw, but several other skirmishes ignited near the Yankees dugout. New York relievers Graeme Lloyd and Jeff Nelson chased a backpedaling Benitez, who threw wild haymakers toward Lloyd, Nelson, and infielder Scott Brosius. There was more pushing and shoving, but things were calming down when Strawberry came from Benitez's left side and attempted to pop the pitcher in the face while he wasn't looking. Strawberry missed his target, smacking the side of Benitez's head before the outfielder tumbled into the Yankees' dugout. Within seconds Mills pounced on Strawberry, landing a right cross to his jaw and bloodying his mouth as several Yankees and Orioles jumped into the melee. "I usually don't talk about it too much," Mills said. "It all happened so fast. I can't remember what exactly happened."

Hoiles was cornered near a camera well and watched the scene unfold. "Strawberry swung at Armando Benitez and went into the dugout, and that's when Alan Mills came off the top rope back down to get Strawberry," Hoiles said. "It was pretty impressive. But here's the thing…We were a very tight-knit group. We had zero problems. We had zero egos. So I think when Mills saw Strawberry go down in the dugout and basically sucker punch Armando, obviously there was action to be taken…To sucker punch is a whole different thing, and I think that's how Mills-y took it."

With his Fu Manchu mustache and icy glare, Mills was already considered a tough guy. And because he was protecting a teammate and because he happened to pummel one of baseball's most controversial characters, Mills will always be treated reverentially by Orioles fans for his moment of pugilism. It overshadowed a solid major league career in which Mills posted a 4.12 ERA in 12 seasons, including nine with the Orioles. "I know there was stuff that I could do besides [punching Strawberry]. But if that's how fans remember me, that's fine. I don't have a problem with that," he said. "I guess I have a reputation of being a tough guy. I'm probably the nicest guy that ever suited up for the Orioles actually. But that's fine. I know who I am and I know the type of person I am."

Mills also knows for sure he's not the toughest pro athlete who ever graduated from Kathleen High School in Lakeland, Florida. That title goes to a Baltimore legend in another sport. "I've been watching Ray Lewis since he was in high school. I've seen it. And he is, in my opinion, the best [linebacker] that's ever suited up," said Mills, who is nearly nine years older than the Baltimore Ravens great. "He should win that comparison, hands down."

72 The Blade

Mark Belanger and Boog Powell didn't think about it as a training tool, a way for a slick-fielding shortstop and a throw-scooping first baseman to improve their craft. They did it to pass the time, have fun, and maybe bruise each other's shins on occasion. The game was called "flip," and it wasn't particularly complicated. Belanger and Powell would stand about five feet from each other and attempt to throw a baseball through the other guy's legs. "We weren't playing a little kiddie game now. We were trying to do anything to get that ball between your legs or hit you on the shin," Powell said. "We would do that for hours and get the most enjoyment out of it. We'd laugh and have a great time, but looking back on it, it was good training—but not necessarily for him because he already had those no-touch hands. When he touched the ball, it was gone. It was right out of his hand."

Belanger played parts of 18 seasons in the majors, 17 with the Orioles, and never once hit more than five homers or drove in more than 50 runs in a season. His career .228 average in 5,784 at-bats is one of the worst in modern baseball history. It hardly seemed to matter. Belanger's career was all about that tiny, pancake-flat glove that he used to snuff the opposition's rallies. He won eight American League Gold Gloves in his career, including six consecutively from 1973 to 1978. "He was so smooth," said outfielder Al Bumbry. "He was one of those kinds of guys who knew all the hitters. He knew our pitching staff and he knew what we had to do to get hitters out and, consequently, he knew where the hitters tended to hit ground balls. So 99 percent of the time he was in position because he rarely ever dove for a ball." Bumbry remembers one game in which Hall of Fame pitcher Jim Palmer, who was known for maneuvering the fielders behind him, motioned to Belanger to slide over a few steps. "Mark looked back and shook his head no. Jimmy kept looking, and Mark kept shaking his head no," Bumbry said. "Finally, Jimmy threw the pitch, and the guy hit a line drive, and all Mark did was reach up and catch the line drive. And Jim just tipped his hat."

Listed as 6'1" and 170 pounds, Belanger was nicknamed "the Blade" for his thin physique. The Blade, though, wasn't flashy like the man he replaced as Orioles shortstop, Hall of Famer Luis Aparicio. Belanger was steady and consistent, the infield glue on perennial playoff teams. "If the ball was hit to Blade, you were out. That's all. If it was hit anywhere he could reach it, you were out," Powell said. "I never ever saw him blow a routine play. Those are things that count more than anything. All shortstops and all infielders can make great plays from time to time. But Blade had wonderful range to his left and he would venture out into center field and catch balls and throw you out. He was special out there."

At the plate it was a different story. He totaled 20 home runs for his entire career and batted over .240 in just three seasons. His best year hitting was in 1969 when he set career highs in runs scored (76), RBIs (50), batting average (.287), and slugging percentage (.345). In a cruel twist of fate, his hitting coach that year, Charlie Lau, was dismissed in the offseason because he was seeking a $2,000 raise, which the Orioles declined. Had he known, Powell said he would have given Lau the raise out of his pocket. "I bet Belanger would have, too, because Belanger hit almost .290 in '69 also, and that was only because of Charlie Lau," Powell said. "The next year the Blade went back to .218."

As Belanger's career progressed, he took on more and more of a leadership role off the field. He became the Orioles' union representative and was one of the few players directly involved in the contract negotiations during the 1981 strike. After that year he became a free agent—his public criticism of Earl Weaver's managing tactics likely led to a separation with the Orioles—and played 54 games with the Los Angeles Dodgers before retiring. Shortly thereafter, he joined the MLB Players Association staff, serving as a player liaison and ultimately the special assistant to executive director Donald Fehr. Belanger stayed with the union until his death from lung cancer at age 54 in 1998. "He was the most organized teammate I have ever been around, and it didn't surprise me that he went to work for the players association after he was done playing," outfielder Ken Singleton said. "Whenever you had a question about any rules or anything, you'd go to him."

Despite his professional nature, there was a fun-loving, mischievous side of Belanger, too. A baseball and basketball star while growing up in Pittsfield, Massachusetts, Belanger loved to take his teammates out on the road in Boston. He once invited Powell to dinner at a place where the waitstaff was intentionally rude as part of its shtick. But he didn't tell the burly Powell that. He wanted to see what would happen. So when the waitress arrived to take Powell's order, the woman sharply asked, "What the [f---] do you want?" "I looked around and said, 'What the hell?'" Powell said. "And then I said, 'I'll take the biggest F'ing steak you got.' Blade just started laughing. I think he almost peed himself that night."

73 The Dark Years: 1998–2011

For those who first experienced Orioles baseball in the initial decade of the 2000s, you deserve an apology. It really isn't supposed to be like that. Teams have bad years. It happens. Things turn around eventually. Well, it took 14 seasons in Baltimore—14 years of dysfunction, backbiting, firings, bad contracts, defections, arrests, and steroid controversies. Most of all, it was 14 years of constant losing. The Orioles' previous skid without a .500 season was three years. But after winning the division and reaching the 1997 American League Championship Series, the Orioles didn't post a winning record or return to the playoffs until 2012. They lost 90-plus games nine times in that span. The drop-off came suddenly after two consecutive ALCS appearances. Then, as former Orioles manager Davey Johnson so eloquently stated: "It all went in the shitter."

A clash with owner Peter Angelos in 1997 led to Johnson's resignation on the day he was named AL Manager of the Year. It was the first indication of the looming downward spiral. Angelos handpicked pitching coach Ray Miller to be the next manager, and Miller couldn't win with the highest payroll in baseball. After that season Rafael Palmeiro, the club's most productive free agent signing, returned to Texas, and general manager Pat Gillick exited after his contract expired. The Orioles hired Frank Wren to be the new general manager and signed recalcitrant slugger Albert Belle for five years and $65 million, the largest contract in club history. The dysfunction ratcheted up a notch. Belle had a heated exchange with Miller, sidestepped work with hitting coach Terry Crowley, sniped at media, and showed displeasure over the club's in-season exhibition games. After two years he retired due to a degenerative hip.

Miller and Wren didn't last that long. Miller lost the clubhouse in April 1999 when he told reporters—after punching a wall in private—to ask the players what was going wrong because "they make all the money." Wren wanted Miller fired several times during the season, but Angelos refused. Both Miller and Wren lost their jobs that October. Wren's departure spun off into its own bizarre chapter. Terminated 11 months into a three-year contract, the Orioles announced the move with a press release that detailed one of Wren's indiscretions: ordering the team plane to take off for the West Coast without star Cal Ripken Jr., who had called Wren minutes before to inform him he was running slightly late due to traffic detours. In retrospect the primary failure of Wren's tenure was the 1999 draft, when the Orioles had seven picks in the top 50 and only one, second baseman Brian Roberts, panned out.

The next July the Orioles dealt away six veterans in five separate trades. They received a haul of 14 players—primarily minor leaguers and untested big leaguers who were supposed to restock the depleted farm system. Only one, Melvin Mora, became a consistent performer. Seeing the shaky direction the club was headed, right-hander Mike Mussina left in free agency, sending the Orioles into a perpetual search for an ace. After Mussina's departure, the Orioles didn't have a starting pitcher make the All-Star team until Chris Tillman in 2013. "It just started to become the whole organization really. Player development, every aspect of the organization was not working well together," shortshop Mike Bordick said. "It wasn't for a lack of effort, I don't believe. I think everyone that was part of the Orioles wanted that winning back and wanted to find the right formula to do that. But it was just lacking, lacking something, leadership maybe. It was hard."

Heading into 2004 the Orioles fired manager Mike Hargrove, hired Lee Mazzilli, and conducted a free-agent spending spree that included bringing back Palmeiro and pitcher Sidney Ponson and signing catcher Javy Lopez and the big fish, shortstop Miguel Tejada, to a six-year, $72 million deal. The first day he arrived at spring training, Tejada, a former AL MVP, proclaimed the losing was over. It wasn't. In 2005, though, the Orioles held onto first place until June 24 and were within a half game of first place on July 18 before a calamitous two-month implosion.

The linchpins of the Orioles' success from 2012 to 2014, Adam Jones (10) celebrates with right fielder Nick Markakis (21) after a 2011 home run against the Toronto Blue Jays.

Seattle Mariners. Markakis and Jones had played with each other before; they were teammates on the 2005 Peoria Javelinas in the Arizona Fall League. Markakis was one of baseball's top outfield prospects at the time. Jones was trying to make the transition from shortstop to center field. "He has come a long way. He has learned a lot," Markakis told *The Baltimore Sun* in 2014. "He is a lot smarter out there now. When he was younger, he was kind of reckless." Through 2014 Jones had four Gold Gloves, and Markakis had won two while playing more games in the outfield together than any other active American League tandem. "I watched both of them come up—young, single, early-20s players in the big leagues trying to find their way as players and as people in general," said former Oriole Brian Roberts. "And to watch the way they have both matured as players and as human beings off the field, family people off the field, it's really been rewarding to see that. What they do on the field pretty much explains itself. They are both models of consistency."

In the four seasons between 2011 and 2014, Jones hit at least 25 homers, drove in 80 runs, and batted .280 or better each year. Markakis batted .270 and hit 10 or more home runs in each of his first nine seasons as an Oriole. Jones said when he signed his record extension with the Orioles in 2012—six years, $85.5 million—he made a promise to himself that he would play nearly every game of the contract because he saw Markakis do that when he agreed to a $66.1 million extension in 2009.

They basically grew up together in the big leagues and shared plenty of moments together. Markakis, who is roughly a year and a half older, became a father first, and Jones sought him out for parenting advice after his first son was born. They both lead relatively boring existences despite the money that they make. "We've got very nice homes, we travel comfortably, but our everyday appearance is normal," Jones said. "Why? Because that's who we are." Some of their passions off the field have intertwined. Markakis has tried to get Jones into hunting with some success. But Jones doesn't try to share his love of technology and social media with Markakis. While Jones was one of baseball's most active Twitter users in 2014, Markakis doesn't even have email. Yes, they are quite different. But the relationship worked. "It's a brotherly love," Jones said. "But even more so, a teammate love."

When Markakis became a free agent after the 2014 season, Jones said he couldn't imagine looking to his left and not seeing his buddy there. "If you cut him open, it would probably bleed a little orange," Jones said. "To see him with some other uniform would be crazy." The unexpected happened in December 2014, when Markakis signed a four-year, $44 million deal with the Atlanta Braves. The Orioles and Markakis were close to a four-year, $40 million pact that November, but the club backed away from negotiations after a MRI showed a bulging disc in Markakis' neck—a remnant of a herniated disc that he had suffered in 2013. The Braves weren't scared off by the medical report, and Markakis, who went to high school in suburban Atlanta, had neck surgery to remove the disc shortly after signing the new deal.

After nearly a dozen years in the Orioles organization, nine in the big leagues and seven with Jones, Markakis became a Brave. "It's a tough decision to leave an organization that you are rooted in," Markakis said. "I wouldn't take anything back from what I did in that organization. I had a great time. I grew as a Major League Baseball player and as an Oriole and I'll always have that."

Markakis took out a two-page ad in *The Baltimore Sun*, thanking fans and the organization for their support and vowing to continue to raise his family in Baltimore County. He also admitted it initially would be strange playing right field without Jones in center. "It's going to be a big adjustment playing next to somebody new. I knew what Jonesy was capable of doing, what he could get to. We couldn't have communicated better out there."

75 Colorful Characters

Maybe it's because the season is so long, and there's so much time to get to know the players, but baseball has had its share of eccentric personalities. So have the Orioles, with Moe Drabowsky, the king of the hotfoot, leading the way. Here are some other colorful Orioles:

Robert Andino

Known for his cocked ballcap and swaggering gait, his walk-off single ruined the Boston Red Sox's playoff hopes in 2011. His scoreboard segment, "Andino at the Movies" showcased his humor. He once quipped "I was traded to Alaska" after being dealt to the Seattle Mariners.

Tony Batista

Begin with the batting stance. Batista stood at the plate with his lead, left leg pointing toward the third-base dugout before the pitch came. He'd do an elaborate, arm-waving prayer ritual at third base after the first pitch of every game. He also convinced teammates to soft-toss sunflower seeds to him while he practiced his swing, believing it improved his focus.

Jackie Brandt

Called "Flakey," the outfielder did a backflip in a rundown and slid into each base during a home run. He once convinced teammates to travel for miles to an ice cream parlor that had an array of flavors. He couldn't make up his mind once there, so he ordered vanilla.

Todd Cruz

When the slick-fielding infielder, whose glove helped the Orioles to the 1983 title, first joined the Orioles he was wearing multiple watches on his wrist. No explanation given. He once was arrested in Canada for falling asleep in a store with watches stuffed in his pocket.

Steve Dalkowski

The 5'11" lefty never made the majors, but "Dalko" may have had the fastest (104 mph) and most erratic fastball ever. He walked 262 and struck out 262 in one minor league year. Off the field, he was just as wild. An old teammate said, "I roomed with a suitcase."

Moe Drabowsky

The Poland native and 1966 World Series hero was dubbed the "Prince of Pranks." The master of the hotfoot—lighting shoelaces on fire—he even victimized commissioner Bowie Kuhn. He'd call an opposing bullpen and order a reliever to get ready.

Kevin Hickey

Once a softball league star, the lefty lived in Triple A Rochester's clubhouse for a season. His Orioles break came in 1989 when the club ran out of pitchers in a spring game. He had been running barefoot wind sprints but put on his cleats and threw three scoreless innings.

Aubrey Huff

While his "rally thong" is part of San Francisco Giants lore, "Huff Daddy" made his goofy mark elsewhere, too. After calling Baltimore a "horseshit town" on a radio show in 2007, Huff wore an "I Heart Baltimore" shirt at the next Fanfest. Boos eventually became cheers.

Kevin Millar

No one talked more than "One Five," which he often called himself in reference to his uniform number. Part of the Red Sox "Idiots" title team, Millar kept that persona going in Baltimore. He was center stage for the "Orioles Magic" video in 2008.

Randy Myers

He had one of the greatest seasons in Orioles history, saving 45 of 46 games in 1997. He was just as intimidating off the field. He kept a grenade in his locker and occasionally cut slabs of beef stick with a machete while sitting in the clubhouse.

Don Stanhouse

He was nicknamed "Full Pack" because manager Earl Weaver would smoke a full pack of cigarettes while watching the righty close out a game. "Stan the Man Unusual" had frizzy hair and a caterpillar mustache and saved 45 games for the Orioles in 1978–79.

Sammy Stewart

He put underwear over his uniform pants to mimic Jim Palmer and threw pantomime to Rick Dempsey in a rain delay. The fun-loving righty reliever also tried to pitch left-handed in a game but wasn't allowed. Drug addiction cost him several years in prison.

Luke Scott

Never shying from conservative opinions about politics and religion, Scott's stance that President Barack Obama wasn't born in the U.S. created a firestorm, prompting general manager Andy MacPhail to defend Scott's freedom of speech, "no matter how goofy you might think" it is.

76 Cartoon Birds, Uniforms, and Caps

The 2009 Orioles dropped 98 games during one of their most horrendous seasons in more than 20 years. But for some fans, the poor results mattered less because "Baltimore" returned to the road jerseys that season. The Orioles were still losing at a dizzying pace, but at least they were finally repping their town again in visiting cities for the first time in decades. Then in 2012, the Orioles made the playoffs for the first time in 15 years. What was the primary reason for the sudden resurgence? Well, the cartoon bird returned to the Orioles' cap for the first time since 1988. It's hard to explain unless you're from Baltimore or a really intense fan, but people in and around Charm City get fired up about the club's uniforms and hats and the tradition they convey.

When the Orioles moved to Baltimore in 1954, they adopted the state bird's color scheme of orange and black, and that hasn't fluctuated in 60 years. But there have been uniform changes —some subtle, some apparently alarming—as the seasons have passed. In addition to cream and gray jerseys, the Orioles added an orange one and a black one that have been used on weekends. There have been redesigns involving the piping and script and the addition and subtraction of patches over the years.

But the change that was cataclysmic for some occurred after the 1972 season. Then-owner Jerold Hoffberger had "Baltimore" taken off the road jerseys for the 1973 season. The Washington Senators had moved to Texas, and the belief was that the club had the opportunity to become more regional. There seemingly always was an undercurrent of support to return "Baltimore" to the road jerseys, but it gained momentum in 2005, when the Montreal Expos moved to the nation's capital and became the Washington

Nationals. With a team in D.C., blue-collar Baltimore really wanted its name back. Managing partner Peter Angelos submitted the proper paperwork with the league office in early 2008. By November, several Orioles were involved in a fashion show at the Inner Harbor, unveiling the new—or old—look. Hundreds of fans turned out for the event.

Once that apparent wrong was righted, there was another focus from uniform-savvy fans: Bring back the cartoon bird. For the franchise's first nine seasons, its cap featured a perched Oriole. In 1963 the team inexplicably changed to a "B." That lasted one year. In 1964 a bird returned. This time it was a chirping one with an open mouth. After two years with that cap, the Orioles made a drastic change in 1966, unveiling a smiling, fat-faced cartoon bird. It was undeniably goofy-looking. And it worked. The Orioles won their first World Series title that year, and, though the caps were altered on occasion, the cartoon bird remained ubiquitous throughout the Orioles' glory years. But in 1988, when the Orioles lost a club-record 107 games, the cartoon bird took the fall. The next season, an ornithologically correct rendition returned to its perch on the team's caps.

The Orioles redesigned that logo twice in the following 22 years, but it was still an actual animal with no trace of artistic goofiness. The Orioles, however, kept losing. For 14 straight seasons, they couldn't get over .500. Then in 2012 a cartoon bird returned. It wasn't the exact same as the old days—the weird orange smudge on its hat, for instance, was replaced with an "O." But nonetheless, the cartoon bird had resurfaced. And with it, of course, the Orioles went back to the playoffs in 2012. Apparently, that's all it took to re-establish winning in Baltimore.

77 Mike Cuellar

When the Orioles traded former American League Rookie of the Year outfielder Curt Blefary and a minor leaguer to the Houston Astros in December 1968, the main player returning to Baltimore was a bit of a mystery, a 31-year-old, veteran left-hander named Miguel Angel "Mike" Cuellar. Most of the Orioles hadn't seen Cuellar pitch live before. He had spent his previous five seasons in the National League, most with the hapless Houston Astros. Almost half of his appearances were as a reliever. "No, we didn't know what we were getting," catcher Andy Etchebarren said. "Once I saw him, I thought we had gotten a pretty good pitcher."

That trade is considered one of general manager Harry Dalton's greatest moves. Cuellar, along with Detroit's Denny McLain, shared the AL Cy Young Award in 1969. In that initial season as an Oriole, Cuellar was 23–11 with a 2.38 ERA, the first of three consecutive years in which Cuellar won at least 20 games, made at least 38 starts, and threw 290 or more innings. Along with Jim Palmer and Dave McNally, Cuellar was part of a trio of starters who were consistently among the best in the majors. In eight years with the Orioles, Cuellar won 143 games with a 3.18 ERA. From 1969 to 1975, he won 139 games, never failing to to amass at least 14 victories per season. Only once in that period did he post an ERA over 3.50. Said Palmer: "139 wins in seven years, do the math. People have no idea how good Mike Cuellar was."

It's not as if Cuellar lacked previous success. As an 18-year-old, he pitched a no-hitter for an Army team in Cuba. He initially made the majors at age 22 with the Cincinnati Reds, but after two less than stellar outings—he gave up a grand slam in his debut—he bounced around the minors and spent a season in the

Mexican League. In 1964 he learned how to throw his trademark screwball and by 1966 he had finished second in the NL in ERA with a 2.22 mark. He was in the majors to stay. The next season he won 16 games for the Astros and made the National League All-Star team, pitching two scoreless innings and striking out his first batter, Orioles third baseman Brooks Robinson. But in 1968 he missed three weeks with a left shoulder strain and ended up with an 8–11 record in 28 appearances while still posting a 2.74 ERA. He was also having financial difficulties and trouble in his marriage.

The Orioles decided to buy low and help him straighten out his personal life. According to John Eisenberg's book, *From 33rd Street to Camden Yards*, Dalton said he sat down with Cuellar and helped him consolidate and minimize his debts by working out deals with some of the creditors. Cuellar also got divorced and later remarried. Pitching and winning became his primary focus. It was Cuellar's complete-game victory in the Game 5 clincher of the 1970 World Series that propelled the club to its second championship. "He was fun to play behind because he would make his pitches, and nobody could hit him," said second baseman Davey Johnson. "When summer came along, and his fastball came alive, he was really unhittable."

Nicknamed "Crazy Horse," Cuellar was one of the quirkiest and most superstitious players the Orioles have ever had. He hated pitching in the cold. (He had a career 4.19 ERA in April and 3.33 or less in every other month.) He would never step on the foul lines, would sit at the same spot on the bench during gamedays, and wouldn't take the mound unless the rosin bag had been removed. He had specific warm-up rituals, including only throwing to coach Jim Frey pregame. He had a lucky ballcap that he once left in Baltimore when the team went on a road trip, and the club had to ship it to him so he could pitch. But it all seemed to work for him.

So did his mystifying screwball that would start out in the middle of the plate to a right-handed hitter and then disappear away. Etchebarren said he'd rarely throw it to lefties. And he didn't have to; his arsenal was much better than just one baffling pitch. "He threw harder than people thought when he came over from Houston before '69. He probably threw 93, 94 [mph]. He had a great curveball, great screwball," Palmer said. "He could get you out so many different ways. And he was tremendously strong. He had the strongest hands that you could imagine. He could take a ball and just make it spin. He would just flip the ball with his hand and make it spin unbelievably."

Cuellar lasted with the Orioles until 1976 and remains fourth on the franchise's all-time list in wins and second in complete games. He signed in 1977 with the California Angels, who were run by Dalton, and lasted just two appearances. He was released days before his 40th birthday. He died in 2010 at age 72 due to stomach cancer.

78 The Rise and Fall of Rafael Palmeiro

I approached Orioles first baseman Rafael Palmeiro in June 2005 with an interview request for a lengthy feature to appear on the front page of *The Baltimore Sun* once Palmeiro secured his 3,000th hit. Palmeiro was standing in his locker, reaching up for something on the top shelf, when he causally asked about my angle. We had known each other for a while and kidded around frequently. So I joked, "Just your typical, Raffy-is-a-baseball-god story." Palmeiro quickly stepped out of his locker and turned. Staring at me, he implored, "Don't write it like that. Please don't write it like that."

I thought he was being humble, though the serious nature of the statement seemed strange. In retrospect I realized Palmeiro had already known about his positive test for the banned steroid stanozolol. Once his appeal was rejected, he was suspended for 10 days, splintering a legacy that he had carefully built. A flowery article in the local paper would only serve to elevate the pedestal from which he was about to tumble. The feature came out in mid-July, two days after Palmeiro doubled in Seattle to become the fourth player in baseball history to reach 3,000 hits and 500 homers. Two weeks later on August 1, 2005, Palmeiro's suspension was announced. It was particularly ironic, considering four-and-a-half months earlier Palmeiro had testified in front of the U.S. House Committee on Government Reform, famously wagging his finger and saying, "I have never used steroids. Period." At the time he was defending himself after former Texas Rangers teammate Jose Canseco had accused Palmeiro, among others, of using performance-enhancing drugs in Canseco's 2005 tell-all book.

When Palmeiro returned in mid-August, Orioles superstar Miguel Tejada was by his side and lifted Palmeiro's left arm, like a referee to a victorious fighter, in a sign of solidarity. That day Palmeiro gave no insight into how the banned substance ended up in his system, saying that his attorneys advised him not to comment. He added, "The time will come soon, hopefully, that I can explain my situation." A month later *The Baltimore Sun* reported that Palmeiro told an arbitration panel that the only explanation for his positive test was that an injection of liquid vitamin B-12 must have been tainted. Searching for an energy boost, he said he asked Tejada for a vial of the vitamin, which isn't a steroid but is only available in liquid form via prescription. It triggered an investigation into the substance and Tejada. Ultimately, no link was confirmed. But Palmeiro's teammates were privately incensed that he would implicate another player. He said that was not the intent, but he never again played for the Orioles or anyone else. He also never backtracked on his story. "I'm not going to change it for the sake of creating a myth," Palmeiro told *The Baltimore Sun* in 2014. "It is what it is. It happened. It's the honest-to-God truth."

Palmeiro played in only seven games following the suspension. In his last, August 30 in Toronto, he wore earplugs to drown out the booing from the Rogers Centre crowd. It was an inauspicious ending to a phenomenal 20-season career in which he compiled 3,020 hits, 569 home runs, 1,835 RBIs, and a .288 batting average. A four-time All-Star, he won three Gold Gloves and two Silver Slugger Awards. Despite gaudy power numbers that began while he was in Texas, Palmeiro didn't look like a slugger—or PED user. He was 6'0", 180 pounds and maintained the same everyman body type throughout his career. "I couldn't believe it with the steroid thing. First of all, I don't think he had a muscle on his whole body," quipped former Orioles manager Davey Johnson. "He was great. I loved him." Palmeiro's teammates were in awe of his flaw-less left-handed stroke. "He had one of the sweetest swings I had ever seen," second baseman Brian Roberts said. "It always amazed me watching it on TV how easy it looked. And then when I saw him in person and played with him, it looked even easier."

Without the positive test, Palmeiro would have made the Hall of Fame. With it, he never received more than 13 percent of the vote and fell off the ballot in 2014 after failing to receive the required 5 percent to stay eligible. Palmeiro became the first casualty of a logjam created by the PED era. His only chance now is selection by the Hall's veterans' committee in the future. "I take full responsibility, accountability for my mistake. It cost me tre-mendously in my life. It ruined my career and now it has ruined my chance of being a Hall of Famer," Palmeiro said in 2014. "I don't blame anybody but myself. I should have known better and I should have trusted no one. You live and you learn. Some lessons are harder than others and this one I'll pay for the rest of my life."

Al Bumbry

Al Bumbry's still not sure why it all clicked in 1971 when he hit .336 in the Northern League and nearly won the batting crown. Two years earlier he had batted .178 in the minors before being forced to temporarily give up baseball. He didn't just leave the game. He left the country and didn't know if he'd make it back alive. Bumbry had to honor his military commitment, which ultimately included nine months as a U.S. Army platoon leader in the Vietnam War.

When he returned he started to hit and stormed through the minors quickly. In 1973, while the war continued in Asia, Bumbry won the American League Rookie of the Year Award with the Orioles by batting .337 with a .398 on-base percentage and 11 triples in 110 games. "All of the sudden, I hit. Don't ask me how and why," Bumbry said. "But I guess I must have matured a hell of a lot from being in the war. I guess it was totally encompassing when you look at the dangers involved in a war and I survived that. Maybe I had a different outlook on baseball. Maybe I was just glad I had gone to Vietnam to serve my country and gotten back unscathed…I didn't hit before I went into the service and I came out and I hit."

Bumbry spent 14 seasons in the majors—13 with the Orioles. He played nearly 1,500 big league games and had a career .281 average with a .343 on-base percentage. His 252 stolen bases were once an Orioles record and are still third on the franchise's all-time list. In 1980 he made the AL All-Star team and became the first Orioles player to reach 200 hits in a season. But his story goes beyond baseball.

Bumbry earned a college basketball scholarship to Virginia State University, where the students had to participate in the Reserve Officers' Training Corps for two years. After his sophomore year, he took his draft physical. "I was playing basketball and did not want to be drafted and be taken out of school," Bumbry said. "So I decided to join the advanced ROTC program that was offered for juniors and seniors." In the advanced classification, Bumbry couldn't be drafted by the military until he completed his schooling and his college basketball career. After that, though, he would be committed to six years of service: two active, two active reserves, and two inactive reserves. Because of his involvement in the program, he'd enter the Army as an officer, a second lieutenant. Active duty, though, meant there was a possibility he would have to go to war. "I was hoping I would not be sent to Vietnam, but, needless to say, I was wrong," he said.

After approximately a year stateside at Fort Knox in Kentucky and Fort Meade in Maryland, Bumbry was sent to Vietnam. Within a few days, he was assigned to a tank patrol in the jungle. The commander told the assembled leaders that they needed to carry out their orders, but their No. 1 priority was the safety of their platoon. Bumbry, who was awarded a Bronze Star in Vietnam, treasured that advice. He's proud that during his leadership his platoon had only two deaths, "and I lost those two because they did something that they were not supposed to do, which was against the rules of engagement, and that's how they lost their lives. But I was there for nine months all total and, the way we operated, I did not lose any men in combat."

He once told his friend and Orioles teammate Ken Singleton that story, but he shared very few other war experiences. "We didn't talk about it all that much because our jobs at the time were playing baseball," Singleton said. "I have a lot of respect for Al just getting back from there and being my teammate. And I'm just happy he did."

Orioles left-hander Scott McGregor said everyone took their lead from Bumbry. He didn't bring up the war, so they didn't ask. As time has gone on, McGregor has heard some of Bumbry's war tales—like what McGregor calls "the leg story." As a tank patrol leader, Bumbry rode up front in the commander's turret with a machine gun before him and the ammunition below. The Viet Cong would shoot rocket-propelled grenade rounds that would pierce a tank's exterior and explode. "You didn't want to have your legs dangling inside," Bumbry said. "So I sat up in that seat that entire time in the tank in basically the fetal position because I did not want my legs to be dangling down in the inside of the tank." It was uncomfortable, for sure, but it may have preserved his baseball career. His success was based on his legs, whether it was stealing bases or dashing after a fly ball. "I think about that now, but I didn't think much about it then. Obviously, my legs were my game. But I wasn't thinking along those lines then," Bumbry recalled.

Known as "the Bee," Bumbry is widely considered the fastest player in franchise history —or certainly one of them. His ability to beat out groundballs led to 158 singles in 1980, still a team record. Another situation beyond his control also shaped that ability. He had been a right-handed hitter in high school but fractured his left wrist when he tried to break his fall during a high jump competition. The wrist didn't heal properly, and it hurt when he swung right-handed. The discomfort wasn't there from the left side, so he switched. "That was a godsend for me in that I could get to first base faster from the left side than the right side. And it turned out pretty well."

Bumbry has often said he's doubly blessed. He survived the Vietnam War without injury and then had a lengthy professional baseball career. He wasn't looking to be a soldier, but those circumstances shaped who he became. "Once I committed to [the Army], it was an obligation that I felt like I needed to do, had to do," he said. "And once I got involved in it, it was full steam ahead. In particular, when I went to Vietnam it was a matter of survival. I don't consider myself an extra strong person, but I know I was a stronger person having gone through that."

80 Closing Memorial Stadium

Even during their down years, the Orioles have been tremendous at ceremonies. When the club had its "Thanks, Brooks Day" on September 18, 1977, and Doug DeCinces pulled third base out of the ground and handed it to Brooks Robinson and said "This is always yours," a fan base blubbered. When 2,131 was unfurled from the Warehouse on September 6, 1995, Cal Ripken Jr. jogged around Camden Yards and intimately celebrated his consecutive games streak with his adoring public. Most Orioles celebrations have been done with professionalism and class. That was epitomized on October 6, 1991. The Orioles closed Memorial Stadium with an unforgettable tribute.

The ceremonial first pitch was a multi-sport affair. Hall of Fame third baseman Brooks Robinson threw a baseball to Cal Ripken Jr., and Hall of Fame Baltimore Colts quarterback Johnny Unitas simultaneously threw a football to then-mayor Kurt Schmoke. It kicked off a tremendously emotional day in which more than 100 Orioles, past and present, were on the field together to say good-bye to the Old Gray Lady of 33rd Street. "It was my home. Baltimore was my home. How does it get any better than that?" said Davey Johnson, the Orioles' former All-Star second baseman who returned five years later as manager.

The game itself was a dud, a 7–1 beating by the Detroit Tigers that closed the Orioles' 95-loss season. The Tigers scored four runs in the first inning against right-hander Bob Milacki, who was chased by the third. "I wish it would have ended better for me and the team," Milacki said, "even though it was a tremendous day at the end of the day." In the ninth with the Orioles down six, closer Gregg Olson picked up one out, and then the bullpen door opened. Mike Flanagan, the bulldog lefty and former Cy Young Award winner who had returned in 1991 at age 39 to be a reliever, trotted in. Trotted is an overstatement. "It took him five minutes to walk in from the bullpen," Milacki said. "That was tremendous, was unbelievable." Flanagan struck out both batters he faced, including Travis Fryman with the last pitch thrown by an Oriole. In the bottom of the ninth, Detroit starter Frank Tanana finished his complete-game victory, getting Ripken to ground into a double play and end 38 years of big league baseball at Memorial Stadium. The sold-out crowd of 50,700 stayed in its seats, understanding something special was looming but not knowing exactly what.

A white stretch limousine drove onto the field, and the ground crew, dressed in tuxedos, dug out home plate and placed it in the limo for a police-escorted jaunt to the site of the new, downtown ballpark. Actor James Earl Jones' distinctive voice cracked the air, as the words from Jones' soliloquy from *Field of Dreams* scrolled on the scoreboard, and the film's haunting instrumental accompanied it. Out of the dugout jogged a solitary figure wearing a pristine, Orioles uniform with No. 5 on the back. With a glove on his left hand, Brooks Robinson took his customary spot at third base, shuffled his feet in the infield dirt, and seemingly prepared to dive back into history to snag a liner. Frank Robinson followed, jogging out to right field and tipping his cap. Then Boog Powell came out to first base, and a teary-eyed Jim Palmer went to the pitcher's mound. The former players began to stream out of the dugout and

Drenched at Memorial Stadium

Writing about October 6, 1991, when the Orioles closed Memorial Stadium and brought back dozens of former Orioles stars, it'd be easy to conclude that there wasn't a dry eye in the place. The truth is one woman had a set of dry eyes, but her clothes were soaked. Susan Johnson, the wife of retired second baseman and former All-Star Davey Johnson, was sitting in the stands left of home plate. "I had never been to a baseball game before," Susan Johnson said. "I go there, and David is down there to be honored, and a pipe broke over my seat and it poured about 30 gallons of sludge water down my jeans and onto these beautiful suede boots."

Susan Johnson left her seat and was taken to a restroom where she gave attendants her clothes to be dried. "I sat in a towel during the whole game in the bathroom," she said. Her husband was one of the first players to come out of the dugout during the now legendary *Field of Dreams* sequence during the postgame ceremonies. Fans cheered Johnson loudly. His wife missed it. "She was naked getting her clothes dried while the game and ceremony were going on," Davey Johnson said. "You can't dream up life's stories, I swear." When she thinks of that day, Susan Johnson laughs. "It was just really, really funny in hindsight," she said. "You would never expect to sit down and have a pipe break over your seat. But I guess that's why it was the last game there."

take their spots on the field. Catcher Rick Dempsey, who was still playing with the Milwaukee Brewers that season, received permission to leave his team to take part in the ceremony. So did pitcher Dennis Martinez, who had thrown a perfect game for the Montreal Expos earlier that July. After the ex-Orioles were in place, the 1991 team took the field with Ripken Jr. receiving his own entrance and cheers. The last one out of the dugout was Hall of Fame manager Earl Weaver. Then Dempsey stood at the missing plate and twisted his body to spell O-R-I-O-L-E-S twice. Those on the field threw souvenir balls into the stands until the scoreboard showed a video of broadcaster and Maryland legend Jim McKay at the site of Camden Yards. Club president Larry Lucchino, Maryland Stadium Authority chairman Herb Belgrad, and some elementary students lowered the Memorial Stadium home plate into its new hole at the downtown construction site. The video then switched to a message from Rex Barney, the longtime public address announcer and voice of Memorial Stadium who was in the hospital after collapsing two days earlier. He ended the recorded part of the ceremony with his trademark, "Thank Youuuu."

With "Auld Lang Syne" blaring and fans crying, Dempsey tucked a pillow into his jersey and did one last pantomime of Babe Ruth hitting a homer, his old rain delay shtick. As he rounded third, he high-fived dozens of old teammates before diving on top of the home-plate hole. It was a perfect send-off for an imperfect but unforgettable stadium. "It was bittersweet," Palmer said of Memorial's closing. "Baseball was going down a different road then. It was about revenue, and you were going to a ballpark with luxury boxes and better seating and more fan-friendly. The thing that made Memorial Stadium so fan-friendly was the teams that played there."

81 Opening Camden Yards

The first pitch ever thrown in a regular season game at Oriole Park at Camden Yards—a ball from right-hander Rick Sutcliffe to Cleveland Indians leadoff hitter Kenny Lofton—occurred at 3:20 PM on Monday, April 6, 1992. The pitch that made that pitch happen, though, occurred roughly four months earlier in a stadium that was only about three-quarters completed. Sutcliffe, a

Camden Yards, Baltimore's beautiful, retro-style ballpark, hosted its first regular season game on Monday, April 6, 1992.

35-year-old veteran free agent and former Cy Young Award winner, had no intention of playing in the American League or on the East Coast. But in December 1991, he received a phone call from a close friend, one of his ex-catchers with the Los Angeles Dodgers. "Johnny Oates called me and begged me to come to Baltimore to talk to him. He didn't say anything about signing with the Orioles or anything like that," Sutcliffe said. "I felt like I owed it to Johnny to at least come here and hear what he had to say."

Oates, the Orioles' second-year manager, took Sutcliffe to the under-construction ballpark near Baltimore's Inner Harbor. They walked into the empty stadium and out to the mound. "'I don't want you to say anything to anybody, but I made up my mind you are going to throw the first pitch in this ballpark,'" Sutcliffe remembers Oates saying to him. "My first thought was, *No, I'm not Johnny. I'm too old to come to the American League. I'm going to try and get closer to home because my daughter is older.*" Oates told Sutcliffe to take some time and look around. Parts of the new stadium reminded Sutcliffe of Wrigley Field, where he had had his best years. Other components were reminiscent of different ballparks throughout the league. He didn't expect a sudden wave of emotion. "I had goose bumps all over my body. I went, 'Wow,'"

Sutcliffe said. "It wasn't more than an hour later we agreed to a one-year deal."

Two weeks before spring training ended, Sutcliffe decided to back out of his clandestine agreement with Oates. After spending all of camp with the Orioles, Sutcliffe was convinced that the team's best pitcher was right-hander Mike Mussina. Although the 23-year-old only had 12 games of big league experience, he deserved the Opening Day start, Sutcliffe figured. So Sutcliffe walked into the manager's office to tell Oates that. "And he goes, 'I know you are not the best pitcher on this team. [Ben] McDonald is better than you, too. Mussina is, and McDonald is. But for us to be good, they need to get off to a good start. And I know when I match you against everybody else's No. 1 guy, you can hold your own.'" That's how Sutcliffe, who won 16 games for the Orioles in 1992, officially received one of the best assignments of his career.

Technically, the first game at Camden Yards was April 3, 1992, when the Orioles beat the New York Mets in an exhibition. But three days later, Baltimore was fully abuzz, an enthusiastic crowd of 44,568 piled into the gleaming palace eventually dubbed "The Ballpark That Changed Baseball." Sutcliffe's excitement was tempered. He was sick. He arrived at Camden Yards that Monday morning with a 103-degree fever. He didn't care. He was pitching.

The first batter he faced was the aggressive Lofton. Typically, Sutcliffe would attempt to throw a first-pitch strike on Opening Day, but he expected Lofton would be looking to ambush a grooved fastball. So he purposely threw his first delivery out of the strike zone. On a full count, Lofton hit a fly ball to right fielder Joe Orsulak for the park's first out. The sold-out crowd roared, and the tone was set. Sutcliffe retired 11 of his first 12 batters. In the fifth inning, Orioles catcher Chris Hoiles broke the scoreless tie with a RBI double, and the Orioles took a 2–0 lead into the ninth. Closer Gregg Olson was warming up, but Oates, who had planned this day months earlier, wanted his old teammate to finish it. Sutcliffe recorded the first two outs on six pitches. Then, on a 1–2 count to Paul Sorrento, he threw an outside fastball with the intent of coming back with a breaking ball to fan Sorrento for the last out. Home-plate umpire Larry Barnett ruined the plan, ringing up Sorrento on the pitch to the delight of the standing, screaming fans. "The umpire calls strike three," Sutcliffe said. "And in my mind I'm going, *No, no. I'll get him on the next one. Don't do that one.*" Still, Sutcliffe had thrown a 110-pitch, five-hit, complete-game shutout to usher in a new era. An Oriole for two seasons, Sutcliffe always will be linked to that day. "I have pitched 10 Opening Days," he said. "This one was, obviously, more special than any other."

Soak in Sarasota

For decades the Orioles pretty much traveled aimlessly in the spring training wilderness, searching for a home and attempting to get out of their old one. After five years in Arizona at their inception, the Orioles moved spring operations to Florida in 1959 and spent 32 springs in Miami. Their home base was Bobby Maduro Miami Stadium, which was located in an area that wasn't exactly a tourist destination. For five years in the early 1990s, the major league nomads bounced around between Florida locales: Sarasota and St. Petersburg. In 1995 they were road warriors without an actual stadium where they could have a home game.

From 1996 to 2009, the Orioles played at dilapidated Fort Lauderdale Stadium while seemingly in perpetual negotiations for either renovation there or relocation somewhere else. Toward the end of their time in Fort Lauderdale, the players were forced to lift weights in a tent in an adjacent parking lot. The club couldn't play night games because stadium officials weren't sure they could shut the lights off once the banks were switched on.

Of all the dysfunction that he wanted to fix when joining the Orioles in 2007, club president Andy MacPhail made finding a better spring home a priority. He couldn't believe that the major league club trained in Fort Lauderdale while the minor league facility was in Sarasota, several hours away. So when a player was sent out of camp, he not only received the indignity of being cut, but then he had a long drive before arriving at minor league camp.

After the Cincinnati Reds announced they were leaving Sarasota's Ed Smith Stadium in order to relocate to Arizona for the 2010 spring training, the Orioles seized the opportunity. Led by executive vice president John Angelos and attorney Alan Rifkin, the Orioles negotiated a 30-year lease predicated on $31.2 million in renovations to Ed Smith Stadium and its complex, which were completed before the 2011 season. Now the Orioles have one of the best spring training sites in the Grapefruit League and an impressive year-round headquarters for its minor league operation. And fans have a reason to migrate south each spring. The ballpark has a seating capacity for nearly 7,500 and can accommodate up to 8,500 fans when standing-room-only is factored in.

The stadium itself is all Orioles—with orange and black trimming and reminders of club lore displayed throughout the facility. There is a state-of-the-art weight room for the players and several well-manicured practice fields, including one with Camden Yards' dimensions. There's also the Earl Weaver Little Field, a half-diamond named after the Orioles Hall of Fame manager and used by instructors working on specific infield drills.

Spring training is always a more laid-back atmosphere than the regular season with a better chance for fans to get autographs or pictures of their favorite players. And when the Orioles aren't playing at Ed Smith Stadium, visitors have plenty of options for things to do in the Sarasota area each March. They can always go to the nearby Twin Lakes Park complex to watch minor leaguers play or check out Orioles' road games, which for the most part are all within an hour's drive. Baseball fans also can take a break and visit the quaint shopping and dining areas in St. Armands Circle or the white sand beaches of the Gulf Coast, including the celebrated Siesta Key.

Matt Wieters

During his tenure as Orioles club president from 2007 to 2011, Andy MacPhail carved a reputation for being conservative and mindful with his words and actions. He never wanted to put undue pressure on an individual or situation. So that's why May 26, 2009, really stands out. During an Orioles broadcast on the team-owned Mid-Atlantic Sports Network, MacPhail made an unprecedented "special announcement" that the club would be promoting phenom Matt Wieters from Triple A Norfolk, Virginia, and starting him three days later, Friday, May 29, at Camden Yards. MacPhail proclaimed that the catcher was ready. "It's time," he said. There was only one purpose for a public announcement about a minor league call-up: create buzz and ticket sales around the 23-year-old's arrival, making it obvious that broadcasting the move was a business—not baseball—decision made by higher-ups.

From a marketing and public relations standpoint, though, it made sense. The Orioles were on their way to a 12th consecutive losing season. It was late May, and they were already last in the American League East, eight games out of first place. Attendance had been tumbling for years, and, on the night of MacPhail's surprising announcement, there were just 10,130 fans at Camden Yards. That ended up being the Orioles' smallest crowd of 2009—home or on the road. As for Wieters, he was in his second year in pro ball but was batting .305 in a 39-game trial at Triple A. And he had been hyped since he was the fifth overall pick of the 2007 draft out of Georgia Tech.

In retrospect, Wieters said he didn't feel any extra pressure that week or that year. "Compared to nowadays, I actually feel like I had it pretty easy—the way some of the kids get hyped to be what they are nowadays and as quick as the information gets out," Wieters said in 2014. "I always had those high expectations for myself, so I never really got wrapped up in what everybody else thought I was going to be or what everybody else saw for me."

What they saw—and said and wrote—was like nothing an up-and-coming Oriole had ever endured. Ben McDonald was the Orioles' only No. 1 pick in 1989 and joined a pennant contender the same year he was drafted. Manny Machado, the third overall pick in 2010, was asked to play a different position and jump from Double A to a playoff team in 2012. Yet, because Wieters was a 6'5", 230-pound switch-hitting catcher with top defensive skills, offensive power, and leadership capabilities, he was the rarest of commodities. And he was treated that way. He fell to fifth in the draft because of perceived contract demands; rumors had been floated that Wieters and his representative, super-agent Scott Boras, were looking for an eight-figure bonus. Ultimately, Wieters agreed to a deal 10 minutes before the deadline on midnight of August 15. His $6 million bonus was the largest ever doled out by the Orioles.

Wieters didn't play pro ball until 2008, but he met all expectations, batting .355 with 27 homers and a 1.053 on-base-plus slugging percentage at High A and Double A that year. His performance earned him *Baseball America*'s Minor League Player of the Year Award—the only Oriole to ever win it. He was considered baseball's No. 1 prospect heading into 2009. The buzz didn't subside easily. *Sports Illustrated* featured him on the cover of its March 15, 2010 issue with the headline, "The Perfect Catch." In baseball circles he was being referred to as, "Mauer with Power," a reference to Minnesota Twins catcher Joe Mauer, the American League MVP in 2009. Then there was the website, mattwietersfacts.com, that posted exaggerations about Wieters' prowess, similar to the quips about martial arts master and actor Chuck Norris. A sampling from the website includes, "Matt Wieters once framed a pitch so perfectly that it counted as two strikes," "Scott Boras hired Matt Wieters as his agent," and "Chuck Norris jokes are based off stuff Matt Wieters actually did."

"I remember all that eyewash. He was the next big prospect, the Jesus Christ of baseball, the switch-hitting Joe Mauer. I remember all of that," said Orioles center fielder Adam Jones. "But one thing about Wieters is that the guy posts—every single day. He is doing one of the toughest jobs, catcher. But the way he goes about it, the way he takes a beating, the size of him. He is what I would want in a player, especially out of a catcher."

Wieters went hitless in his debut on May 29, 2009, but he served his first purpose. The announced crowd at Camden Yards that night was 42,704; it was estimated that more than 10,000 tickets were sold on the day of the game. That night's attendance was higher than the three previous contests at Camden Yards combined. Wieters picked up his first hit the next day in his sixth big league at-bat. It came against Detroit Tigers ace Justin Verlander. Most impressive, it was a triple. (In his next five seasons, the lumbering Wieters tripled just twice more.) That hit against Verlander perpetuated the hopes that this guy would one day lead the Orioles back to the playoffs. In a sense, he did. But he wasn't alone. He was surrounded by emerging talent, and that made a huge difference when the Orioles ended their postseason drought in 2012. "We were all young. When I came up guys like Nick [Markakis] and

Jonesy had a few years in, but we were still all young and learning together," Wieters said. "So it wasn't like, 'Okay, we are going to call up this young rookie and we're going to hope he's going to carry this team of veterans.' We were all learning together and we are all at similar stages in our careers."

By his second full season in 2011, Wieters was an All-Star and Gold Glover. He achieved the same accolades in 2012 and put together three straight seasons of 22 or more homers from 2011 to 2013, though his average dipped to a career low of .235 in 2013. Wieters rebounded with the best start of his career in 2014, hitting .308 with five homers and a .500 slugging percentage in 26 games. It looked like his offense had caught up to his defense, but Wieters was shut down with a right elbow injury in May that eventually required season-ending Tommy John surgery. The injury, which may have first occurred when he was a closer at Georgia Tech, robbed him of his second postseason in three seasons.

Instead of leaving the team and rehabbing on his own, Wieters returned after his surgery to experience the 2014 playoff run with his teammates. "When you have to sit out and watch, it hurts even more. I think being around the team definitely helped me," Wieters said. "I don't ever see myself being able to sit at home and watch on TV."

Orioles manager Buck Showalter said losing Wieters to injury was certainly an on-field blow. But having his presence and knowledge on the bench throughout the year was essential. "He's just been a consistent voice. You are looking for things that are the same. You don't want to wave around in the wind. Matt is a rock emotionally," Showalter said. "Teammates know where Matt is. They are not going to get, 'I don't want to talk to you today. I've had a bad day.' Matt's always on the even keel. But underneath that is a lot of emotion and a lot of toughness."

84 The Reign of Peter Angelos

No owner in Baltimore sports history has ridden the roller coaster of public opinion like Orioles managing partner Peter G. Angelos. He has been a savior, a pariah, and somewhere in between. Former Baltimore Colts owner Robert Irsay never had the peaks like Angelos; former Orioles owner Jerry Hoffberger never had the valleys. A brilliant trial lawyer who made a portion of his fortune in successful asbestos litigation, Angelos was a rags-to-riches triumph when he and a group of local investors purchased the team in August 1993 for $173 million. Baltimore was not yet a decade removed from Irsay sneaking the Colts to Indianapolis in the middle of the night. That was a gut-punch to the city, and the initial fear at the time was that Washington-based attorney Edward Bennett Williams may try to move his Orioles to the nation's capital. When Williams' estate sold the club in 1988 to New York financier Eli Jacobs, a lease for the yet-to-be-constructed Oriole Park at Camden Yards already was agreed upon. Still, Jacobs was viewed as another interloper. So when Angelos secured the club at bankruptcy auction, it marked the first time a Baltimore resident owned the Orioles since Hoffberger in the 1970s. Charm City rejoiced.

Born in Pittsburgh to Greek immigrants, Angelos was raised in blue-collar East Baltimore, where his father ran a tavern. Angelos went to the University of Baltimore's School of Law, was valedictorian of his class, and earned a reputation for defending the working man. In 1995 he received high marks for his refusal to employ replacement players during baseball's strike. He also was lauded for his keen interest in the team. He often talked to local media, speaking like a fan and even criticizing specific moves by Johnny Oates, the manager he inherited. Before the 1996 season, Angelos hired two successful baseball men who had been minor league teammates decades earlier in the Orioles farm system: general manager Pat Gillick and manager Davey Johnson. They were charged to return glory back to the sagging franchise and, with Angelos opening his checkbook, they did. The Orioles made the playoffs in 1996 for the first time in 13 years and then won the American League East and reached the American League Championship Series for the second consecutive season in 1997. But by then Angelos' public persona was changing.

In July 1996 Gillick intended to trade pitcher David Wells and outfielder Bobby Bonilla, but Angelos vetoed the separate deals, saying he owed it to the fan base to try and win. The Orioles rebounded and made the playoffs. Critics said that move embold-ened Angelos and led to more intense meddling; supporters say Angelos owned the team, and it was his prerogative to reject his employees' suggestions. The following year, in the Orioles' best season in a decade, Angelos' relationship with Johnson and Gillick continued to deteriorate. That November, Johnson resigned on the day he was named AL Manager of the Year in a dispute with Angelos.

They differed on the specifics of the rift, but, regardless, Johnson was gone. "Me and Gillick, we built that team and we put Baltimore back on the map, and [Angelos] was mad at me for doing it," Johnson said. "What kind of deal is that?" It was the second high-profile defection under Angelos; wildly popular but occasionally critical radio broadcaster Jon Miller was not retained after the 1996 season. Gillick left after his contract expired at the end of 1998, and a revolving door of managers and general manag-ers kept spinning. In a period of 14 losing seasons from 1998 to 2012, Angelos employed seven different managers and seven differ-ent front-office leaders. Angelos and his sons, John and Louis, were harshly criticized for the club's woeful performances and instability.

Although the Orioles were typically in the middle third of MLB payroll during the losing streak, Angelos was vilified for not spending more. When he did spend, those players underachieved. An anti-Angelos rally was held during a 2006 game at Camden Yards, and in 2009 *Sports Illustrated* named him as baseball's worst owner. By then Angelos had faded out of the public eye, rarely granting interviews and rarely seen publicly at Camden Yards despite still attending games in his private suite. "I felt like he got a really bad rap for a team that was losing," said former Orioles second baseman Brian Roberts. "That can't all be put on the owner."

In 2007 Angelos personally and clandestinely recruited and hired Andy MacPhail, a longtime baseball executive whose father once ran the Orioles. MacPhail, who had previously worked with Angelos during MLB labor negotiations, championed a rebuilding effort with an emphasis on restocking a depleted farm system. In 2010, with the endorsement of the owner, MacPhail hired proven manager Buck Showalter to take over on-field duties. MacPhail left amicably following the 2011 season, and Angelos hired Dan Duquette to be the club's new vice president. Showalter and Duquette led the Orioles to the playoffs in 2012 and again in 2014.

When Angelos entered the clubhouse following a 2012 playoff win, he was greeted enthusiastically by the players—with several lining up to meet him. Closer Jim Johnson presented the owner with a game ball from one of his franchise-record 51 saves. By 2014 Angelos' organization was thriving with a competitive payroll, a strong on-field product, a vibrant Camden Yards, and a regional TV network that was created as a concession to Angelos when the Washington Nationals moved into his territory in 2005. The octogenarian owner may never return to the hero status he held in 1993, but the club's rebound may have altered public sentiment toward him, at least somewhat. "He has a great heart, he takes care of his own, and that's what stands out to me. That

side of him that I know most people don't know or get to see,"
Roberts said. "It's been hard for him. Any time you hear people
bashing you, and it may be unwarranted, it's tough."

Alomar's Ugly Incident

In 2011 second baseman Roberto Alomar was elected to the
National Baseball Hall of Fame on his second try, representing the
Toronto Blue Jays, a club he played with for five seasons and led
to two World Series titles. Alomar spent just three seasons with the
Orioles but was arguably the best player on those star-studded 1996
and 1997 clubs that lost in the American League Championship
Series. And the most famous—and infamous—moment in Alomar's
wonderful career came as an Oriole: spitting in the face of umpire
John Hirschbeck. "That shouldn't define Robbie in any way," said
former Orioles outfielder Brady Anderson. "He had a bad 10 or 15
seconds."

With the Orioles needing a victory to make the playoffs, the
mild-mannered Alomar was batting in the first inning September
27, 1996 in Toronto. On a full count, Hirschbeck, the home-plate
umpire, called strike three on an outside fastball from Blue Jays
right-hander Paul Quantrill. Disgusted, Alomar griped about the
call. Hirschbeck told him to keep quiet, and, according to Anderson,
Alomar responded by saying, "Just play," as he was walking away.
But that was enough for Hirschbeck, who ejected Alomar. And the
ugliest on-field moment in Orioles history unfolded. Alomar and
Hirschbeck erupted in a war of words with Hirschbeck allegedly
hurling slurs at Alomar. Manager Davey Johnson stepped between

the two, but Alomar tilted his head and spit in the umpire's face. The vitriol continued afterward when Alomar said Hirschbeck had become increasingly bitter after one of his sons had died from Adrenoleukodystrophy (ALD) and another had been diagnosed with the terminal genetic disease. When Hirschbeck heard about the comments the next day, he charged into the Orioles clubhouse to find Alomar before being restrained by a fellow umpire.

Alomar was immediately suspended five games at the start of the following season, meaning he would be able to finish out 1996 and participate in the playoffs. The lenient punishment, which included a $50,000 fine to go toward ALD research, was heavily scrutinized in and out of the sporting world. It, however, was an important ruling for the Orioles. The next day in Toronto, Alomar hit a 10th inning homer to give them a 3–2 win, clinch the AL wild-card spot, and send the club to its first postseason appearance in 13 years.

The next April, Alomar and Hirschbeck shook hands before a game in a public show of reconciliation. They didn't really mend fences for another couple of years but have since bonded. Alomar has voluntarily donated money and given his support in the fight against ALD. Years later, when Hirschbeck was diagnosed with testicular cancer, Alomar immediately called to check in on him. In turn, Hirschbeck was a vocal supporter of Alomar's Hall of Fame candidacy. "Me and John are great friends. He forgave me. We keep talking as friends. I know his family. I know his kids," Alomar said. "At times it gets blown out of proportion, but we move on. I hope some people can move on the same way John and I did."

On the field, Alomar was a maestro with the glove and bat. He made the All-Star team in each of his three seasons with the Orioles, winning the All-Star Game MVP in 1998. He won two of his 10 Gold Gloves and one of his four Silver Slugger Awards as an Oriole. "At second base, he could make plays nobody could make. Super smooth, super coordinated, super intelligent. As a basestealer, unbelievable. As a baserunner, unbelievable," Anderson said. "He had a knowledge of the game and a skill for the game that few players have."

Alomar's .312 batting average is the highest mark for any Oriole in modern-franchise history with at least 1,200 at-bats. "He could almost will things to happen," said Buck Showalter, who managed against Alomar. "Okay, the club needs a home run here; there's a home run. Oh, I need a stolen base; here's a stolen base. He's also one of those guys that you swear he was hitting every inning."

Although it will forever be marked by the spitting incident, 1996 was one of the finest seasons of Alomar's 17-season, seven-team career. In the first two months, he batted .397. He ended up hitting .328 with a .938 on-base-plus-slugging percentage, 22 homers, 94 RBIs, and 17 steals, one of the best all-around years in club history. Really, he did everything in his first two seasons with the Orioles before having a down year by his standards in 1998. He left that offseason as a free agent and joined his brother, Sandy Jr., on the Cleveland Indians.

Alomar was inducted into the Orioles' Hall of Fame in 2013. During the announcement of that honor, he discussed the spitting incident. "I wish it wouldn't have happened," Alomar said. "It's a cloud that I have to live with."

86 Grand Slamming with Hoiles

There was no grand plan, no secret philosophy that made Orioles catcher Chris Hoiles so good when he came to the plate with the bases loaded. It was very much the opposite. "Guys get jacked up a little bit when they get in that situation and they start trying to do too much with the ball, and that's when they start getting into trouble. So I was just trying to simplify things, use the biggest part of the ballpark, try to hit a fly ball, and stay away from a ground ball that would lead to a potential double play because of lack of speed on my part. Take it as another at-bat. I think that's what helped me out mostly."

Hoiles spent parts of 10 seasons in the majors, all with the Orioles, before a degenerative left hip condition ended his career. He batted .262 with 151 homers, a .366 on-base percentage, and threw out 28 percent of would-be base stealers. Pitchers liked to throw to him because of his preparation and big target.

He was, by all accounts, a solid major league catcher. Load the bases, though, and he became something more: an RBI machine. In 77 plate appearances with the bases loaded, Hoiles drove in an impressive 75 runs. That includes six walks and 13 sacrifice flies while striking out just 12 times and hitting into only one double play. In 57 official at-bats, he hit .386 with a phenomenal .842 slugging percentage—the second best mark in an Orioles uniform behind only Hall of Famer Eddie Murray in statistics compiled since 1974. "I guess I never really stopped to think about it as far as the magnitude of what I actually did. I didn't even know I was second to Eddie Murray in that category. So to sit back and hear some of the stuff that's coming out years later after I retired, it makes me proud to be able to say I was able to do that in clutch situations."

Hoiles hit eight grand slams in his Orioles career, and his accomplishments with the bases juiced in two different games will follow him forever. The video board at Camden Yards shows Orioles' historic highlights during each homestand, and Hoiles is always featured—whether it's his walk-off grand slam to beat Norm Charlton and the Seattle Mariners on May 17, 1996 or his two-grand-slam game against the Cleveland Indians on August 14,

1998. Only seven Orioles have ever hit game-ending grand slams; only three have ever hit two grand slams in one game. Hoiles is the only Orioles player to do both. (Frank Robinson had a two-slam game for the Orioles and a walk-off grand slam for the Cincinnati Reds.) According to home run stats guru David Vincent, a two-slam day has happened only 13 times in baseball history, and three times an Oriole has done it: Jim Gentile in 1961 (in consecutive innings), Robinson in 1970 (also in consecutive innings), and Hoiles in 1998. "To even be mentioned in the same breath as Frank and Jim offensively with what they've done in the game and what they did for the Orioles is a huge honor on my side," Hoiles said. "When I hit it, I was the ninth one [in MLB history], and the Orioles had three of them at that time. When I heard that it made it even more special."

The game at Camden Yards against the Mariners in 1996 was a wild one. The Orioles had leads of 7–2 and 9–6, but Seattle scored five runs in the eighth, capped by an Alex Rodriguez grand slam against Alan Mills. The Orioles got one back in the bottom of the eighth, but a Jay Buhner two-run homer against Mills made it 13–10 heading into the bottom of the ninth. With two on and two out, Charlton walked Cal Ripken Jr. to load the bases for Hoiles. With a full count, Hoiles launched a split-finger fastball several rows into the left-field seats for a stunning 14–13 victory in a not-so-tidy four hours and 20 minutes. It was the 42nd hit of the night. "I remember it was a long-ass game first and foremost," Hoiles said. "I understood the magnitude of it, of scoring four runs and winning the game for us as a team. But I didn't quite understand the magnitude historically at the time. I think the biggest thing was just helping the team win a ballgame."

His performance in Cleveland two years later wasn't nearly as dramatic. His third-inning grand slam against Charles Nagy gave the Orioles a 7–1 lead. "Charles at that time was pretty nasty, but

Slamming Company

Players with Two Grand Slams in Same Game

Name/*Team*/Date
Tony Cloninger *Atlanta Braves* (07/03/1966)
Nomar Garciaparra *Boston Red Sox* (05/10/1999)
Jim Gentile *Baltimore Orioles* (05/09/1961)
Chris Hoiles *Baltimore Orioles* (08/14/1998)
Tony Lazzeri *New York Yankees* (05/24/1936)
Bill Mueller *Boston Red Sox* (07/29/2003)
Jim Northrup *Detroit Tigers* (06/24/1968)
Frank Robinson *Baltimore Orioles* (06/26/1970)
Jim Tabor *Boston Red Sox* (07/04/1939) Game 2
Fernando Tatis *St. Louis Cardinals* (04/23/1999)
Robin Ventura *Chicago White Sox* (09/04/1995)
Josh Willingham *Washington Nationals* (07/27/2009)
Rudy York *Boston Red Sox* (07/27/1946)

Game-Ending Grand Slams for the Orioles

Date/**Name**/*Versus*/Score
(07/07/1970) **Brooks Robinson** against *New York Yankees* 6–2
(05/22/1976) **Ken Singleton** against *Detroit Tigers* 8–4
(08/08/1982) **Terry Crowley** against *Kansas City Royals* 10–6
(08/24/1982) **Joe Nolan** against *Toronto Blue Jays* 7–3
(05/17/1996) **Chris Hoiles** against *Seattle Mariners* 14–13
(05/04/1999) **Harold Baines** against *Chicago White Sox* 9–5
(04/18/2013) **Matt Wieters** against *Tampa Bay Rays* 10–6

Players Who Have Hit Two Grand Slams in One Game and Ended Another Game with a Grand Slam

Name/*Team*/Date of Two Grand Slams/Date of Game-Ending Slam
Nomar Garciaparra *Boston Red Sox* (05/10/1999, 09/02/1998)
Chris Hoiles *Baltimore Orioles* (08/14/1998, 05/17/1996)
Jim Northrup *Detroit Tigers* (06/24/1968, 05/17/1968)
Frank Robinson *Baltimore Orioles* (06/26/1970,) *Cincinnati Reds* (08/20/1962)
Robin Ventura *Chicago White Sox* (09/04/1995, 07/20/1991)

I was just looking for a ball to drive, and he hung a split-fingered fastball and I got all of it and I was able to drive it halfway up the left-center field bleachers at Jacobs Field," he said. The Orioles were up 11–2 in the eighth when Hoiles faced Ron Villone in the same situation. He jumped on a full-count fastball and jacked it down the left-field line. "Even though the game was handily out of reach, as a hitter you don't want to throw at-bats away. So I didn't have any other thought except to drive in maybe another run or two and keep the same philosophy as I always did with the bases loaded," Hoiles said.

That game was particularly special. Hoiles grew up in Ohio, about two hours from Cleveland, so he had his own cheering section; he estimates between 30 and 40 friends and family members were there. Plus, Hoiles had been dealing with the hip issue for a while and knew his career might be inching toward the end. He homered just three more times in his career after that night. So to deliver that kind of performance in chronic pain was especially rewarding. When pushed on the subject, Hoiles said he probably would take the two grand slams over the walk-off because it meant he came through twice in a big way for his team.

The answer doesn't surprise those who played with Hoiles. "He's just a humble guy. He never talks about himself. He's an ole country guy, a simple guy that could play. You'd never know all the stuff he has done just by talking to him," said former Orioles starter Bob Milacki. "I mean you couldn't not like this guy. And the type of hitter he was on top of that just made him all the better."

87 Eddie Murray's Timely 500th Home Run

You have to forgive Hall of Famer Eddie Murray for initially not knowing the exact day in which his buddy Cal Ripken Jr. broke Lou Gehrig's hallowed consecutive games played streak. Murray was with the Cleveland Indians when Ripken made international news on September 6, 1995, by playing in his 2,131st consecutive game.

The following July, the Orioles traded for the 40-year-old Murray. Although those 1996 Orioles benefited from Murray's leadership and his switch-hitting presence at designated hitter, the trade was also clearly a strong public relations move. Murray had starred with the Orioles for 12 seasons, but the club was rebuilding after the disastrous 1988 campaign, and Murray's relationship with Baltimore and its fans had soured. So before the 1989 season, Murray was dealt to the Los Angeles Dodgers for a package of three players who never made an impact with the Orioles.

By the summer of 1996, Murray wanted out of Cleveland, and the Orioles wanted him to hit his milestone 500th home run in their uniform. On July 21 the Orioles shipped pitcher Kent Mercker to the Indians for Murray, who was nine short of 500 at that time. He hit eight more homers for the Orioles heading into September and was temporarily stuck at 499 when the Orioles began a homestand on September 6. Murray arrived at the Camden Yards clubhouse that afternoon with a feeling that he would be hitting No. 500 against the Detroit Tigers in front of the home fans. He shared his prediction with Ripken. "That particular afternoon I remember nobody really talked to me. I came in, and the first thing I told Cal was, 'I'm going to do it tonight,'" Murray said. "He goes, 'What?' I said, 'I'm going deep tonight.'"

That was the end of the conversation. Ripken was going to let Murray figure it out himself that the date already held certain significance for the organization and its fans. The two Orioles went out to the field together for warm-ups that afternoon, and Murray did his first wind sprint. He then looked up toward the Camden Yards video scoreboard. "And they've got Rip up on the board. September 6th. I go, 'Oh, hell no.' And he goes, 'Yep, you already said it,'" Murray said. So not only was Murray on record with his pal that he was going to hit a homer, but also he had the pressure of trying to do it on the initial anniversary of Ripken's record-breaking consecutive games feat.

And the task got a little trickier as the night wore on. The remnants of Hurricane Fran made their way up the East Coast, delaying the game for about two hours and 20 minutes. The crowd was announced at 46,708, but roughly half had left by the time Murray stepped up to the plate in the seventh inning against right-hander Felipe Lira. Murray hit a first-pitch, split-fingered fastball into the right-field bleachers above the grounds crew shed to become the third player in baseball history and first switch-hitter to

Orioles' connections to 500th home runs

Players Who Hit No. 500 as an Oriole
Frank Robinson versus Detroit's Fred Scherman at Memorial Stadium—*September 13, 1971*
Eddie Murray versus Detroit's Felipe Lira at Camden Yards—*September 6, 1996*

Players Who Hit No. 500 Against the Orioles
New York Yankee **Mickey Mantle** versus Stu Miller at Yankee Stadium—*May 14, 1967*
Minnesota Twin **Harmon Killebrew** versus Mike Cuellar at Metropolitan Stadium—*August, 10, 1971*
Boston Red Sox **Manny Ramirez** versus Chad Bradford at Camden Yards—*May 31, 2008*

have at least 500 home runs and 3,000 hits. The homer tied a game in which the Orioles eventually lost after 2:00 AM in 12 innings. But Murray kept his promise to Ripken by 13 minutes; his homer left the yard at 11:47 PM on September 6.

Murray knew the homer was coming, but the Psychic Friends Network didn't have such prescience. The fan who caught the 500th home run ball reportedly sold it for $280,000 to Baltimore businessman Michael Lasky, who had started the Psychic Friends Network of 1990s infomercial fame. "Obviously, his company wasn't that good or he wasn't that good or otherwise he would have had somebody sitting there [waiting for the homer]," Murray joked in 2014.

The ball landed in Section 96, Row 7, Seat 23. We know this because—to commemorate Murray's home run—that seat is now the rare orange seat in a sea of green. It is one of only two seats in the ballpark that are orange. The other is in the left-field bleachers—section 86, Row FF, Seat No. 10—and is where Ripken hit his 278th homer as a shortstop on July 15, 1993, passing Ernie Banks for first on the all-time list at the position.

Murray's milestone dinger was the second of three 500th career home runs achieved in Baltimore. The first was September 13, 1971 at Memorial Stadium and was hit by Oriole right fielder and Hall of Famer Frank Robinson. It was similar to Murray's in that it was against the Tigers, wasn't accomplished until late into the night, and not a whole lot of people were there to witness it—or at least not as many who claim to have been there.

Robinson's blast to left field against Tigers left-hander Fred Scherman occurred with two outs in the bottom of the ninth in the second game of a doubleheader—roughly around 11:45 PM. The announced crowd was a paltry 13,292, and certainly all of them didn't stick around for the ninth inning of a blowout that Detroit won 10–5.

289

The other 500th home run hit in Baltimore was by Boston slugger Manny Ramirez against the Orioles on May 31, 2008 in the seventh inning of a 6–3 Red Sox victory. Ramirez hit the first pitch from Orioles submariner Chad Bradford into the right-field stands at Camden Yards.

Fan Favorites

Thousands of players have worn Orioles uniforms throughout the years, and it's impossible to give them all their own chapters. Here are some who had an impact on the field and a strong connection with the fans off of it.

Harold Baines

Owning one of baseball's sweetest swings, the left-handed designated hitter batted .301 in parts of seven seasons with the Orioles during an illustrious 22-season career in which he compiled 2,866 hits. A native of Easton, Maryland, he went to St. Michael's High School.

Steve Barber

The hard-throwing lefty was the club's first 20-game winner (1963) and a member of the Kiddie Korps that energized the Orioles in the early 1960s. It didn't hurt that he was a local product, too: a native of Takoma Park, Maryland.

Don Baylor

The club knew what they had in the intense, power-hitting outfielder who was supposed to be a building block. But the temptation to land Reggie Jackson was too much. So the Orioles traded Baylor to the Oakland A's in 1976. He became the American League MVP for the California Angels in 1979.

Mike Boddicker

There was nothing special about his repertoire, but Boddicker sure could pitch. With his foshball, a screwbally change-up, Boddicker is the club's last 20-game winner (1984). His departure in 1988 also helped: he was dealt to the Boston Red Sox for Brady Anderson and Curt Schilling.

Mike Bordick

The pride of Maine, Bordick is forever known as the guy who moved Cal Ripken Jr. to third base. Ripken endorsed the switch because he respected Bordick's defensive abilities and work ethic. In 2002 Bordick set a record for consecutive errorless games at short with 110.

Don Buford

He was a man without a position, but he became one of baseball's best leadoff hitters. The speedy, 5'7" Buford settled in at left field and scored 99 runs on three straight World Series teams. In 1969 he became the first player to open a World Series with a homer.

Wally Bunker

The right-hander won 19 games at age 19 in 1964, the year the city's mayor proclaimed the Memorial Stadium mound, "Baltimore's Bunker Hill." At 21 he threw a complete-game shutout in the 1966 World Series, but arm trouble ended his career at 26.

Terry Crowley

An outfielder by trade, Crow made his living getting big hits. His career average was .250, but he hit .295 with a .390 on-base percentage in "high leverage" situations and had 109 career pinch-hits. As a longtime Orioles hitting coach, he was called "The King of Swing."

Rich Dauer
A first-round draft pick in 1974, Dauer hit just .257 with 43 homers in 10 seasons, all with the Orioles. But he was a gritty second baseman whose three RBIs led the Orioles to a Game 4 victory in the 1983 World Series.

Mike Devereaux
The slick fielding center fielder routinely scaled walls for jaw-dropping defensive plays. He could hit, too. In 1992 he had career highs in homers (24) and RBIs (107). His "fair or foul" homer in July of 1989 is among the most famous shots in club history.

Andy Etchebarren
A career .235 hitter, Etch caught in four World Series and was a two-time All-Star. He also dove into a swimming pool and pulled out a potentially drowning Frank Robinson. (See sidebar.) And he owned the thickest, most distinctive eyebrows in club history.

Jay Gibbons
The red-haired slugger with the Popeye arms and quick wit was one of the brightest spots during the Orioles' dark years in the 2000s. He couldn't have been more gracious to fans, but his image took a hit when he was named in the Mitchell Report as a steroid user.

Bobby Grich
His best offensive years came with the California Angels, but Grich made his early mark as an Oriole. In seven seasons in Baltimore, Grich won four Gold Glove Awards and the hearts of young female fans, who loved the Southern Californian's surfer good looks.

J.J. Hardy

It took two unheralded pitchers to acquire Hardy, who was coming off injury in 2010. He became a Gold Glover and Silver Slugger and signed two extensions to remain an Oriole. Public address announcer Ryan Wagner's "J...J...HAR-DEEE" is a staple at Camden Yards.

Catching Frank

Andy Etchebarren spent a dozen years behind the plate for the Orioles, but his greatest catch may have been at a private pool party in August of 1966. The team had gathered at the home of Leonard Ruck, a local funeral home director who was good friends with pitcher Steve Barber. It was an off day, and the team was partying together when players started throwing each other in the pool, which went from a shallow three feet to five feet to nine feet quickly.

Star outfielder Frank Robinson, who had just joined the Orioles in a trade from the Cincinnati Reds months earlier, had switched from regular clothes to swim trunks because he didn't want to get thrown into the pool. He went in himself and was wading in the shallow end, when it suddenly dropped off. Robinson didn't know how to swim.

Etchebarren and second baseman Davey Johnson were on the side of the pool when they saw Robinson struggling. "I just saw him down there, saw him thrashing his hands, but I didn't know he couldn't swim," Etchebarren said. "So I went to get him, and the first time he grabbed me around the neck and I wasn't ready for that."

Etchebarren said he pushed away from Robinson, went up for air, got his breath, and went back down again for the future Hall of Famer. He knew Robinson wasn't messing around. Etchebarren, with some help from Johnson and others, dragged Robinson out of the pool safely. "He wasn't in good shape. He was laying on the side of the pool, coughing up water," Etchebarren said. "But he ended up making it, thank God."

At least one Oriole didn't see the incident unfold. Earlier, first baseman Boog Powell had attempted to throw reliever Moe Drabowsky into the pool. Powell slipped, hit his head, and received a gash above his right eye. He went to the hospital to get it stitched up.

Six weeks later the Orioles were world champions for the first time.

Dennis Martinez

The majors' first Nicaraguan, Martinez never fully realized his potential in Baltimore, partially because of alcohol addiction. He turned his life around and compiled 245 wins, including a perfect game for the 1991 Montreal Expos. He's been warmly welcomed back.

Billy O'Dell

A two-time All-Star in five seasons with the Orioles, the left-hander was wildly cheered when he entered the 1958 All-Star Game at Memorial Stadium. He threw three perfect innings for the save. No other Oriole has pitched in an All-Star Game at home. (Sorry, Mike Mussina.)

Joe Orsulak

He was your solid, average ballplayer, but he played as if his hair was on fire, and fans loved him for that. Orsulak took the extra base, threw out runners, and laid out for catches in the outfield. In five seasons with the Orioles, he hit 35 homers, stole 31 bases, and batted .281.

Brian Roberts

The ultimate baseball rat, the little second baseman was the son of a collegiate baseball coach. He turned himself into a two-time All-Star, a tremendous leadoff man, and the most popular Oriole before injuries and his Mitchell Report inclusion became part of his legacy.

B.J. Surhoff

No one competed harder than Surhoff, who had 2,326 career hits despite dealing with injuries at the end of his career. He was an understated cog on the great teams of the mid-1990s and gained fan bonus points for breaking down publicly when he was traded away in 2000.

Miguel Tejada
One of the most talented and energetic Orioles ever, his 150-RBI season in 2004 stands as a club record. But there was always drama following the shortstop, whether it was demanding a trade or the swirling steroid accusations punctuated by the Mitchell Report.

Breaking the Color Barrier

When Joe Durham was a 23-year-old rookie outfielder for the Orioles in September 1954, he made just one road trip: to Chicago, where he stayed in one hotel while his teammates were in another. As the club's only African American ballplayer at that time and the second to play for the new franchise, Durham said he didn't worry about segregation, even in the big leagues. "It didn't bother me because I was always a person that went along with the punches," Durham said. "I did what I had to do. I came to play baseball and not to be some political, outspoken person."

Besides, Durham said, he was familiar with the blacks-only Evans Hotel; he had stayed there while he was a member of the Chicago American Giants of the Negro Leagues. That's who Durham played for before signing a minor league deal prior to the 1953 season with the St. Louis Browns and owner Bill Veeck. When Veeck was forced to sell the franchise, the Browns moved to Baltimore, and Durham became an Orioles farmhand, making his major league debut on September 10, 1954. He said he had no problems with his Orioles teammates or the Memorial Stadium fans. "It was fine. I think I was accepted by most of the players," Durham said. "I didn't have any transportation to get to and from the ballpark, so I'd go down Pennsylvania Avenue and my man [pitcher] Don Larsen would pick me up and take me to the stadium. We all got along just fine."

Durham wasn't the first African American to play for the Orioles; that distinction goes to left-handed pitcher Jehosie "Jay" Heard, a former World War II veteran who played in the Negro Leagues for the Birmingham Barons, among other clubs. Heard, who was listed at 5'7", 155 pounds, won 16 games for the open classification Portland Beavers in 1953 and had his contract purchased by the Orioles in the December before their first season in Baltimore.

Heard was with the big league club to start the 1954 season but pitched only twice. The 34-year-old broke the Orioles' color barrier and made his major league debut by retiring all four batters he faced in relief during a blowout loss to the Chicago White Sox on April 24. He didn't pitch again for more than a month, finally facing the White Sox at Memorial Stadium on May 28. He allowed five earned runs in two innings, including a grand slam to Chicago third baseman Cass Michaels in the first game of a doubleheader. Heard never pitched in the majors again; he was sent back to the Pacific Coast League and never returned. He played three more years in the minors, including two seasons with the Havana Sugar Kings, a Cincinnati Reds affiliate, in Cuba before retiring. He died in Birmingham, Alabama, in 1999.

The Orioles could have had a much higher profile pitcher break their color barrier. Hall of Famer Leroy "Satchel" Paige pitched in 57 games and made four starts for the St. Louis Browns in 1953, posting a respectable 3.53 ERA at age 46, though he may have been older than his listed age. Paige had a close relationship with Veeck, and when Veeck sold the team, Paige was out of a job. The sense was that the new club in Baltimore didn't want their first black player to be as flamboyant as Paige, one of the great characters in baseball history. It would have been his second turn

Baseball Hall of Famers Who Played in the Negro Leagues in Baltimore

Roy Campanella—Baltimore Elite Giants
Leon Day—Baltimore Black Sox
Pete Hill—Baltimore Black Sox
Biz Mackey—Baltimore Black Sox and Baltimore Elite Giants
Satchel Paige—Baltimore Black Sox
Mule Suttles—Baltimore Black Sox
Ben Taylor—Baltimore Black Sox
Willie Wells—Baltimore Elite Giants
Jud Wilson—Baltimore Black Sox

in Baltimore. He pitched for the Baltimore Black Sox of the Negro Leagues in 1930.

Durham played in 10 games for the Orioles in 1954, getting his first hit in his September 10 debut with a single in the bottom of the ninth off Washington's Mickey McDermott. Durham then scored his first big league run—a game-winner—on a RBI single by Frank Kellert.

Durham's first home run—the first by an African American Orioles player—came in the sixth inning of the second game of a doubleheader at Memorial Stadium on September 12. When he hit it against Philadelphia Athletics lefty Al Sima, Durham said he thought it would go out. But he said he never considered it would be a watershed moment. "I didn't realize the significance of that home run when I hit it," Durham said. "But I had a great feeling rounding the bases."

After the game Durham said a woman was waiting to give him the home run ball, which he still has 60 years later. Durham spent the next two years in the U.S. Army, then returned to the Orioles in 1957, but never felt like he got a fair shake from manager Paul Richards. Playing sparingly, he batted just .185 in 177 plate appearances over 77 games. He spent six games in 1959 with the

St. Louis Cardinals as a Rule 5 pick but was sent back to the Orioles. He never returned to the big leagues after that, remaining with the organization for years as a minor league player and coach and member of the front office.

Durham and Heard paved the way for an organization that has had several African American stars over the years, including Frank Robinson, Paul Blair, Eddie Murray, Ken Singleton, and Adam Jones. Baltimore's connection with great African American ballplayers, however, reaches beyond the Orioles. Baltimore hosted two Negro League teams, the Black Sox from 1916 to 1934 and the Elite Giants from 1938 to 1950. Hall of Famers who called Baltimore home during those years included Paige, Roy Campanella, and Leon Day.

90 Leading the League in Babies

As good as Melvin Mora was in his 10 seasons with the Orioles, including hitting a franchise-best .340 in 2004, his most incredible statistic is in life: five babies, all at once. "I don't know if I laughed, if I cried, if I was jumping up," Mora said about when he first learned his wife, Gisel, was pregnant with quintuplets in 2001. "One thing I know is I was checking my wallet to see if I could take care of all those kids." When the Moras married, they knew they wanted a big family. Fatherhood was important to Mora, whose dad was killed in Venezuela when Mora was just a young boy. Gisel already had four-year-old Tatiana from a previous marriage, but she had had difficulty getting pregnant that time. So the couple decided, after six months without results, Gisel would try fertility drugs. The Moras knew multiple births were a possibility; they just weren't prepared to hit the infant lottery.

On July 28, 2001, while Mora was in Anaheim, California, with his team, he received a 3:00 AM phone call. Gisel was going into labor three months prematurely. She had had premature labor before, but this time doctors at Johns Hopkins Hospital felt they needed to deliver—and deliver immediately. It was a risky proposition. The babies would be tiny; the survival rate for all five was not encouraging. "I expected to be in the hospital with her when she delivered the babies," Mora said. "It was difficult because I wasn't there." After a cross country flight, he arrived at his wife's hospital room to find incubators everywhere and 20 members of the medical staff working. Then he heard laughter. "It made me relax," he said. "Everyone was fine."

That was just the beginning of the battle. The five children—girls Genesis, Rebekah, and Jada and boys Matthew and Christian—were between one-and-a-half and two-and-a-half pounds. Mora could slip his size 11 NLCS title ring to the shoulder of each infant. All five were placed in the neonatal intensive care unit and would remain in hospitals for months. There were feeding tubes and respirators. There were infections, lung complications, and surgery to repair a hole in Christian's small intestine. It was an ordeal times five. All the while, Mora was playing baseball, trying to make a lasting impression on a team he had just joined the previous year after being traded by the New York Mets. "You'd get no rest and then you'd have to face a pitcher like Pedro Martinez or Andy Pettitte," Mora said. "You have to be strong mentally and physically to face those guys. For me, mentally I was strong, but physically I was weak. I'd have to go to certain places in the clubhouse to try to get some sleep for maybe a half an hour [before games] if I could."

By that offseason the children were home. Physically and developmentally, they were on track for a normal life—or as normal as the lives of quintuplets who are the children of a major league ballplayer could be. The five—and their big sister—became celebrities at Camden Yards, wearing matching Mora T-shirts and being carted around in a humongous stroller. As the infants grew into toddlers and pre-schoolers, Mora emerged as one of the best players on the Orioles. His average jumped from .233 in 2002 to .317 in 2003, when he made his first All-Star team. After bouncing around the infield and outfield, he was given the third-base job at the start of 2004 and flourished offensively and defensively. His .340 average that year stands as a franchise record. "To see him come out and do his job the way he did, especially during those first few months when he was spending the night at the hospital and not getting much sleep and taking care of his wife and the kids, I have so much respect for him and the way he handled it and the way he embraced the community," said Mora's longtime teammate, Brian Roberts. "That's really what people want their guys, their players, to do. To feel like part of the city. Not everybody can do that, but Melvin, he was incredible."

Mora, who last played in the majors in 2011, lives in Fallston, Maryland, with his wife and a half-dozen teenagers. He said it's not as bad as it sounds. "It's fun. My wife makes sure they are really organized. When it's time to go to bed, everybody goes to bed. Nobody stays behind. We put everybody on the same schedule, and they have made our lives easy." When he ponders his baseball career, he thinks the frightening uncertainty in 2001 allowed him to become a better player. "When the hurricane passes, you can do whatever you want to do. My pressure [in baseball] was gone after my kids were born," he said. "I didn't know if they would survive or not. So when I went through that, I knew I could get through anything. I thought playing baseball was tough. No, having kids in an incubator in a hospital—that's tough."

91 Two Games Against Cuba

It was the ultimate spring training road trip. In March 1999 the Orioles played primarily in Florida, with one exception: a game in Havana against a Cuban All-Star team on March 28. It was the first time a major league squad had played in Cuba since 1959, when communist dictator Fidel Castro took over the country. Orioles managing partner Peter G. Angelos had tried multiple times to arrange a home-and-home baseball exhibition with Cuba, but his requests were rejected. In 1999 travel restrictions to Cuba were eased under the Clinton administration, and Angelos secured permission to go. The organization had three weeks to make the trip happen. Roughly a week before their regular season opener, the Orioles stepped off chartered planes in Havana. "Once you landed you didn't know what you were going to get yourself into or what was waiting for us when we got there," said catcher Chris Hoiles. "But once we got there and noticed their culture and noticed how well-received we were, it was really a cool experience." Hoiles said he remembers walking into a compound with Castro present and armed officers everywhere. "Being able to shake Castro's hand and meet all of his people, it was cool in one aspect," Hoiles said. "But it was very unnerving in another because they're dressed in full military uniforms with pistols on their belts."

Shortstop Mike Bordick said once the game began—the Orioles won 3–2 on a RBI single by Harold Baines in the top of the 11th inning before a crowd of about 50,000—it was business as usual. But as part of the pregame pageantry, Castro, followed by several assistants carrying large briefcases, greeted the Orioles at the visiting dugout. Bordick said there were rumors that the man was a

Castro double and the briefcases held machine guns. Later, Castro sat in the stands between Angelos and baseball commissioner Bud Selig. The Orioles treated the game as a season tune-up. Right-hander Scott Erickson, one of the club's top starters, allowed one run in seven innings. The lineup was representative, though it was missing superstar Cal Ripken Jr., who remained in the U.S. due to the death of his father. Pitcher Juan Guzman, a Miami resident, asked for and received permission to skip the trip. "It was at the point in spring training where guys were starting to get their timing and everything and wanted the challenge of playing against a quality opponent," Bordick said. "We wanted to go show that we were a real good team and represent Major League Baseball and the country. There was a lot of pride in that, and you could tell."

That wasn't the case for the second game, played on May 3, a misty night in Baltimore. It was supposed to be an Orioles off day, and the team, already in last place in its division at 7–17, wasn't thrilled with the timing. "It's really hard to throw an exhibition game into the heart of a season. You can't afford for a guy to get hurt. Every game matters. I think a lot of guys kind of felt that way," Bordick said. "You still wanted to put your best foot forward and compete. Unfortunately, I don't know that everybody was on the same page like we were in spring training." An announced crowd of 47,940—not including anti-Castro protesters outside of Camden Yards—witnessed a lackluster 12–6 loss to the Cuban All-Stars. The Orioles started right-hander Scott Kamieniecki, who was on the disabled list with a strained hamstring and hadn't pitched in the big leagues since the previous August. None of the club's top seven pitchers appeared in the contest. The Orioles' starting first baseman was rookie Calvin Pickering, who hadn't yet played in the majors that season. He made three errors. Surly right fielder Albert Belle waged a silent protest, not swinging at 11 straight pitches at one point. He chose not to shake hands with the giddy Cuban team afterward.

The contrast in enthusiasm was stark—especially when designated hitter Andy Morales hit a ninth-inning home run, waving his arms high in the air and blowing kisses to the exhilarated Cuban fans as he rounded the bases. The second most memorable moment was when Cuban umpire Cesar Valdez body-slammed a protester who ran onto the field. For days after the game, the Orioles were criticized by the media and players—including New York Yankees stars David Cone and Mariano Rivera—for not giving a better showing. "I remember it just being a tough situation," Bordick said. "I remember getting heat from other players about it being embarrassing." Initially, nothing came from the diplomatic venture except that it was a showcase for Cuba's love and commitment to baseball. In December 2014, however, President Obama re-opened diplomatic relations with Cuba. And the Orioles' 1999 trip was referenced as an historic venture and important cultural exchange. "We saw how baseball is a huge sport over there," Hoiles said. "And now we have seen some of the players that have left Cuba and have come over here and have made a huge splash in Major League Baseball."

92 Attend Opening Day

My mother and father, like most parents, always put an emphasis on education. Unless you were really sick—and I mean lighting-up-the-thermometer sick—you were going to school. It was the kids' responsibility, and my parents made almost no exceptions. They weren't buying any excuses—except for one day in early April each year; that's when my parents looked the other way. Playing hooky on the Orioles' Opening Day was tolerated in my household and pretty much throughout Maryland.

The baseball home opener in Baltimore is an unofficial holiday. Good luck filling your classrooms or getting full production out of your workforce. Every year—even when the Orioles are terrible— Opening Day is a shoulder-to-shoulder celebration. In Camden Yards' history, there's never been a season opener that wasn't a sellout. Partially it's tradition; partially it's that the Orioles do the festivities right—with balloons and fireworks and, at times in the past, flyovers by fighter planes.

One of the Oriole-specific traditions is always a hit with the fans—and a moment of brief panic for the players. Each year the Orioles roll out an orange carpet from the warning track to the infield, and the players run down it as each is introduced. It gives the fans a way to show their appreciation to each individual, though a couple players have been booed during those introductions over the years. The players aren't as concerned about the fan reaction as they are about the possibility of tripping on the carpet, tumbling onto the field and making sports blooper highlights for eternity. Several Orioles warned rookie infielder Jonathan Schoop about that potential catastrophe before 2014's Opening Day, and he said, despite his excitement, he was planning to be very careful while completing the run. Orioles manager Buck Showalter joked afterward that he viewed Schoop's entrance on the orange carpet differently: "I think Jon was floating on it. He didn't have to worry about tripping."

First pitch on Opening Day normally doesn't occur until 3:05 PM, which gives fans plenty of time to get "prepared" for the festivities. Although pretty much all restaurants and watering holes around downtown are packed on Opening Day, the place to be is Washington Boulevard, just beyond left field. Pickles Pub and Sliders Bar and Grille are the traditional meeting spots for thousands of fans. Pickles, at 520 Washington Boulevard, states it's only "a home run away," while Sliders, at 504 Washington Boulevard, has estimated it is 771 feet from home plate. Good luck getting inside either bar on Opening Day. But the street in front of both is shut down and replaced by tents where you can buy drinks and witness a sea of people in black and orange eager to see the first home W of the season.

Manny Machado

From the moment in 2010 when the Orioles drafted the fresh-faced kid from a tiny private school in Miami, there was a certain buzz in Baltimore. Think for a moment about some of the Orioles shortstops over the years: Rookie of the Year Ron Hansen, Hall of Famer Luis Aparicio, eight-time Gold Glove winner Mark Belanger, Hall of Famer Cal Ripken Jr., sure-handed All-Star Mike Bordick, former MVP Miguel Tejada, and Gold Glover and Silver Slugger J.J. Hardy. The shortstop lineage is impressive. Yet when the Orioles selected 17-year-old Manny Machado with the third pick—the second highest in franchise history behind only No. 1 overall Ben McDonald in 1989—he came with more hype than any of his predecessors.

The anticipation was that Machado would move through the system quickly and could make an impact before he was 21. And he did that—with a twist. In 2012, with the Orioles attempting to make their first postseason in 15 years, the Orioles were set at shortstop with Hardy. But they had a major hole defensively at third base with Wilson Betemit and Mark Reynolds fumbling their way through the position. So the Orioles made an unconventional move. They promoted the 20-year-old Machado from Double A Bowie to play third base in a pennant race, though he was hitting

Third baseman Manny Machado, who patrols the corner as well as anyone in the game, displays his deft fielding during a 2014 contest against the St. Louis Cardinals.

just .266 and had played only two games at the position in his pro career—both at Bowie in 2012.

Adam Jones admitted he and his teammates initially were a little surprised by the promotion. "He wasn't down there just tearing the cover off the ball," the Orioles center fielder said. "But down in the minors, it's not all about the numbers. There are guys down there that hit .350 that never get up here, and there are guys that hit .260 and come up here. It is the approach and the attitude that he took toward the game that is the reason he got called up so early. He understood what we were doing and he just fit himself right onto this team. And he has turned himself into a hell of a ballplayer and a big part of our mission."

It's fair to say Machado wasn't intimidated by the bright lights. He was called up August 9, 2012, and made his debut that night with two hits, including a triple in his second big league at-bat against Kansas City Royals left-hander Will Smith. That was an appetizer. In his second Orioles game, Machado homered in consecutive innings against Kansas City right-hander Luke Hochevar. Just 35 days after his 20th birthday, Machado became the youngest player in major league history to hit multiple homers in either his first or second major league game. He's the youngest to have a multi-homer night for the Orioles. Jones pushed Machado out of the dugout for a curtain call that night. "It was the best feeling ever," Machado said. "The crowd here loves me, and for them to support me like that after my first home run, it just felt great." Said Orioles manager Buck Showalter: "It's one of those nights that you're really honored and lucky just to watch. I look at it more from a city of Baltimore standpoint. He'll put it behind him and realize there's another challenge tomorrow."

Machado answered every challenge in 2012, playing great defense at his new position and hitting .262 with seven homers in 191 regular season at-bats. He also hit a home run in the postseason against the New York Yankees. His first full year in the majors was even more impressive. In 2013, he batted .283 with 14 homers and an American League-best 51 doubles, but it was his defense that catapulted him into stardom. He won the AL Gold Glove at third base and the AL Platinum Glove for best defender at any position. He seemingly made a jaw-dropping play every night. His best was on July 7 in Yankee Stadium when he actually bobbled a grounder into foul territory and then unleashed a rocket while nearing the stands to get Luis Cruz running to first. MLB.com named it the play of the year for 2013. "Opponents get wowed by it, but we see it all the time," Jones said. "There's nothing that really amazes me anymore. But I take ground balls with him sometimes at third and I can't really explain it, just how smooth he really is. It's a pleasure to see over there at third base."

With the pleasure, though, also has come some pain. On September 23, 2013, Machado collapsed while running to first base at Tropicana Field. He tore the medial patellofemoral ligament in his left knee, ending his season. He needed surgery to repair it and missed the first month of the 2014 regular season. He struggled some in his return but was starting to regain his form when he was involved in two incidents in June with the Oakland A's. On Friday, June 6, 2014, he jawed with Oakland third baseman Josh Donaldson after Donaldson made a hard—but clean—tag on Machado, who stumbled to the ground. Two games later A's reliever Fernando Abad threw two consecutive pitches inside at Machado; the second time Machado flung his bat, and it landed near third base. Benches cleared, but no fight ensued. Machado was ejected and ultimately suspended five games. Initially, he said the bat slipped from his hands, but later he apologized publicly for the incident. When he returned from suspension, he immediately started hitting and playing great defense.

Disaster struck again, though, on August 11, when he collapsed in the batter's box at Camden Yards after swinging at a pitch. He had partially torn the same ligament—this time in his right knee. He was forced to have another season-ending surgery—and one in the midst of a pennant push. It crushed Machado. "I didn't want to do the surgery because I knew what we have here," Machado said. "I know how this team is. I know how important this thing is to all these guys in here. So me being down sucks. I want to be out there playing every day and giving it my all."

There's an obvious concern that two serious knee surgeries by age 22 could hamper such a promising career. But Machado believes that the abnormalities in his knees have been fixed and he should be able to resume playing at a high level. But, he admits, the period between September 2013 and August 2014 has tested him. "This is the biggest obstacle I've ever done in my entire life. It's been tough, but it's just part of life," Machado said. "There are a lot of roller coasters in life, and you've just got to ride it. You've got to ride it out and stay mentally focused and strong. And at the end of the day, an outcome will always be there. And, hopefully, the outcome is a great one."

The Truck Driver and the Rusty Nail

Right-hander Dave Johnson's story is so ridiculous, so improbable that it belongs in a baseball novel—except it all happened. Johnson drove a tractor trailer full time for three years after graduating from Overlea High School in Baltimore County while pitching in a well-respected men's league. He attended an open baseball tryout—it was on a Saturday, so he didn't have to ask off work—and his performance there eventually led to pitching at the Community College of Baltimore. Despite excelling collegiately, he wasn't drafted. Instead, he agreed to a minor league deal with the Pittsburgh Pirates; his signing bonus was a steak dinner. He made it to the big leagues in 1987 with the Pirates, pitched five games in relief, and became a minor league free agent after the following season.

Like Son, Like Father

As the Orioles' 2012 "Buckle Up" season progressed, the comparison between it and the "Why Not?" 1989 Orioles campaign was inevitable.

The 2012 team was trying to make the playoffs after a franchise-worst stretch of 14 losing seasons; the 1989 club attempted to make the postseason after rebounding from a franchise worst 54–107 record in 1988. Both teams were filled with young, unheralded talent and a sprinkling of cast-offs from other organizations who made significant contributions.

On August 8, 2012, 24-year-old right-hander Steve Johnson, a local kid from Kingsville, pitched six strong innings to beat the Seattle Mariners and pick up his first major league victory in his first big league start and second Orioles appearance. It marked the 23rd anniversary of another Baltimore County right-hander—Steve's father, Dave—who pitched a complete game against the Minnesota Twins, securing his first major league win for the Orioles in that magical 1989 season.

Yes, a father-son combo earned their first big league victories on the same date 23 years apart in a pennant race for their hometown team. Both did it in their second game with the Orioles after beginning their pro careers with another organization. "It's something I was thinking about for a long time: get my first win and have [my dad] here," Steve Johnson said that night. "And the way those days worked out—23 years to the day—it's just special. It's all I can really say about it. It means a lot to me."

Steve Johnson ended up going 4–0 with a 2.11 ERA in 12 games with the 2012 Orioles, who made the playoffs but lost to the New York Yankees in the American League Divisional Series. Dave Johnson was 4–7 with a 4.23 ERA in 14 starts for the 1989 Orioles, who lost to the Toronto Blue Jays in the final weekend of that season.

The Orioles acquired the hometown kid in a seemingly inconsequential minor league trade in March 1989 just before the improbable "Why Not?" season began. His Orioles debut that August was almost canceled by rain. He had to pay his own airfare to Boston because there was a mix-up with his ticket. When he arrived at Fenway Park that day, security wouldn't let him in initially because he couldn't prove he was a player. (He had no Orioles gear since he had spent spring training with the Houston Astros.) He signed his first Orioles contract in the Fenway Park clubhouse bathroom next to the urinals and stalls. His first warm-up pitch sailed into the opposing team's bullpen because he was afraid he was going to hit bullpen coach Elrod Hendricks, who had momentarily looked away. And yet none of it could top the sheer weirdness of the legendary "rusty nail." "The whole, 'stepped on the nail' thing, the 'Why Not?' season, that last weekend, and the magnitude of the Saturday game," Johnson said. "That was really my whole career in a nutshell."

Johnson was a poster boy for the "Why Not?" club that—after a league-worst record in 1988—should have been terrible again in 1989. But with an influx of new personnel—many, like Johnson, were from baseball's scrap heap—the 1989 Orioles battled the Toronto Blue Jays to the final weekend of the season. With the pennant on the line, the Orioles and Blue Jays met for a three-game season finale with the Jays clinging to a precarious one-game lead. Johnson had given the Orioles a big lift after he was called up August 1 as a 29-year-old rookie to pitch the second game of a doubleheader. After getting a no-decision in that game at Boston, Johnson went 4–1 in his next five starts with three complete games. He notched two complete-game victories over the American League's best hitting teams, the Minnesota Twins and the Red Sox, and was named the AL Pitcher of the Week in his second week with the Orioles.

He, though, struggled some in September, and at the end of the month, Orioles manager Frank Robinson told Johnson and fellow rookie right-hander Pete Harnisch that whichever one pitched well in a series in Milwaukee would get the Saturday start in Toronto. Harnisch, the 23-year-old, former first-round pick, lasted into the seventh inning and allowed just three runs in a win against the Brewers. Johnson, who hadn't won in a month, allowed four runs in four and two-third innings in his loss to Milwaukee.

So Harnisch was slated to start Saturday against the Blue Jays in what would ultimately be a do-or-die contest for the resurgent Orioles. They had fallen two games behind the Jays with two to play after losing a 2–1 heartbreaker in 11 innings on Friday night. After that game Harnisch was walking back to the hotel and stepped on a nail—in Orioles lore it will always be a rusty nail—and because he couldn't put full weight on his foot, he had to be scratched for the crucial Saturday start. No one told Johnson, who arrived at the park Saturday morning to find two baseballs in his cleats, Hendricks' traditional signal to indicate the day's starter. Johnson thought Hendricks made a mistake, so he put the balls back in the coach's locker, only to find the baseballs in his shoes minutes later. Johnson began looking for Hendricks when he ran into pitching coach Al Jackson, who told him about Harnisch and the nail. "I kind of played it off, like 'Okay, no big deal.' Meanwhile, whooooo," said Johnson, who began tapping his heart to show how nervous he was that day. "Here we are two games down with two to go and we need to win this game to stay alive. And I'm starting."

In the first inning, Johnson walked Lloyd Moseby, the leadoff hitter, and then allowed a two-out, seeing-eye single to George Bell to give the Blue Jays a 1–0 lead. As he walked off the mound, Johnson dropped his head, distraught that he was letting down his team. When he reached the top step of the dugout, he was met by an enraged Robinson. "He basically said, 'Get your head out of your ass. I need you to give us a good six or seven innings right now. Let's go,'" Johnson recalled. "It was like a wake-up call." Johnson allowed just one more hit and one walk through the next six scoreless innings. Entering the eighth he had a 3–1 lead and was putting an exclamation point on the most improbable season in franchise history. But he walked the first batter in the eighth and was pulled for lefty Kevin Hickey, who walked the only batter he faced. Mark Williamson entered and surrendered two RBI singles and a sacrifice fly. In a blink the Orioles lost 4–3, and their magical "Why Not?" year was over. The Orioles won the final game in Toronto, but finished two games behind the Blue Jays in the AL East.

In 1990 Johnson led the Orioles with 13 wins and was second on the club to Harnisch in starts (29) and innings pitched (180) while posting a respectable 4.10 ERA. After an injury-riddled and ineffective 1991, the hometown hero was released by the Orioles. He pitched in six games in relief for the Detroit Tigers in 1993 to cap his career. Eventually a radio and TV broadcaster in Baltimore, Johnson pitched in just 77 major league games, but his rags-to-riches story in 1989 was one of the most inspirational in club history. "Most people don't realize I led the team in wins the next year or where I came from before that. As far as people in Baltimore know, I was a truck driver from Middle River, and they summoned me to pitch because Pete stepped on a nail," Johnson said. "It didn't really work that way. But there's no question that defined my career as the whole blue-collar thing."

95 The International League Orioles

For 52 years from when the American League Orioles left in 1902 until the St. Louis Browns moved to Baltimore in 1954, the Orioles were a minor league franchise. It was a tremendous one that was well-respected throughout the game and beloved by its fan base. In fact, Baltimore's exuberance for the minor league Orioles—specifically in 1944—is probably the reason the city was such an attractive landing spot for the majors a decade later. The architect of the minor league Orioles was Jack Dunn, a former major leaguer and the man who discovered Babe Ruth. The minor league Orioles initially played in the Class A Eastern League from 1903 until 1912, when the minors were reshuffled and the EL moved up to become the Class Double A International League. Starting in 1919, Dunn built a mini-dynasty with his club winning seven straight International League titles and posting 100 or more wins each season.

That 1919 club was led by third baseman Fritz Maisel, one of several local products who Dunn signed. The 1920 club won its final 25 games. The 1921 squad was even more dominant, winning 27 in a row and ultimately being named by MLB.com as the second greatest minor league team of all time. That group featured Jack Bentley, a first baseman and left-handed pitcher who won the Triple Crown at the plate and went 12–1 with a 2.35 ERA on the mound, earning the Sandy Spring, Maryland, native the nickname, "Babe Ruth of the minors." Bentley pitched in the 1923 and 1924 World Series for the New York Giants. The 1921 Orioles club also included 31-game winner Jack Ogden as well as a second year pro who was 25–10 with a 2.56 ERA in 313 innings pitched. That 21-year-old left-hander was Robert Moses Grove from Lonaconing, Maryland. Lefty Grove eventually was sold to the Philadelphia Athletics for $100,600 and won 300 games in a 17-season Hall of Fame career.

After a 101-win season in 1926 that did not culminate in a title, the International League Orioles took a step backward. But they returned to glory in one of the more tumultuous and rewarding baseball seasons in Baltimore sports history. The 1944 club was led by manager Alphonse "Tommy" Thomas, a Baltimore native who pitched for Dunn's Orioles in the 1920s and for 12 years after that in the major leagues. In the early morning hours on Fourth of July of 1944, a fire destroyed the all-wood stadium—which was initially built for the Federal League Baltimore Terrapins in 1914—and everything in it. The flames were so immediate and intense that some feared the stadium had been bombed as part of a World War II strike. The club was forced to play on the road for 12 days and returned to the cavernous football field, Municipal Stadium on 33rd Street, the predecessor to Memorial Stadium. According to *The Baltimore Sun*, Municipal Stadium had a left-field fence that was 260 to 290 feet from home plate, but it was more than 500 feet to right-center. The club thrived at its new home. The Orioles ended up backing into the International League pennant when they lost their season finale while Newark dropped a doubleheader. The Orioles then beat Buffalo and Newark in the playoffs and defeated Louisville of the American Association to win the Junior World Series and become the city's darlings. Catcher Sherm Lollar, who turned 20 that season and ultimately made seven major league All-Star teams, led the offense along with first baseman Bob Latshaw, second baseman Blas Monaco, third baseman Frank Skaff, and outfielders "Howitzer" Howie Moss, Stan Benjamin, and Felix Mackiewicz. Red Embree, who pitched eight years in the majors, was the Orioles' ace, winning 19 games with a 3.20 ERA.

The most enduring aspect of that team was its unmatched popularity. The first game of the 1944 Junior World Series at Municipal Stadium drew 52,833 fans, a very significant number since the final game of the major league World Series was played on the same day at Sportsman's Park in St. Louis between the Browns and the Cardinals. That one drew just 31,630. It was the impetus Baltimore needed to promote itself as big league ready. Within a few years, Municipal Stadium had been reconstructed, leading to the new Memorial Stadium. And within a decade, the Browns were headed to town. The IL Orioles returned to one more Junior World Series, losing to Columbus in 1950, but it was the 1944 team—and a disastrous fire—that sparked big time baseball's return.

Cult Heroes

These aren't the best players. But when their names are mentioned, an Orioles fan can't help but smile a little bit. Maybe it was one game or one season, but these guys earned their way into the collective memories of Orioles fans.

Jeff Ballard
Only once in his five seasons with the Orioles did the lefty from Montana have a winning record or an ERA under 4.00. But what a year he had in 1989, going 18–8 with a 3.43 ERA and finishing sixth in the American League Cy Young voting. He majored in geophysics at Stanford.

Dave Criscione
The Orioles' ultimate one-hit wonder, the reserve catcher played in seven games in his big league career, all for the Orioles in 1977. He was 3-for-9, and his lone home run was a walk-off in the 11th inning against the Milwaukee Brewers. It was his only big league RBI.

Clint Courtney

Nicknamed "Scrap Iron," he may have been the first blue-collar type to connect with Orioles fans. The 5'8" catcher with the circular glasses hit the first homer in a regular season game at Memorial Stadium in 1954. He had three, one-season stints with the Orioles.

Eric Davis

He spent just two seasons and 173 games with the Orioles in his 17-season career, but his battle with colon cancer in 1997 was an inspiration. His pinch-hit, ninth-inning home run in Game 5 of the 1997 American League Championship Series prompted Rafael Palmeiro to say to Davis, "You're my hero."

Sam Horn

He made his club debut on Opening Day 1990 with four hits, six RBIs, and two, three-run homers. The 6'5", 240-pound left-hander was supposed to be the first to hit the B&O Warehouse with a homer. He didn't, but he had 42 longballs in three years with the O's.

Chito Martinez

The only Belize-born player to make the majors, Martinez was promoted to the Orioles in July 1991 and hit 13 homers in 216 at-bats. The Orioles promoted him for Rookie of the Year by sending selected voters bags of Cheetos. He hit five homers in his next two seasons.

Randy Milligan

At 6'1", 230 pounds, "Moose" Milligan looked like a typical power-hitting first baseman, but never hit more than 20 homers in a year. He was an on-base machine, compiling a .388 on-base percentage in four seasons. He also hit the first grand slam in Camden Yards history.

Darren O'Day
A sidearmer who honed his delivery in a beer league, he became a key reliever in 2012. Fans serenade him with "O'Dayyyy, O'Day, O'Day, O'Day," when he pitches. His family surname, Odachowski, was changed before he was born, making him "a fake Irish Polish man."

Jeff Reboulet
The utility infielder spent 12 seasons in the majors and had just 20 regular season homers. But his lone postseason longball in Game 4 of the 1997 American League Division Series against nasty left-hander Randy Johnson gave the Orioles a 2–0, first-inning lead and helped them clinch the series.

Floyd Rayford
Known as "Sugar Bear" or "Honey Bear" for his lumpy physique that resembled a cereal box cartoon character, Rayford was a catcher/third baseman who hit 18 homers in 1985. He once missed the team bus after a teammate—likely Cal Ripken Jr.—locked him in a bathroom.

Lenn Sakata
The club's first Hawaiian-born player spent six seasons with the Orioles, hitting .233 with 21 homers. His walk-off homer in the 10th inning on August 24, 1983 that came after he was forced to catch—and Tippy Martinez picked off three Toronto runners—is a franchise classic.

Larry Sheets
Picked ahead of Cal Ripken Jr. in 1978, the Virginia native hit 36 homers in parts of his first three seasons. Then, in 1987 at age 27, the outfielder batted .316 with 31 homers and 94 RBIs and looked like a star in the making. He hit 27 homers for the rest of his career.

John Shelby

T-Bone spent seven seasons with the Orioles and returned to coach years later. His lasting legacy was "the Throw" in late September 1982 in Milwaukee. He caught a fly ball to center and, in one motion, unleashed a rocket home for a double play that kept pennant hopes alive.

John Stefero

A Mount St. Joseph's High School product, the reserve catcher had four RBIs in 11 at-bats in 1983. Two were walk-off singles in consecutive games against the Brewers. Former Brewers owner Bud Selig joked that Stefero and Criscione gave him nightmares for decades.

Jim Traber

The Whammer grew up in Columbia, Maryland, and went to Wilde Lake High School. He grabbed legendary status in July 1986, when he subbed for an injured Eddie Murray and had five homers and 14 RBIs in his first 10 games. He hit 13 homers in 1986 but just 14 more for his career.

Mickey Tettleton

It's hard not to love a strapping, muscular catcher who admitted that he ate Froot Loops every morning. Tettleton played three years for the Orioles, including his breakout 1989 in which he hit 26 homers, made his first All-Star team, and won a Silver Slugger Award.

Koji Uehara

He was the first Japanese pro the Orioles had ever acquired and he assimilated well to Baltimore. He broke down in tears when he was traded to the Texas Rangers in 2011, though that trade was a boon for the Orioles, who received Chris Davis and Tommy Hunter.

Jerry Walker

The right-hander pitched in four seasons with the Orioles and made the All-Star Game in 1959. One outing from that season stands out: a 16-inning, complete-game, 1–0 shutout of the Chicago White Sox. He allowed six hits and three walks and faced 55 batters.

Villains

Baltimore isn't Philadelphia, but it's still an East Coast city that likes to be heard. The fans will boo—usually opponents they feel have slighted the city. But they'll get on their own guys, too, especially if they are underperforming or disrespectful. These are the men who really got an earful. Others—such as Mike Mussina and the Angelos family—have their own chapters.

Albert Belle

No star in club history was more coldly received than the surly slugger, who signed a five-year, $65 million deal in December 1998 and only fulfilled two seasons before retiring due to a degenerative hip condition. Fans couldn't root for him; media couldn't talk to him.

Armando Benitez

If he'd only thrown his fastball instead of hanging a slider to Tony Fernandez in Game 6 of the 1997 American League Championship Series, maybe he wouldn't be on this list. But he was blamed for losing that series and lost more points when he purposely hit Tino Martinez, igniting a brawl in 1998.

Glenn Davis
The Orioles gave up Steve Finley, Curt Schilling, and Pete Harnisch for Davis' power bat; he hit just 24 homers in three injury-riddled, star-crossed seasons that included a neck injury, a broken jaw while breaking up a bar fight, and a liner off his head while in the dugout.

Richie Garcia
The umpire who didn't see what the rest of America did: a kid reaching over the right-field wall at Yankee Stadium and deflecting a potential out into a Derek Jeter home run in Game 1 of the 1996 ALCS. What really irked O's fans is that he signed autographs the next day.

Cito Gaston
The Toronto Blue Jays manager was roundly booed during and after the 1993 All-Star Game at Camden Yards. He chose to pitch his own closer, Duane Ward, in the ninth over Orioles ace Mike Mussina, who warmed up in the bullpen. Animosity ensued.

Reggie Jackson
I grew up in Baltimore, and Jackson was the first player I was taught to boo. The Orioles had to give up Don Baylor to get him in 1976. He then held out for a while and left for big bucks from the New York Yankees that offseason. Then he excelled for the Yankees.

Jeff Maier
I met Maier years after he was a 12-year-old kid who turned the Jeter fly ball into Orioles-Yankees' history. He's a polite, humble man; O's fans don't care. He did something inappropriate, cost the Orioles a win, and was celebrated in Gotham as a hero.

J.C. Martin
His run up—and out of—the base line in the 1969 World Series' Game 4 at Shea Stadium on a bunt interfered with Pete Richert's throw to give the Mets a gut-wrenching win. After 1969 he never played in Baltimore again, so he was never officially improperly treated.

Terry Mathews
The stocky reliever became a lightning rod at Camden Yards in 1997; he was booed when he entered games to the point where he couldn't be used at home. "I don't look like a ballplayer," he said in 1997. "I'm sorry God didn't bless me with an Eric Davis body."

David Ortiz
The Red Sox slugger abused Orioles pitching over the years. He also terrorized a phone in the visiting dugout at Camden Yards, bashing it to pieces. And he once charged Orioles reliever Kevin Gregg for pitching inside, inciting a mini-brawl at Fenway Park.

Sidney Ponson
An Aruba native and Orioles homegrown product, Ponson was gifted but never reached his potential. His off-field antics included punching a judge at an Aruba beach in 2004, for which he was initially jailed. After his second DUI arrest in 2005, he was released by the O's.

Sister Sledge
The 1979 World Series hero, Willie Stargell, was too decent and honorable to be a villain. So Baltimore's bitterness from that heartbreak is targeted toward the disco/R&B group that sang "We Are Family," the Pittsburgh Pirates' theme song. It'll never get play in Maryland.

Struggling relievers

Whether it was Eddie Watt after giving up a homer in the 1970 World Series or Mike Gonzalez, who was booed running down the carpet during the 2010 home opener, Orioles fans have little tolerance for relievers who serve up homers or can't throw strikes.

Mark Teixeira

There was faint hope the Severna Park, Maryland, product would choose his hometown team in free agency and lead them back to respectability. Instead, he took a mega-deal from the Yankees and then said he went to Orioles games as a kid wearing a Don Mattingly jersey. *Ouch.*

Alan Wiggins

The troubled infielder was suspended separately for drug use and an altercation with teammate Jim Dwyer. Wiggins never fit in with his teammates and rarely seemed alert on the field. In 1986 he fell for the hidden-ball trick. Fans were done with him after that.

Earl Williams

The 1971 National League Rookie of the Year was so coveted by Earl Weaver that the Orioles dealt away four players, including Davey Johnson, for him. The catcher's numbers fell, he and Weaver spat, and fans treated him harshly before he was dealt back to the Atlanta Braves.

98 Road Trip to the Minors

It would be a pretty intense road trip to undertake all at once. You might want to spread it over a week. Sure, you can take the easy way out and make five separate trips, but trying it all at once is both impressive and doable. It's roughly 600 miles total, and no single leg is longer than four hours in normal traffic.

Here's what you do: start in Aberdeen, Maryland, 35 miles northeast of Charm City. Spend one night there, then head south past Baltimore, but stop before you get to Washington, D.C.—this is a Baltimore book after all—and stay in Bowie, Maryland. Then take a trip to the beach toward local tourist hotspot Ocean City, Maryland. You can dip in the waves for an hour or two. But remain focused. Towel off, get back in your car, and go to nearby Salisbury, Maryland. Keep that Eastern Shore vibe going the next day by traveling down to Norfolk, Virginia. (You've already seen the ocean; you don't need to go to Virginia Beach, but, hey, it's your road trip, so you make the call.) After leaving Norfolk, find your way back onto Interstate 95, head north, and then go west to end up in Frederick, Maryland. (At 235 miles from Norfolk to Frederick, this is the longest jaunt.) Once you leave Frederick, head back to Baltimore and end your excursion at Camden Yards. And you will have done it: five of the Orioles' minor league affiliates and the big leagues all in one trip.

So maybe that's a little adventurous, but the point is if you want to see an Orioles minor league game, they are all within a four-hour or so drive from Baltimore (except the rookie level Gulf Coast League in Sarasota, Florida, but we're assuming you've already been to spring training—see Chapter 82—so you're exempt from that one). A minor league driving odyssey wasn't the point when the

Orioles began assembling their affiliates close to Baltimore. But the franchise loves the idea that fans can watch players all the way up through the system. And plenty of fans do. "There are quite a few fans that come to mind—or their faces at least come to mind—that you've seen literally since the beginning because the stadiums are drivable," said Orioles catcher Caleb Joseph. "You may have to take a weekend trip to come to Norfolk, but from Aberdeen to Delmarva, Frederick, and Bowie and then to the big leagues, there are quite a few familiar faces."

Before getting called up from Triple A Norfolk in May 2014, Joseph was in his seventh season in the minors, all in the Orioles system. He's played at every level except Low A Delmarva. "It is really enjoyable as a player to be able to see those same people that were supporting you and encouraging you from the very beginning

Easy Access

Having all of their affiliates within a short drive was part of a concentrated effort by the Orioles. It's better for shuttling players back and forth between levels—something that has become a common practice in recent years—and it's better for the fans who want to follow a prospect's path to the majors.

Here is a list of Orioles affiliates, their leagues, ballparks, cities, and the distance that each one is from Camden Yards.

Triple A: Norfolk Tides, International League, Harbor Park, Norfolk, Virginia, *230 miles*

Double A: Bowie Baysox, Eastern League, Prince George's Stadium, Bowie, Maryland, *28 miles*

High A: Frederick Keys, Carolina League, Harry Grove Stadium, Frederick, Maryland, *50 miles*

Low A: Delmarva Shorebirds, South Atlantic League, Arthur W. Perdue Stadium, Salisbury, Maryland, *115 miles*

Short A: Aberdeen IronBirds, New York-Penn League, Ripken Stadium, Aberdeen, Maryland, *35 miles*

Rookie Level: Gulf Coast League Orioles, Gulf Coast League, Ed Smith Stadium, Sarasota, Florida, *996 miles*

all the way to the very top," Joseph said. "They can experience the road with you, and there's some sort of enjoyment that they get, too, to watch you go through the entire process and make it to the big leagues."

As far as stadiums go, the jewel of the Orioles' minor leagues is in Aberdeen, birthplace of Orioles Hall of Famer Cal Ripken Jr., whose family owns the club. Ripken Stadium is part of the overall Ripken Baseball headquarters, which includes youth fields and a baseball academy. The stadium has sold out every game since it opened in 2002, the year after Ripken retired from the Orioles. "You can get really spoiled in Aberdeen your first year," Joseph said. "You kind of come into pro ball, and one of your first experiences is playing in front of 6,500 people or so, and you have that Ripken aura."

If Joseph had to pick a favorite spot in his minor league journey, it might be Frederick, because he enjoyed the town, and the stadium was often packed with energetic fans. He spent four seasons in Bowie, where he made some close friendships and played on what he believes is the best manicured field in the minors. Delmarva may have the most eclectic crowds. Salisbury's Arthur W. Perdue Stadium—named after the founder of the multi-billion-dollar chicken processing company—draws in beach tourists who want to fit baseball into their vacations.

Norfolk has a big city feel for a minor league town, partially because it boasts the largest naval base in the world. So Joseph said there were things to do on off days like tour old warships. Plus, there was another huge reason Norfolk was a good place for a baseball lifer like Joseph—and for the fans who love watching prospects. "When you get to Norfolk, you know you are really, really close to making it to the big leagues," he said.

30–3 Defeat

It was supposed to a happy day for the Orioles. They held a press conference before their August 22, 2007 doubleheader against the Texas Rangers at Camden Yards to announce they were taking the interim tag off manager Dave Trembley, who had endured more than two decades in the minors to reach that plateau.

In the stands that day was recently signed first-round pick Matt Wieters, who was arguably the most hyped prospect in the club's history. Wieters would be introduced to the crowd during the first contest and then walk through the clubhouse and meet the current Orioles in between games.

But something quite remarkable happened on that supposedly feel-good day in an otherwise forgettable Orioles season. The Rangers absolutely, positively pummeled the Orioles in the first game. The Orioles were leading 3–0 heading into the fourth inning; the Rangers then scored 30 consecutive runs after that. The joke that week was that the Orioles fell to 0–1 in their history in games in which the opponent scored 30 or more unanswered runs.

It was the most given up in one big league game since June 29, 1897, when the Chicago Colts beat the Louisville Colonels 36–7. The Rangers set the largest margin of victory in one contest since the turn of the 20th century. When you're making modern-day baseball history, you know it's special. "It's been a long day," Trembley said at the time. "Whatever we threw, they hit it. They say hitting's contagious, and that certainly was the case in the first game. I've never seen anything like it."

Unfortunately for the Orioles, after that three-hour, 21-minute shelling, they had to go out and play a second game. They lost that one 9–7, allowing 39 runs while scoring 10 in one day. After a nine-run sixth inning with the Orioles trailing 14–3 in the first game, Wieters turned to his father and said, "No way are we going into that clubhouse." Richard Wieters, a former minor league pitcher, agreed. The Rangers actually scored in only four of the nine innings in the 30–3 rout: five in the fourth, nine in the sixth, 10 in the eighth, and six in the ninth.

Starting pitcher Daniel Cabrera allowed six runs in five innings, and he by far received the gold pitching star in the game for the home team. Reliever Brian Burres allowed eight earned runs in two-thirds of an inning; Rob Bell gave up seven runs in one and one-third innings, and veteran Paul Shuey was touched up for nine runs in two innings. The Rangers hit six homers in the game; Jarrod Saltalamacchia and Ramon Vazquez each hit a homer against Cabrera and against Shuey.

Texas had 29 hits, and six of the nine starters had at least three apiece. The Orioles actually compiled nine hits and committed only one error. It's just that the Rangers couldn't stop feasting on the Orioles' pitching. "People are going to laugh about it and say, 'Is that even possible?' or 'How did that happen?'" Orioles second baseman Brian Roberts said at the time. "That's just the way it is. It was just one of those nights. It's not like we were a joke. We didn't kick balls around, make 15 errors. It was just one of those nights where nothing went right for us, and everything went right for them."

100 Behind the Scenes

There are plenty of people who shaped the Orioles—or who had a lasting effect on the organization—who never threw or swung at a big league pitch. Here are some of them:

Herb Armstrong

A longtime baseball executive who helped the minor league Orioles move to 33rd Street after their park burned down in 1944, he became the big league club's first business manager. The organization's annual award for non-uniform personnel is named after him.

Monica Pence Barlow

She was the first female public relations director in club history. Her death at age 36 in February 2014 became a source of inspiration for the team's playoff run that season. For more than four years, Barlow handled her daily job duties while privately fighting lung cancer.

Frank Cashen

A Baltimore native and former sportswriter, he was hired by Jerry Hoffberger to be publicity director of two racetracks and the National Brewing Company. He became executive vice president of Jerold Hoffberger's Orioles, overseeing business operations in 1965 and then serving as general manager from 1971–75.

Pat Gillick

He led the Toronto Blue Jays and the Philadelphia Phillies to World Series titles as GM. He got close with the Orioles in 1996 and 1997, but the club lost both times in the American League

Championship Series. He left when his contract expired in 1998 due to a rift with owner Peter Angelos.

Jim Henneman

A Baltimore native and longtime sportswriter, he covered decades of Orioles games, off and on, from 1961 until 1995. He's been one of the primary official scorers at Camden Yards since 1997. It's believed no one alive has seen more Orioles games in person.

Jerold "Jerry" Hoffberger

He was instrumental in getting the Orioles from St. Louis to Baltimore in 1954. He bought controlling interest in the club in 1965 and held ownership throughout the club's glory years before selling to Washington attorney Edward Bennett Williams in 1979.

Phil Itzoe

Before his death in 2010, Itzoe was the longest-tenured traveling secretary of any of the four major sports teams. He spent 41 of his 45 years in the organization supervising the club's travel. Prior to that, Itzoe worked as the club's assistant public relations director.

The MacPhails

Lee MacPhail Jr. joined the Orioles in 1958 and helped shape the club, setting the wheels in motion for the Frank Robinson trade before leaving in 1965. His son, Andy, took over in 2007 and returned it to respectability by acquiring young players such as Adam Jones.

Jon Miller

From 1983 to 1996, he was the Orioles' radio voice, taking over for legend Chuck Thompson. Known for his sharp wit, Miller's contract wasn't renewed because he wasn't pro-O's enough for ownership or because he wouldn't reduce his national TV commitments. Or both.

Hank Peters

The longest tenured general manager in club history, he oversaw the second wave of Orioles greatness from 1975–1987. Among his biggest contributions was the 1976 trade with the New York Yankees that brought in Rick Dempsey, Scott McGregor, and Tippy Martinez.

Jim Russo

Considered the Orioles' "super scout," he worked for the organization from 1954–1987 and is credited with endorsing amateurs such as Jim Palmer and Boog Powell. He once said his proudest accomplishment was his report that helped the Orioles sweep the Dodgers in 1966.

Pat Santarone

The head groundskeeper at Memorial Stadium from 1969 to 1991, he was considered one of the top in his field. But he was best known for his annual tomato-growing competitions beyond the left-field foul line with manager Earl Weaver.

Pitching coach trio

A coaching staff can be volatile, but for the Orioles' first 31 years, they had just three pitching coaches: Harry Brecheen (1954–1967), George Bamberger (1968–1977), and Ray Miller (1978–1985). Miller had two other stints as O's pitching coach and one as manager.

Trainers

No club has had more continuity in its training staff. Baltimore has had three head athletic trainers in its modern existence:

Eddie Weidner, who took over full time with the 1923 minor league Orioles through 1967; Ralph Salvon, 1968–88; and Richie Bancells, 1988 to present.

Tylers

Umpires attendant Ernie Tyler worked 3,819 consecutive games before snapping his streak to attend Cal Ripken's 2007 Hall of Fame induction. Sons Jim and Fred are longtime O's clubhouse managers. Jim left the home clubhouse to take over his late father's job in 2013.

Acknowledgments

Because this is my first book, I never knew how many people were actually instrumental in making one happen. This one, specifically, was created by a village, since so many shared their insights. First, I'd like to thank Tom Bast of Triumph for approaching me with the idea and my editor, Jeff Fedotin, for his suggestions, his polite deadline reminders, and for working around my crazy baseball schedule. To make this project work, I needed to talk to as many Orioles, past and present, as possible. Bill Stetka, the club's alumni director, was instrumental in facilitating that and in providing me with historical perspective. PR whiz John Maroon came through for me as always and so did the Orioles' 2014 public relations staff, specifically Jeff Lantz, Jay Moskowitz, and Amanda Sarver. I was approached to do this book the week my friend, O's PR director Monica Barlow, passed away. The project provided me with a needed distraction at the time.

I was pleasantly surprised how gracious the past and present Orioles were in affording me time. Many were excited. One current Oriole high-fived me when he found out he had his own chapter. I interviewed roughly 50 players and staff members; most of the interviews were one-on-ones, but a few came from the 60th anniversary reunion press conference. That was like Christmas Day for me. So a humongous thank you to: Brady Anderson, Harold Baines, Mike Bordick, Al Bumbry, Chris Davis, Doug DeCinces, Rick Dempsey, Dan Duquette, Joe Durham, Andy Etchebarren, Jim Gentile, Rene Gonzales, Adam Jones, Chris Hoiles, Billy Hunter, Tommy Hunter, Dave Johnson, Davey Johnson, Caleb Joseph, Tito Landrum, Manny Machado, Nick Markakis, Dennis Martinez, Tippy Martinez, Ben McDonald, Scott McGregor, Bob Milacki, Alan Mills, Melvin Mora, Eddie Murray, Mike

Mussina, Darren O'Day, Gregg Olson, Jim Palmer, Milt Pappas, Boog Powell, Brian Roberts, Brooks Robinson, Frank Robinson, Gary Roenicke, Billy Ripken, Cal Ripken Jr., Joe Saunders, Buck Showalter, Ken Singleton, Steve Stone, Rick Sutcliffe, Tony Tarasco, and Matt Wieters. Powell, Hoiles, Singleton, and the incomparable Palmer were particularly giving of their time. Marty Bass and Wayne Kaiser helped me better understand the culture of Section 34.

Before I agreed to do the book, I needed approval from my bosses at *The Baltimore Sun*. I really appreciate the trust shown by Dean Jones Jr., Ron Fritz, Trif Alatzas, and Sam Davis. They trusted I could juggle this without affecting my daily baseball coverage. Thank you for the leap of faith. As a kid growing up in Baltimore, covering baseball for *The Sun* is a dream. When I was hired in 2005 by Randy Harvey, for whom I'm eternally grateful, I immediately joined a tremendous fraternity of sportswriters, a lineage of current and former employees I would put up against any in the country. I tapped into the newspapers' archives and the minds of that group. Thanks to Kevin Cowherd, John Eisenberg, Eduardo Encina, Jim Henneman, Mike Klingaman, Roch Kubatko, Ken Rosenthal, Peter Schmuck, Childs Walker, and Jeff Zrebiec. Special kudos to my current *Sun* baseball team of Ed, Pete, and Dean for their support and understanding while I ran this marathon. A hat tip to my Camden Yards press box family, as dysfunctional as it may be, for allowing "the book" to dominate, well, everything: Mel Antonen, Rich Dubroff, Britt Ghiroli, Dave Ginsburg, Craig Heist, Brett Hollander, Jim Hunter, Luke Jones, Steve Melewski, Ted Patterson, Pat Stoetzer, Gary Thorne, Mark Viviano, Casey Willett, David Wilson, and Alejandro Zuniga. I must single out Dubroff, who at times seemed more energized about this project than I was. Authors that have survived the grind and dispensed advice and/or camaraderie: Nick Cafardo, Cowherd,

Eisenberg, Tom Haudricourt, Maureen Mullen, Gerry Sandusky, Dave Sheinin, and Susan Slusser.

One of the think-tanks I used was John Mongan's terrific staff of attendants in the Camden Yards press box. They took the "homework" I gave them seriously; my thanks to Mark Allen, Jim Bronakoski, Phil Dell'Uomo, Richard Dietrich, John Lowensen, John Mongan, and Mike Mooney. My formal research started with Eisenberg's phenomenal oral history of the team, *From 33rd Street to Camden Yards* as well as Patterson's *The Baltimore Orioles*. I leaned heavily on baseball-reference.com, my favorite website in the universe, and received help from home run/ejection historian David Vincent; Bill Arnold of Sports Features Group; John Odell and Matt Rothenberg of the National Baseball Hall of Fame and Museum; John Ziemann of the Babe Ruth Birthplace and Sports Legend museums; and Elias Sports Bureau. Bob Rambo of Martin Library in York, Pennsylvania, and Dennis Ford provided me with some important resource material. So many others have been supportive throughout this process, including Ron and Shirley Peters, the Plotkin family, the Edwards family, the Craft family, Jim Geary and the BDHL boys, Tom Moore and the NWBL boys, and my old Calvert Hall and Etown cronies.

Most important, I need to thank my family, who are accustomed to me being work-obsessed throughout the summers. This obsession, though, ate through October and well into November. The looming deadline forced me to miss the destination wedding of my awesome niece, Katie. Because of the Orioles' postseason run and the book, I also attended fewer of Grace's soccer games, Annie's newspaper meetings, and Alex's cross country meets than I desired. My three children will always be my greatest priorities; this work thing is a passing fad.

My father, Jerry Sr., often said he regrets working so much and not spending more time with his kids. Rubbish. He serves as a wonderful example: a hard-working, kind-hearted, moral man.

He also happened to marry a saint. No one had a bigger impact on me than Ann Connolly, who read countless stories to me as a child and encouraged me to dream big. I miss my mom every day. I thank God daily that I was blessed with such tremendous parents, siblings, and children. Mostly, I thank God for the gift of my beautiful wife, Karen, who is my best friend, my editor, my everything.

Sources

Books

Ain't The Beer Cold by Chuck Thompson with Gordon Beard, 1996, Diamond Communications, Inc.

The Baltimore Orioles: Forty Years of Magic from 33rd Street to Camden Yards by Ted Patterson, 1994, Taylor Publishing Company.

Cal, Tribute to an American Hero by the *York Daily Record*, 2001, Triumph Books.

From 33rd Street to Camden Yards, An Oral History of the Baltimore Orioles by John Eisenberg, 2001, Contemporary Books, McGraw-Hill.

Oriole Magic by Thom Loverro, 2004, Triumph Books.

Rex Barney's Thank Youuuu by Rex Barney with Norman L. Macht, 1993, Tidewater Publishers.

Tales from the Orioles Dugout by Louis Berney, 2004, Sports Publishing LLC.

100 Things Reds Fans Should Know & Do Before They Die by Joel Luckhaupt, 2013, Triumph Books.

Newspapers, wire services, and publications

Associated Press

Baltimore Orioles media guide

Chicago Tribune

Los Angeles Times

St. Louis Post-Dispatch

The Baltimore Sun

The New York Times

The Washington Post

The Washington Times
The York Dispatch and Sunday News
United Press International
York Daily Record

Websites

Baberuthmueseum.org
Baltimoresun.com
Baseball-almanac.com
Baseballhall.org
Baseballprospectus.com
Baseball-reference.com
ESPN.com
Lasportshall.com
MLB.com
Minorleaguebaseball.com
Retrosheet.org
SABR.org
Wikipedia.org